George Soros

A Life in Full

George Soros

A Life in Full

———

SURVIVOR, BILLIONAIRE, SPECULATOR,

PHILANTHROPIST, PHILOSOPHER,

POLITICAL ACTIVIST,

NEMESIS OF THE FAR RIGHT,

GLOBAL CITIZEN

Edited by Peter L. W. Osnos

Platform Books
Harvard Business Review Press

Cover design by Maryellen Tseng and Stephani Finks

Book design by Jane Raese
Set in 11.5-point Baskerville

Editorial production by Christine Marra, Marrathon Production Services. www.marrathoneditorial.org

Library of Congress Cataloging-in-Publication Data
Names: Osnos, Peter, editor.
Title: George Soros : a life in full / edited by Peter L. W. Osnos.
Other titles: George Soros (Harvard Business Review)
Description: Boston, MA : Harvard Business Review Press, [2022] | Includes index.
Identifiers: LCCN 2021021732 (print) | LCCN 2021021733 (ebook) | ISBN 9781647822798 (hardcover) | ISBN 9781647822804 (ebook)
Subjects: LCSH: Soros, George. | Capitalists and financiers—United States—Biography. | Philanthropists—United States—Biography. | Hungarian Americans—Biography. | Jews—United States—Biography.
Classification: LCC HG172.S63 G36 2022 (print) | LCC HG172.S63 (ebook) | DDC 332.6092 [B]—dc23
LC record available at https://lccn.loc.gov/2021021732
LC ebook record available at https://lccn.loc.gov/2021021733

Contents

Introduction

Peter L. W. Osnos

THE NAME GEORGE SOROS IS WORLD FAMOUS. And yet the man himself is surprisingly little understood.

Depending on who or where you are, describing Soros is likely to elicit different answers. He has even more identities than he has lived decades, now into his tenth.

In addition to survivor, billionaire, speculator, philanthropist, activist, author, nemesis of the far right, and global citizen, there is husband, father, and, to an extent he may not even realize, friend.

The first eight of these are Soros's public profile, and they are the focus of this book. Over the years, attempts have been made to write George Soros's biography, but no single account of his life can capture its extraordinary, multifaceted character. The writers whose work appears in this volume have approached Soros from the perspective of those whose expertise in their fields have enabled them to provide a description of his activities and—to the extent possible—the motivation for them and their impact. There will be places where the narratives overlap; think of these as interlocking pieces of a puzzle covering a vast area. Some essays may not altogether reach the same conclusions. On a canvas this wide, this is perhaps inevitable. And with so much to cover, there may well be less of some activities than of others. But the breadth of these portrayals is considerable.

Essential to this process was that the writers have complete confidence in their independence of judgment, along with the responsibility to be accurate and fair-minded—while also recognizing that anyone writing about another person will bring his or her own experience to the task.

The essays are not intended to describe in detail how Soros's activities and initiatives have developed over the decades. Suffice to say that the paths have not always been smooth. In finance there are straightforward measures of outcome—money spent, money earned, profit and loss.

In philanthropic areas, success or failure is more difficult to assess because there are few clear metrics. Have the efforts and expenditures provided the desired results? When situations and personalities require changes to be made, how are these handled? The answers to these questions—especially at the Open Society Foundations and Central European University, among the most ambitious philanthropic commitments of modern times—are yet to come.

These institutions have been founded by Soros, funded by Soros, and are ongoing. All the essays in the book are portrayals of George Soros's experiences and vision and how he uses his wealth. He does seek counsel, advice, and information from other people. But the ultimate decisions have been and will continue to be his, as long as he can make them. This is not always popular.

So, this volume has been compiled with the assurance that it would be the best possible representation of George Soros's life we can achieve. And he and his family did not read it until it was completed. I have guided the project with the assistance of Paul Golob, the estimable editor who has worked with me to bring the essays to final form. The opinions expressed, as the saying goes, are those of the authors. It will not be surprising if Soros's critics find some fault with the essays.

My own dealings and fascination with Soros began in the 1980s, as he became involved with human rights issues, particularly Human Rights Watch. As a former journalist in the Soviet Union, Eastern Europe, and Southeast Asia (including the war in Vietnam), and by personal instinct, I was also an advocate and interpreter of human rights issues.

In 1997, I founded the publishing house PublicAffairs, whose very first list included Soros's book *The Crisis of Global Capitalism: Open Society Endangered*. All his books that have followed were likewise published by PublicAffairs, as well as in dozens of countries around the world.

My latest publishing venture, Platform Books LLC, is copublishing this book with Harvard Business Review Press to assure the broadest possible reach for the book in the world marketplace.

In a book of my own, *An Especially Good View: Watching History Happen*, I reflected on George Soros and our engagement over the years. I made the case that Soros was one of three individuals who were instrumental in the ultimate demise of the Soviet empire. The others were the great Soviet scientist and dissident Andrei Sakharov and Pope John Paul II. Sakharov, because of the universal acclaim for his humanism and democratic beliefs; John Paul, because he became the symbol throughout Eastern Europe of defiance of Kremlin orthodoxy; and Soros, because the combination of principles and wealth enabled him to back the avatars of Western open society where they did not exist.

As the Soviet empire entered its final stages before dissolving in 1991, Soros was in many ways the capitalist fantasy of all latter-day communists—a very, very rich man. What the Soviets and Eastern Europeans did not recognize about Soros was that his genius for making money was matched by his passion for the "open society" as defined by the philosopher Karl Popper. In the years of *glasnost* and *perestroika* and the early years of the post-Soviet era, Soros created an infrastructure of civil society organizations and support for democratic ideals and education.

What the communists and their successors missed was that Soros was subversive to their ideology, a radical as well as a billionaire.

Increasingly after 2000, as the politics of these countries deteriorated after early hopefulness, pressure on the open society enterprises grew. The record of the post-Soviet era is still unfolding. Nonetheless, an entire generation of people saw what was possible in progressive reform.

In the years since, Soros has continued to refine his guiding philosophical and financial thesis called "reflexivity"—the way events and trends influence how markets sway, often with unintended consequences. Knowing how to make the right early calls was a source of Soros's genius and enormous wealth.

In particular, the great international recession of 2008–9 was widely seen as a validation of his sense of how market distortions such as subprime mortgages can convulse economies. Soros was very proud of his open society philanthropy and activism. But I think he took exceptional pleasure in finally being recognized for his philosophy.

Over the years, Soros became a major nemesis to the global extreme right wing, which has deployed a mix of conspiracy theories and anti-Semitic tropes to discredit his activities on behalf of progressive causes and civil society. The bizarre notion that he is a mastermind of everything the right-wingers around the world reject is nonsense. The attacks are not easy to ignore, especially when a bomb was placed in the mailbox at his home in Bedford, New York.

Yet Soros has displayed extraordinary equanimity (at least as I could measure) in almost every way. Michael Vachon, his savvy longtime adviser on media and politics, said one evening as we sat at dinner, "George, no one is ever going to feel sorry for you" having to endure the slings and arrows of fame and fortune.

What did bother Soros, I thought, was that in his homeland of Hungary, the autocratic leader Viktor Orbán, who had once studied at Oxford as a Soros-funded fellow, made Soros the focus of his nativist political strategy. In time, I came to understand the significance of Soros's personal heritage: that the influence of his father, Tivadar, in the war years was a basis for his own daring and risk-taking in finance and in life generally.

All this and a great deal more is discussed in these essays. Each of the writers is a highly respected expert in the aspect of Soros's life and work they are exploring.

The opening essay is by Eva Hoffman, whose early years in Poland, in the immediate aftermath of World War II and the Holocaust, give her a particular understanding of Soros's experiences during that time and the impact on his life. Her own admired books prepared her for this account of his background and early years.

Sebastian Mallaby is a writer who can, with extraordinary clarity, explain the development of Soros's career as a speculator (Soros's own term), his instincts about how to amass wealth, and how he has shaped the modern world of finance.

Darren Walker, as the president of the Ford Foundation, is a preeminent twenty-first-century philanthropic leader. He is also a Black man and proudly gay. Walker explains Soros's approach to philanthropy, how it fits into today's world, and why it has been so meaningful to him and others who have been underserved and victims of racism and bigotry.

Gara LaMarche led the launch of the Open Society Foundations' work in the United States. As president of the Democracy Alliance, LaMarche has joined in Soros's involvement with US politics and was fully aware of the relentless attacks of the far right, startling in their crudeness and falsehoods. LaMarche combines a career in civil liberties and human rights with an acute awareness of political strengths and failings.

Ivan Krastev is of the generation that emerged after the fall of the Soviet empire, which enables him to write with a measure of distance about how Soros took on the challenge of bringing open society principles to places it had not been and the frustrations that were perhaps, in retrospect, inevitable.

Michael Ignatieff is an acclaimed author who deploys his philosophical ideas to practical application in institutional leadership. As the former rector of Central European University, an institution founded by Soros, he has seen the great asset it can be as well as the difficulty in fulfilling its vision.

Orville Schell, one of the world's foremost experts on China, helped guide Soros in his interactions with the ascendant superpower. With his equally brilliant wife, the late Baifang Schell, he became an adviser to Soros and, in the process, a confidant.

Leon Botstein is a scholar, a college president for nearly fifty years, and a well-known orchestra conductor with a deep appreciation of the identities that have defined George Soros: as a Jew, as a survivor, and as an innovator in many fields of consequence. Botstein is an exceptionally astute interpreter of Soros's persona and his place in history.

This book is not a philanthropic exercise. It has been funded by a private entity that is backed by Soros's wealth (though not by his Open Society Foundations). That money will be repaid from revenues the book accrues. In other words, this book is a business venture of an unusual kind, and given the subject, this should not be altogether surprising.

As I wrote at the outset, no book can be sufficiently broad to describe every aspect of Soros's life. There are parts that only he can truly examine—his approach to family, for instance—and insights that are only his to share. What you have in this book is, as nearly as anyone can do it, George Soros's life in full.

I WOULD LIKE TO THANK several people for their role in making this book a reality: George Soros and his wife, Tamiko Bolton, for their cooperation with this book from the outset; Michael Vachon for his assistance at every stage; Christine Marra for her role as production editor; Bill Warhop for his copyediting; Adi Ignatius at Harvard Business Review Press and his colleagues for being wise and encouraging copublishers; and Paul Golob for his always superb editing. And of course I would like to thank Susan Sherer Osnos, my wife and partner in Platform Books.

George Soros

A Life in Full

Origins

Eva Hoffman

GEORGE SOROS IS A MONUMENTAL FIGURE whose outsize dimensions can be measured in many ways: in the sheer size of his fortune, in the international impact of his human rights and pro-democracy work, and in the success of the various causes he has supported.

All this we more or less know. But what do we know of George Soros as a person? Is it possible to envisage him as a child, or an adolescent boy? I doubt that many people's imagination would extend that far. Like many world-famous figures, Soros, to those who don't know him personally, is a kind of abstraction, or a brand, rather than a living, breathing, emotionally complicated (as which one of us is not?) human being.

And yet, of course, George Soros was once a child; and as it happens, his childhood was extremely eventful. It was also—and for more than personal reasons—powerfully formative. Soros was born in Budapest in 1930; when World War II broke out he was nine years old. During the months of 1944–45, when Hungary was invaded and occupied by Germany, he turned fourteen. For those who are at all acquainted with the course of World War II, these dates speak volumes. They mean that George's childhood and early adolescence coincided with the most cataclysmic event of the twentieth century, which, moreover, wrought its greatest ravages in Eastern Europe, and particularly to its Jewish populations. And yet, several decades later, in his foreword to *Masquerade*, his father's memoir of those years, George Soros, reflecting on his wartime childhood and particularly its most dangerous period, wrote, "It is a sacrilegious thing to say, but these ten months were the happiest times of my life. We were pursued by evil forces and we were clearly on the side of the angels because we were unjustly persecuted; moreover, we were trying not only to save ourselves, but also to save others. . . . What more could a fourteen-year-old want?"[1]

Later still, when I asked ninety-year-old George (during a COVID-bound Zoom conversation) if he still stood by those startling sentences, his first response was to joke that his memory isn't very good anymore, and that he "only remembers the future." "I think more about the future," he added. "And also, I happen to be very happy now." To hear this from a person of his age is wonderfully inspiriting—even inspiring—and it is possible that his capacity for happiness was also seeded in his early years. Eventually, George said that he stood by his "sacrilegious" statement; and I think those sentences about his wartime childhood provide quite a few clues to who he is and who he has become.

For those who lived through World War II, and especially through the Holocaust, that experience of ultimate danger and survival affected everything that came after: personal fate, inner life, views of the world, and the shape of character. This was true for George and his older brother, Paul, no less than for their parents. But for all of them, there was life before, which had its shaping influences as well. It is perhaps hard for most of us to imagine life in "the Other Europe" in the early part of the twentieth century; but prewar Budapest, where Paul and George grew up, and where their parents spent a good portion of their lives, was a beautiful *Mitteleuropean* city, situated on two sides of the Danube, its former grandeur as part of the Austro-Hungarian Empire inscribed in its splendidly ornate parliament building, its long and complex history readable in its many monuments, its epicurean character palpable in its luxuriant public baths and in its many cafes, which especially before the war were sites of intimate conversation and lively political discussion.

Prewar *Mitteleuropa* was a much less puritan or work-driven part of Europe than its Western regions, never mind North America. It was also home to highly sophisticated cultures. In his own memoir, written in America in the 1990s, Paul Soros, born four years before George, remembers that in the city of his youth, despite "the hateful undercurrents" of nationalist chauvinism and anti-Semitism, "political discourse, literature and sports flourished, as did theatre, music, opera, in a cosmopolitan atmosphere that, despite our best efforts and greater material resources, we were not able to match for our children."[2]

Culture matters—and Tivadar Soros, George's father, was a very *Mitteleuropean* personality. He was a lawyer by training, multilingual, worldly, well read, and well informed; but by the time the 1930s came around, he had forsworn hard work and spent much of his time in those pleasant baths and cafes, eating delicious pastries in good company, and undoubtedly flirting as well. This was true of many Hungarians of his class and financial means; but as George pointed out in conversation, in Tivadar's case there was an important difference: before his turn to this easy-going lifestyle, his father had lived through his own life-changing experiences of extreme danger and survival.

These are worth dwelling on, if only because of their impact both on Tivadar's actions during World War II and on George's imagination and later attitudes. In condensed summary, Tivadar's time of trial followed on his volunteering to fight in the Austro-Hungarian army in World War I. He apparently took this step not out of patriotism, but because he didn't want to miss out on the adventure. But if adventure was his aim, he eventually got more of it than he bargained for. After a period of relatively easygoing soldiering, he was captured by the Russians and interned in a prisoner-of-war camp in Siberia. While there, he managed, rather amazingly, to publish a newspaper called *The Plank*; he also used the time to bolster his knowledge of Esperanto, a "universal" language invented at the end of the nineteenth century, which became the *lingua franca* of various international movements. Tivadar would remain engaged in the Esperanto movement and its publishing house until late in his own life; *Masquerade* was first written in that language. George's internationalist tendencies had good family precedents.

Tivadar's period of captivity, however, also included more grimly instructive incidents. During his internment, he witnessed the execution of a "prisoners' representative" after some captives managed to escape. This led to his refusal to accept such a position himself, and to the lesson—very useful during the war to come—that it doesn't always pay to be prominent. Instead, realizing that the situation was increasingly hopeless, he proceeded to organize a mass escape. This involved travel by "train, raft, mule, and pony"[3] and an unfortunate geographical mistake, which meant that for a while, the escapees found themselves unintentionally headed toward the Arctic Ocean. Once they reversed tracks, Tivadar's journey home took several months and involved various dangers and privations, possibly including torture; but eventually he made his way to Moscow—by that time, the capital of postrevolutionary Russia—and then, through further guile and deception, back to Hungary.

One can easily imagine the impact such true tales of danger and derring-do had on the impressionable young minds of his sons. As George put it in his foreword, "I learned the art of survival from a grand master."[4] World War I, Esperanto, and his father's adventures were part of George's prehistory—even if they were deeply internalized and vividly present in his imagination. But for Tivadar, these were apparently adventures enough. In George's view, his father, after living through the Russian revolution, came back a changed man. Before his escapades, he was apparently an ambitious young man, trained as a lawyer and eager to achieve great things; afterward, he was simply happy to be alive. He decided to devote himself to enjoying life rather than to more conventional achievements—especially since money didn't seem to matter to him very much. In his foreword, George says that his father was the only man he knew "who systematically decumulated his assets."[5] Mind you, much later, George did something analogous, on a much larger scale, when he decided to stop devoting himself to making money and to dedicate his time to worthwhile causes instead. That was when he was already very much his own man; but perhaps one can discern his father's influence in this radical and highly unusual step as well.

Tivadar's easygoing lifestyle was greatly facilitated by marriage to his second cousin, Erzebet Szucs, whom he met when she was just sixteen. Marriages of such close relations may seem unusual or even dubious to us today, but in that earlier age, and especially among Jewish families, they were not uncommon. Erzebet was ten years younger than Tivadar, and, according to her oral memoirs, fell in love with him at first sight, giving up her ambition to acquire a college education in order to enter into a relationship with him. She was a very different character from Tivadar: quite timid, given to spiritualist tendencies, and suffering from nervous states and occasional ulcers. She also brought to the marriage considerable material assets. Her father, Mor Szucs, was a successful businessman until he was diagnosed with paranoid schizophrenia at a late age, nurturing the unfounded conviction that his wife was unfaithful to him with his business partner. Given his state, he could no longer manage his wealth. Instead, Tivadar was put in charge of his businesses, which included a famous fabric shop as well as properties in Budapest, Vienna, and Berlin; he received a management fee for various transactions and accumulated a very satisfactory income without putting in too many working hours.

This too was part of George's significant history. His own story began in the interval between the wars, with what can fairly be described as a happy childhood. His earliest years don't seem to have been marked by any unusual drama, but one important event occurred in 1936, when he was six years old, and his parents decided to change the family name from Schwartz to "Soros." This was not an uncommon practice among educated and assimilated (or at least acculturated) Hungarian Jews; but it is also possible that Tivadar stayed alert to worrying developments in Germany and that his decision was driven by a sense of potential danger. In 1936, anti-Jewish laws had not yet been enacted in Hungary, but Tivadar, who was multilingual and politically savvy, listened to the BBC's German broadcasts, and probably read newspapers in German as well as Hungarian (perhaps in those sociable cafes, where newspapers were kept on hand for customers). Most of all, he knew how to read the signs of the times. If George could say, several decades later, that his family was different in its attitudes from other Hungarian Jews—in ways that soon came to have crucial consequences—this was because of Tivadar's Russian education, and what it taught him about totalitarian systems. He undoubtedly followed the rise of the Nazis in Germany and Austria, and was aware that the infamous summer Olympics that year took place under the sign of the swastika. In another vein, Erzebet argued for a name change as well, so that her sons would not be stigmatized, especially since George was beginning school that year. The choice of the particular name might have had some added significance. "Soros" means "next in line" in Hungarian, and possibly indicated a symbolic passing of the baton by Tivadar to his sons. In addition, Tivadar would have known that in Esperanto, the word "soros" is the future tense of the verb "to soar"—a connotation that undoubtedly appealed to him.

Apart from such serious events, life for George and his older brother in their early years was easygoing, pleasurable, and full of vigorous physical activities. In the 1930s, the family spent their summers on Lupa Island, an outcropping on the Danube just outside Budapest that could be reached only by water, and which featured a small number of summer cottages, about half of them owned by middle-class, acculturated Jewish families. The Soros "cottage" was a small but striking, Bauhaus-style villa, designed by the well-known architect Gyorgi Farkas, who was a family friend. There were two tennis courts established on the island at Tivadar's initiative, where George probably acquired his passion for tennis (at the age of ninety, he still plays three times a week), and his parents had a small stand where they sold coffee and pastries, which became popular with the island's vacationers and the numerous rowers who passed alongside the island. (Erzebet was trained in making Gerbeaud pastries, made famous by a renowned Budapest cafe.) George spent a lot of time kayaking in the Danube, and he and Paul were allowed to swim in the deep river by themselves from an early age, to the surprise of many onlookers.

But apparently, leisure and pleasure were not sufficient for George, and in an endearingly childish version, he began to show philanthropic tendencies early on. While vacationing on the island, he established a newspaper called *Lupa News*, and according to a local reminiscence by a rather more conventional journalist, dated December 1939, nine-year-old George was this publication's author, editor, reporter, and distributor, using his earnings from its sales to contribute to worthy causes. In the journalist's account, the "apple-faced smiling little guest" visited his quarters in order to donate money "to the Finns. They are fighting a freedom fight now, Daddy said."[6] Whether Daddy also suggested the donation is not recorded in the annals of history, but his influence on George was clearly discernible in this gesture.

Perhaps one can also discern early signs of George's business instincts (as well as his self-confidence) in an anecdote recounted to Tivadar by a stationery shop owner in Budapest and recorded in Erzebet's later recollections. After coming into the store one day, George looked around and decided that the goods were not displayed to the best advantage. He then proceeded to advise the rather astonished shop owner on how to rearrange things—advice which the man apparently followed and did not regret.

On Lupa Island, Tivadar played with his own and other children as if he were one of them. He invented a cry—"Papuuaa!"—by which they could summon each other, as if they were brave Indian warriors. He also recounted an ongoing story—a sort of children's serial—called "Amosarega," about a miraculous machine whose name combined beginnings of the words for "airplane," "motorcycle," "car," and "garage," and which could be magically converted into any of these things. According to an account by Michael Kaufman in his biography of George Soros, "Tivadar would, for example, inform the boys that he had received a call from Mahatma Gandhi in India who, it seemed, needed their help. In that case, as he told it, he and the brothers first flew to Central Asia and then, after turning Amosarega into a car, drove over the Hindu Kush, talking their way out of difficulties among the fierce Pathans as they headed toward their rendezvous with Gandhi."[7] Such tales kept his young listeners in a state of enchantment and, without any overt didacticism, provided incidental lessons in geography and important issues of the day.

Of course, no idyll is complete without its difficulties. Aside from play and pleasure, there was, during George's childhood, a webwork of less overt family relations, and these were—the word follows almost inevitably—complicated. In her later reminiscences, recorded in a long interview, Erzebet was full of wonder at Tivadar's love of his children, from babyhood on. "I've never seen a man love babies so much," she said, describing her husband as being almost more maternal than she was.[8] He loved to hold his baby sons, to play with them and, later, to teach them and guide them. And yet, many decades later, the ninety-year-old George touchingly remembered that, as a child, he felt his father didn't love him enough. "I never understood why he liked my brother more than me," he said. "He was the favorite." Paul, according to George's reminiscences, was the forceful personality, the one who merited their father's attention. Was this simply sibling rivalry, and the younger child's almost inevitable insecurity? Probably—and George eventually became convinced that he was much loved by his father as well. Still, it is testimony to the depth of those earliest emotions that they continued to thread their way through George's psyche for so long—and in the face of so much contradictory experience and information.

Reinforcing this picture, there are George's remarks in the afterword to his brother's memoir, published in 2006. "Let me add some of my own reminiscences," George wrote. "As children we were not on the best of terms. He liked to torture me. I would complain to my parents but they would ignore my complaints for lack of independent evidence. This was my first encounter with injustice in the world and it must have played a role in shaping the objectives of my foundation; we took a strong stand against torture."[9] This is even more astonishing: that George, in his later years, could trace the roots of his important political ideas and his morally informed stand against torture to childish scare games is, again, testimony to the force of early feelings—or perhaps George's unusual ability to understand the relationship between his subjectivity and his values.

The resentment George felt toward his older brother did not go unreciprocated. Paul wasn't at all happy about the arrival of a younger brother on the scene when he was four years old, and throughout their childhood years he continued to regard George as something of a nuisance. Eventually, however, brotherly relations improved. "I thought I would never forgive him," George continues his afterword, "but Paul, being the torturer, did not hold any grudges against me. When I left Hungary for good at age 17, Paul gave me his best, green flannel suit. I was touched. He has been a good brother ever since."[10]

That was later; but when they were growing up, there was, aside from brotherly rivalries, a division of parental attachments. In her reminiscences, Erzebet told her interviewer that George "got very much love from me because it was easy to love him. He was not resisting or stubborn like Paul."[11] During boat trips or their frequent ski excursions, George always ended up staying close to her, while Paul accompanied Tivadar. These weren't planned decisions, she adds, but somehow it seemed to happen. George, recollecting this in conversation, confirmed that his older brother had an uneasy relationship with his mother. Erzebet, he said, was "very didactic"; and Paul, being a strong-willed and tough kid, resented this. "I was much more malleable," George said. "I considered myself a softie."

But if he had a good relationship with his mother, he positively "adored" his father. "Mother also adored him," he added. Tivadar's philosophy of child-rearing was the opposite of Erzebet's: it was to instill strong principles in his sons, while leaving them maximum autonomy—and perhaps this allowed George to differ from his father on one important matter, which was the way in which Tivadar treated Erzebet. George was apparently aware, even at a young age, of his father's flirtatious and perhaps philandering tendencies. In conversation, he recalled that he once saw his father walking arm in arm with a young woman, which was disconcerting. And when a family friend asked young George, "What kind of a man is your father?," George replied that he was "a married bachelor." For an adult, such a reply would have been witty and slightly damning; but for a young child, it surely suggested not only precocious perceptiveness, but some unease.

Erzebet, in her reminiscences, remembers that George was very upset when his parents had fights; even several decades later, he recalled an incident in which his mother, in a fit of anger, set off in a rowboat by herself. George went after her and brought her back. Speaking to his biographer, Michael Kaufman, about this, George said that "I expressed it at the time to my parents, saying I loved them both—but I really disapproved of my father for the way he treated my mother. . . . There were big fights between them. And there was sexual tension."[12] For a young child, this was both unusually sensitive, and courageous; in our conversation, George told me candidly that he struggled with the question of his father's character—and whether he was a strong or a weak man—for quite a while. His doubts sprang from his suspicion that Tivadar married Erzebet not for love but because her family's properties enabled his easygoing lifestyle. George's skepticism ceased when he witnessed his father's tireless efforts to protect his family in time of great danger; but his ability to question and criticize his adored father implies a strong sense of personal morality, from which a more developed ethics can grow.

Whatever the complexities of marital relations, Erzebet's own most vivid memories from the prewar period are of family excursions, particularly in Germany or the Austrian mountains, which she recollected as occasions of pure pleasure. The whole family loved to ski, and Paul later took it up as a competitive sport. It's unclear when George began skiing, but from early on, he was enchanted by the beauty of mountainous landscapes. "That's God's mountain!" Erzebet remembers him saying, as he contemplated a snow-covered peak—a lovely observation for a child to make. In 1938, however, a trip to Germany delivered an upsetting revelation. In a pub where they stepped in for a drink, there was a big sign: "NO JEWS ALLOWED." Erzebet's reaction is worth quoting: "I wanted to turn my back and go out; it was a terrible feeling. Institutionalized: No Jews Allowed. And Tivadar said, 'You are a foreigner, that's not for you.' But it was a terrible feeling so we didn't stay, just two or three days I think."[13]

The incident was a foreshadowing of things to come all too soon in Hungary itself. The Hungarian experience of World War II was exceptionally complicated, and, in its last phases, exceptionally appalling. In the 1930s, the Kingdom of Hungary, as it was then known, relied on trade with the future Axis powers of Italy and Germany for recovery from the global Great Depression, and for help in settling some territorial disputes—a matter of great importance for a country that, after World War I, lost the greater part of its territory in the Treaty of Trianon, a settlement imposed on it by the Allies and long remembered as the "Trianon trauma." In 1940, partly because of its geopolitical situation, and in the hopes of recovering some of its lost territory, Hungary entered into an alliance with the Axis powers. The pact was negotiated by the prime minister, Béla Imrédy, apparently with some initial reluctance. But there were also early signs that when required, the Hungarians proved themselves to be very willing executioners. In 1941, when Hungarian forces participated in the invasion of Yugoslavia and the Soviet Union, their exceptional cruelty was noted even by German observers. For other Hungarians, however, the compromises involved in the pact were unacceptable; and the country's subsequent prime minister, Count Pál Teleki, killed himself not long afterward.

Neither Teleki, however, nor any other politicians were willing to protect Hungarian Jews from the country's increasingly vicious anti-Semitism. In 1938, the first "Jewish laws" were enacted, granting citizenship only to those who could prove that they were resident in Hungary before 1914. Severe quotas were imposed on Jews in certain professions; and in order to continue practicing law, Tivadar was required to recruit a non-Jewish partner for his office. In 1941, when George began high school (adopting an option which allowed such early entry), Jewish pupils were segregated in separate classes; in the same year, Paul had to transfer to a newly established all-Jewish school.

Anti-Semitism was now not only a matter of personal prejudices—it was, in Erzebet's perceptive word, institutionalized; and that made all the difference. How people feel or what they say in the privacy of their homes is one thing; what they are permitted to do by law or official encouragement is quite another. Not many Jewish citizens of Hungary could provide proof of long-term residence, since there was no need for such documents in the decades and centuries before—and the consequences were dire. In 1941, several thousand Hungarian Jews were deported from the countryside to the Ukraine, where atrocities had already begun. Indeed, they were probably among the earliest groups of people subjected to methods of persecution and mass murder, which we have come to know as the Holocaust. In a rare instance of what we might call denial—or at least, a refusal to face facts head-on—Tivadar, in his autobiography, acknowledges that "untouched directly by such calamities, we felt that we were somehow above them. Our final line of defence was not to believe that such barbarisms were happening at all."[14]

Of course, even if Tivadar and others had confronted such facts squarely, they could not have done very much about them. The denial was undoubtedly reinforced by the odd atmosphere of simultaneous menace and normalcy that, after the initial burst of murderous cruelty, prevailed in Hungary until 1944.

This was, paradoxically, the effect of the pro-Axis alliance, which meant that until 1944 Hungary did not suffer war on its territory. Indeed, for most of its inhabitants, it remained a relatively safe country, in which life could continue uninterrupted—if, for the Jewish part of the population, hardly undisturbed. From the beginning of the war, the atmosphere of anti-Semitism, especially among the part of the population belonging to the pro-Nazi Arrow Cross Party, was becoming more toxic, and its expressions more routine. Still, in Budapest itself there were, as yet, no active persecutions or violence directed at the Jewish population. For the Soros family and their friends, there were bridge games every Sunday, maids in spacious apartments, meetings with friends in cafes, and the sense, deriving perhaps from middle-class complacency, that nothing terrible would happen to them.

It is evidence of the odd normalcy in abnormal times that, in 1943, George decided to go through the Jewish ceremony of initiation into adulthood—a bar mitzvah. His decision was entirely self-motivated; certainly his father, with his policy of giving maximum autonomy to his children, did not steer him in this direction. Having grown up in an earlier generation, Tivadar was closer to traditional Jewish life, and more aware of its customs and habits—as well as the ubiquitous Jewish jokes, some of which he offers in a chapter of *Masquerade* called "A Little Jewish Philosophy"—but he was not himself religious in any conventional sense. Indeed, he was apparently quite syncretic in his spiritual readings, which included the Koran and the Bhagavad Gita, a book called *The Story of Christ*, and Martin Buber's *Jewish Legends*. As for Erzebet, she was actively opposed to any display of Jewishness, although she had spiritualist tendencies of a rather occult sort.

George's decision to undertake the studies necessary for a bar mitzvah was all the more surprising since he was apparently a middling student during his high-school years—perhaps paradoxically because of his self-confidence rather than its lack. He simply didn't care very much and clearly didn't think his fate would depend on good grades. But he was initiated into several languages, including German, English, and French, as well as some Latin and Esperanto. If this seems quite exceptional to us, it probably wasn't so for Hungarians of his social class. Hungarian does not belong to any of the major categories of European languages and is extremely difficult for foreigners to learn. Therefore, educated Hungarians have had to learn other languages—which, in my experience, they pick up with impressive ease. George also wrote stories and poems throughout his early years, which suggests an active inner life and a drive to express it, or perhaps make sense of it.

Hebrew, however, was not among the languages included in his school curriculum, and he attended Hebrew classes on his own initiative. His bar mitzvah did not include the extensive rituals or parties we now associate with such events, but took place in an almost empty synagogue, where he read the appropriate section of scripture and was formally initiated into male Jewish adulthood.

In long retrospect, George said his decision was prompted by a brief but intense period of interest in spiritual matters. He thought a lot in those days about the ultimate questions of death and the meaning of existence—which, he added, seemed to him natural for someone his age. It undoubtedly was; but given the circumstances, translating such interests into practice was a strong gesture. Clearly, even at a young age, George felt an impetus to give his inner convictions expression and meaningful enactment, something that can be discerned in his later humanitarian and political work.

George decided to have his bar mitzvah at a time when it was still relatively safe to do so; but not long after, everything changed, changed utterly. In March 1944, Hitler summoned Hungary's regent, Miklós Horthy, for a conversation in which he informed the country's ruler that Hungary's allied status no longer held and that Germany intended to occupy Hungarian territory. No armed resistance was possible, not only because the Germans were so much stronger, but also because a faction of the Hungarian government itself was pro-Nazi. Tivadar, like most others, learned about this startling turn of events from the news, but initially it was difficult to appraise its implications. On the Sunday when the announcement was made, the weekly bridge game went on as usual, although the latest developments were the subject of lively discussion as well as some indignation about the lack of resistance on Horthy's part.

Soon after, however, the informal grapevine delivered more shocking news. Even as the bridge game was in progress, it was learned that prominent politicians and journalists (presumably of a more liberal or left-wing persuasion) had been arrested, and that Polish refugees—undoubtedly trying to flee from their deeper circles of the inferno—were to be deported. After the guests left, Tivadar turned from the Hungarian radio, which continued with its usual fare of light music, to the BBC's transmission from London, where the occupation of Hungary was the lead story—apparently, delivered in several languages. On the radio, this sounded like just another news item; but he immediately grasped something that many others—for far too long—didn't. "I had the feeling," he wrote in his memoir, "that no radio could convey the real news—the death sentence of a million Jews." There was also a broadcast from US president Franklin D. Roosevelt appealing to Hungarians to help Jewish people in the face of the collective death threat that Nazi occupation clearly spelled for them. Given the ambiguous role the United States played in the Holocaust—its refusal to take in refugees, or to intervene—it is striking that Tivadar felt this was a "poignant and human statement, the first touch of humanity I had heard all day."[15]

By the time of the Nazi invasion, the Allied powers were pressing Hungary to end its Axis pact and to do more to protect its Jewish population; but it was too little too late. In an expressive phrase used by George, the progress of the Holocaust in Hungary is difficult to understand, because—in contrast to events in Poland, for example—it happened in a sudden "crescendo" of violence in the final year of the war. Indeed, reading about the speed of change from seeming normalcy to mass murder, about the relentless determination of the leading Nazis to complete the process of extermination in Hungary with ruthless efficiency, and about the cooperation of numerous Hungarians in carrying out this gruesome task is—even after all that we now know of the Holocaust—horrifying to the point of implausibility. It's difficult to take in. Perhaps it is no wonder that many ordinary, upstanding Jewish citizens were unprepared to deal with the events. Of course, news of the horrors that had been unfolding in Poland since the war's beginnings had reached people in Hungary, but if Tivadar chose to ignore such developments, then so, undoubtedly, did everyone else. Hungary's Axis alliance also contributed to creating a false sense of safety; that, after all, was its point. And indeed, even on the evening of the Nazi takeover, events were happening only on the radio. Budapest itself remained quiet, with no invading armies in sight.

Tivadar, however, aside from his grasp of the news' terrible implications, understood something that many others didn't: he knew that he needed to be afraid. This may seem paradoxical, but a sense of danger and its realistic appraisal was, at that terrible time, crucial to survival. It meant that, at least, you could try to make provisions to protect yourself. In Tivadar's case, the instinct for danger was honed during his Russian captivity and escape, and although in *Masquerade* he says that on the day when the Nazi invasion was announced he didn't want to appear "afraid or defeatist," he tried to convey to his family the perils they were facing and the need to protect themselves. As we contemplate the Holocaust from our long distance, and with all the retrospective knowledge of the range of responses to that atrocity, I think it should go without saying that Tivadar's grasp of ultimate danger, and his fear in the face of it, was not a sign of cowardice but, on the contrary, of a wiser courage.

The grip of fear, however, was followed by a cool-headed appraisal of the new situation and what it meant for him and his family. In long retrospect, what George found admirable about his father during the time of utmost danger was that he "managed to overcome his fears—and to appear fearless; to make it a happy experience for us." "Happy," once again, may seem like an incongruous word, but to clarify, George added that even if his father sometimes felt fear himself, "he managed to give me the sense he knew what he was doing—that I was in safe hands—and this gave me a sense of happiness." Perhaps also the sense of safety provided by his father's protection allowed George to feel that facing danger was his own adventure; his own great game.

For Tivadar, however, there were literally life-and-death decisions to be made. After considering several possibilities, he decided that the only way to save himself and his family was to disguise their identities and to live as non-Jews. This decision was indirectly aided by the actions of the Jewish Council, set up by the Germans immediately after the invasion and consisting of Jewish community leaders. The role of Jewish Councils in the Holocaust has been a much-debated subject—and none has come under more scrutiny or criticism than the one established in 1944 in Budapest. These organizations were created in effect to act as representatives of the Nazi authorities within Jewish communities, and to make the new rulers' work easier. The leaders of such bodies were faced with agonizing decisions about which actions would save—or lose—the greatest number of lives; but in Budapest, the council's leaders complied with the Nazi orders all too eagerly, in the hope of saving themselves and their families. In *Masquerade,* Tivadar states his views on this sorry episode unequivocally. "When systematic persecution of Jews began," he writes, "it was carried out not by the Germans, nor by their Hungarian lackeys, but—most astonishingly—by the Jews themselves. . . . There was nothing the Germans could request that they were not ready, without a second's thought, to provide."[16]

George had his own brief encounter with the council, when he was required by its representative to deliver a "summons" to addresses housing Jewish inhabitants, ordering them to report to a "Rabbinical Seminary" with a blanket and food for two days. When Tivadar asked his son if he knew what this meant for the people responding to the summons, George responded that he thought they would be interned. This was perceptive, although he could not yet understand what might follow from internment; Tivadar, however, could, and he instructed George to deliver the summons, but to tell people not to obey the order.

But the tragic fact was that people did obey—including large numbers of Jewish lawyers, who subsequently perished in concentration camps. The habit of trusting official authorities was apparently deeply ingrained, but the collusion of the Budapest Jewish Council with the Nazis enabled and aided this, with awful consequences. Indeed, the role of the Council seems even more dubious in retrospect, as information about a document called the Vrba-Wetzler Report has come to light. This eyewitness account by two escaped inmates from Auschwitz described what was taking place in that concentration camp, including details of the gas chambers. Some decades after the war, a former employee of the Council, Gyorgi Klein, wrote that he saw the report when it was delivered to his boss in 1944. After reading it, he managed to avoid boarding a train which would have taken him to Auschwitz. The Council, however, did not tell the Jewish community about the report—probably for fear of losing favor with their Nazi overseers. When I talked about this with George, he said, in a tone that suggested the gravity of what he was saying, that "this was a tragedy of the Holocaust," since the Jews who went along with the Council's directives were in a sense "willing victims"—a real tragedy, he added, that was very difficult to articulate. Indeed, in the aftermath of traumatic histories, shame and humiliation are the most difficult emotions to contend with.

Tivadar's own well-justified anger at the Jewish Council never subsided, and he had no intention of answering its summons, or indeed waiting for it to reach him. Instead, he proceeded to find ways to provide false identity papers for various family members. He had no doubt about the rightness and the necessity of such a decision; and yet he felt that if he was going to follow it through, he needed to address "the moral problem of breaking the law." His reflections on this are worth quoting: "I felt fully entitled, morally and legally, to disobey the state when it threatened me unjustifiably," he says in his memoir, and then goes on to extend moral questions to the international order. "Not only does every state have a right to intervene in the internal affairs of another state if that state violates fundamental human rights, but it has a moral responsibility to do so. . . . We all of us have an obligation to help the helpless when their human rights are violated and when atrocities are perpetrated against them."[17]

Undoubtedly, such reflections were prompted by the failure of the Allies to come to the aid of less powerful countries, or to intervene in the horrors of the Holocaust. And surely one can see the influence of Tivadar's ideas on George's later activities—most notably the Open Society Foundations, which were established within authoritarian states to enable oppositional free expression and sometimes action. In conversation, George reiterated that his father "wanted me to form my own views." And yet, he added, "I am his faithful copy."

Following the Nazi betrayal, events unfolded with lightning speed. When Germany occupied Hungary, the invading troops included a division led by Adolf Eichmann, who arrived there to supervise the deportation of Jews to Auschwitz. To cite just one terrible statistic, between mid-May and the beginning of July 1944, more than 434,000 Hungarian Jews were deported to Auschwitz and murdered in gas chambers. Historians have apparently wondered at the pace of the transports, given the gruesome fact that the gas chambers and crematoria at Auschwitz were already struggling to cope with the numbers of inmates to be "processed," and that the war was clearly drawing to a close. But surely, that was precisely why the "crescendo" of the Hungarian Holocaust gathered its speed and pitch: Eichmann and his fellow executioners wanted to finish the job before it was, from their point of view, too late.

Initially, the situation was worst in the countryside, where ghettos were set up immediately as gathering places for deportation to Auschwitz. Tivadar had reports of these events from people who had managed to escape, and he says that he felt them deeply. He also noted the spate of suicides that took place immediately after the Nazi takeover, and the instant rise in denunciations of Jews. And yet *Masquerade* mostly reads more like a suspenseful thriller than a narrative of traumatic events.

Throughout the terrible period following the invasion, Tivadar continued to search for ways of protecting his family from discovery as Jews. This involved two basic strategies: creating or finding hiding places, and obtaining papers to prove non-Jewish identities for each of his family members, and in some cases, for other people as well. (George estimates that Tivadar may have helped about fifty people in these ways.) The task of obtaining false but credible identity papers for people of different ages and genders involved a gesture of goodwill from a manager of a property Tivadar administered, who provided an initial set of personal documents—as well as some failed attempts—but eventually, Tivadar's search brought him in contact with a forger of genius who was willing and able to provide perfectly plausible papers for all the members of the Soros family, and a few friends as well.

Once convincing papers were obtained, Tivadar decided that various family members would live in different places to minimize chances of discovery. In some cases, this involved approaching people whom he knew—for example, the building manager who had given him the identity documents—and trusting them not to betray their Jewish tenants, even if they were aware of their real identities. Approaching such potential helpers in the first place involved a degree of risk; but Tivadar was a quick and discerning judge of people's character. He often made instant and instinctive decisions about whom to trust—and who might prove unreliable or buckle under the strain. Fortunately, he never made major mistakes.

Eventually, Tivadar decided to live in the building whose manager he knew well, and which he chose partly—even then!—for its proximity to a good restaurant and convenient access to a swimming pool (where he continued to meet his sons throughout the next months). He also found a roommate named Lajos Kozma who happened to be one of the most renowned architects in Hungary, and the two converted their living quarters into a well-designed hiding place.

Aside from providing family members with false identities, Tivadar decided that it was safer for them to live separately. George, through the mediation of a barber who was fond of him (he seemed to have a talent for endearing himself to people), was placed with a man named Baufluss, who was officially assigned by the Hungarian Ministry of Agriculture to provide inventories of confiscated Jewish estates. Baufluss (who had a Jewish wife) was mostly away from Budapest, leaving George unhappily alone. On one occasion, realizing that his fourteen-year-old charge was having a hard time, he took George along on a trip to the countryside, where he was working on a very grand estate of a Jewish aristocrat who preferred to leave with his family and his life, rather than preserve all his wealth. While there, Baufluss even allowed George to ride horses around the estate. (Several decades later, this was the source of a bizarre CBS television program in which George Soros—by that time a renowned figure, as well as the target of exceptionally vicious anti-Semitism—was accused of helping the Nazis to confiscate Jewish property. Needless to say, George was entirely baffled by this line of attack, but the baseless charge was repeated on a number of occasions in the fringe right-wing media, to George's great dismay.)

Paul decided early on not to respond to his draft notice when he reached the age of eighteen—a decision that Tivadar typically left up to him, and which turned out to be possibly life-saving, as many young recruits, including one of Paul's close friends, never came back. Instead, he found more or less satisfactory flats for himself. The member of the family whom it was most difficult to protect was Erzebet's aging mother, whose response typified an extreme form of denial. She did not believe that the occupiers were doing anything more than moving people from place to place, or that deportations culminated in the gas chambers. "Such things simply aren't possible," she said, and Tivadar notes that in some sense she was right: such things shouldn't be possible. She did, for a while, accept being placed in a hotel, but after several weeks she came back to her apartment, claiming that she wanted to clean it out. She eventually accepted a safer place in a building where she knew some people, but Tivadar suspected that her visit to the apartment was to protect her furniture and other possessions—a motive he saw in others as well, and of which he was rather scornful, especially when it led to greater dangers.

But it was Erzebet, the most psychologically fragile member of the family, who had the closest brush with danger. She was living in a suburban country cottage under a pseudonym when she was visited and interrogated by two policemen. Given her proneness to nervous states, she might well have succumbed to anxiety, or even panic. But instead, she entered a state often described by people who have experienced moments of deadly danger: in her recollections, she said that it was as if she were standing beside or above herself, observing what was going on with almost preternatural serenity. She calmly answered all the questions put to her, in accordance with her false identity papers, and allowed the increasingly flustered policemen to inspect her premises, watching them as they struggled to fill out a report on their visit—after which, with some apologies, they left. Later, she said that this was her own finest hour. She passed the hardest of tests with flying colors and was proud of it. Not that she could maintain this state for long—this is also well known from accounts of extreme experiences—but it's possible that she became less afraid of being afraid. After moving to another location near Lake Balaton, partly to be close to a young woman she was fond of, she even delivered a message alerting another person of danger; but her stay there was mostly safe and included some bucolic moments of mushroom picking and other rural activities.

In fact, Erzebet's descriptions of life in the countryside led George to decide that he would like to live there as well, and he moved to a place nearby—although, following Tivadar's principle of family separation, he stayed in a different location. Neither of them was informed on, or met with immediate danger in subsequent months, but being Jewish required constant alertness. When members of the family did meet in public places, they addressed each other by their pseudonymous names, and when George fell ill with tonsillitis, his mother judged it too dangerous to summon the local doctor since he was a member of the Arrow Cross—and in a state of undress, George's Jewishness would have been easily discerned.

George, however, soon recovered, and his need for pleasure and company returned. Village life was pleasant, but he soon got bored with it and moved in with the Prohászka family, whom he met through

Baufluss on that later misunderstood trip, to their home in Buda hills (across the Danube from the main part of Budapest). These sympathetic and apparently entirely unprejudiced people were Christian Royalists who added George to their small family and who, in Tivadar's words, "lavished on him all the parental love he missed and really still needed."[18] The affection was apparently reciprocated, and in a thoughtful gesture, George told Tivadar that "the Prohászkas are so good to me—I'd really like to do something for them. Perhaps we could do rounds of the drugstores and try to buy some baby-food."[19] Tivadar agreed, and after discovering better-supplied suburban drugstores, he reciprocated the Prohászkas' care of his son by delivering large supplies of this hard-to-find product.

Tivadar's own situation, in the meantime, was once again made precarious by a political development that, among all the Nazi-occupied territories, was unique to Budapest: the creation of so-called Jewish Houses. This was a tactic similar to that used earlier in Theresienstadt, a concentration camp in the Czech territory where the Nazi authorities managed to convince a Red Cross delegation that it was a legal and in fact quite pleasant internment camp. In Budapest, instead of creating a ghetto, which would have been a clear sign of oncoming extermination, the Nazi overseers recruited the Jewish Council to prepare an inventory of houses owned by Jews—a task the Council fulfilled with alacrity—which were then marked with a yellow Star of David. The entire Jewish population of Budapest, consisting of about 150,000 people, was crammed into these quarters. The building where Tivadar and Kozma were staying was among the so-called Yellow Star houses, which meant that, in order to keep up their disguise, they had to move to another place.

At the same time, the international community began, however belatedly, to take some action, and in Budapest, several embassies designated their own safe houses for Jews—although Tivadar decided it was best to stay away from those as well. Perhaps this was because he saw the deadly scams perpetrated on Jewish people whose desperation may have made them even more credulous. In one incident, a large number of Jews boarded a plane that was supposedly going to take them to Cairo, and even yielded their watches before take-off. None of these unfortunates returned alive, and in *Masquerade*, Tivadar expresses a combination of chagrin and contempt for their naivete.

Among the few heroic figures to emerge from this dark history, the best known was Raoul Wallenberg, a Swedish diplomat and special envoy to Hungary who used his position at the Swedish Legation in Budapest to issue Protective Passports to Jews and shelter them in houses designated as Swedish territory. On one occasion, he appeared personally at the railway station in Budapest and insisted, using all his official powers, that the people on the train, who he knew were bound for concentration camps, should be allowed to disembark. He suc- ceeded in this, and in saving thousands of Jews, before vanishing and most probably being killed in a Soviet prison himself. The mystery of his disappearance has never been fully solved, despite repeated attempts to do so after the war—but his legend, and monuments to him erected in various countries, lives on.

Less well known but no less courageous was Carl Lutz, a Swiss diplomat who held posts in the United States and what was then Mandatory Palestine before serving as the Swiss vice-consul in Buda- pest from 1942 until the end of the war. In that position, he cooper- ated with the Jewish Agency and, through a deal with the Hungarian government and the Nazis, obtained eight thousand safe-conduct documents, which enabled Jews to emigrate to Palestine, and which he deliberately applied to families rather than individuals. Altogether, he is credited with saving sixty-two thousand Jewish lives. A memorial to him has been erected next to the US embassy in Budapest.

The endgame of the war and the Holocaust in Hungary was as infernally complicated as its previous progress. In *Masquerade*, Tivadar follows it in detail, in all its political twists and sudden turns, as he learned about it through the street grapevine and the BBC's German- language broadcasts. The roller coaster began on October 15, with Admiral Horthy declaring the end of Hungary's alliance with the Nazi regime, which, he said, had betrayed its promises to his country, and announcing an armistice with "our former enemies"—i.e., the Allies.

For people like Tivadar and many others, this announcement was met with euphoria. But this was short-lived, as the news delivered the next turn of events: the takeover of the government by the fascist Arrow Cross Party, under the leadership of Ferenc Szálasi. Even a realist of Tivadar's stripe didn't initially want to believe this; he knew that Arrow Cross rule spelled utter disaster for the Jewish population of Budapest. As soon as Szálasi came to power, tens of thousands of Jews were sent to the Austrian border in death marches; most forced laborers in the army were deported to Bergen-Belsen, among other places. Two ghettos were now established in the city—one ostensibly under the protection of neutral international powers—and Arrow Cross raids and mass executions took place brazenly in both. The one achievement of the diplomats overseeing the "Small Ghetto" was to issue a few thousand safe-passage documents out of the Hungarian inferno to its inhabitants. In addition, although exact estimates are hard to come by, Arrow Cross guards murdered upward of seven thousand Jews, who were either herded and shot into the Danube in January 1945 or killed by more conventional methods. Coming so close to the end of the war and the fascists' inevitable defeat, this was surely one of the most vicious acts of "gratuitous violence," in Primo Levi's phrase—that is, violence committed not in the aims of conquest or victory, but purely to wipe out the identity, or the very existence, of a group, as well as individual victims.

Nevertheless, for the Soros family, protected by their assumed identities, life briefly continued almost as before, although with a new awareness of the surrounding horror. On the day of the Arrow Cross takeover, Tivadar met his wife and older son for their scheduled rendezvous at the Cafe Mienk. Erzebet, alias "Julia," was clearly very upset and broke into tears when a group of Jews being herded by Arrow Crossers marched nearby, with their arms up in the air. Paul supported his father in urging her to go back to the country, saying, "We men can get by easier here."[20]

Toward the end of December, the now allied Russian and Roma-
nian troops surrounded and raided Budapest, ushering in a period
of violent struggle within the city itself. Tivadar, noting the collapse
of a major bridge between Buda and Pest, summoned George back
to Pest, judging that it would be much harder to come back later.
Even then, however, their personal adventures weren't quite over.
The violence hadn't yet reached their part of the city and for a while,
Tivadar continued his daily visits to Cafe Mienk, where he noted a
large presence of young Frenchmen, who presumably had escaped
from imprisonment or an internment camp in France and somehow made their way to Hungary, which may have been, for them, a
safer place. Observing them for a while, Tivadar was impressed by
their *esprit*, their elegance, and their ability to attract good-looking
young women. Impressed enough, in fact, to make them part of a
bold venture in which George was recruited as his father's interme-
diary. This involved a valuable gold bracelet entrusted to Tivadar by
an acquaintance who was hard up and asked if he could sell it for
her at a good price. Tivadar judged, correctly, that the French boys
might be interested in such a transaction; he also decided that it was
safer to send George on this errand than to go himself. Decades later
George explained, with just a hint of apology, that his father did this
because a young boy was less likely to be arrested, but Tivadar must
have had great faith in his son's ability to judge the situation as well.
Indeed, on this occasion, George had to make the kinds of instant
decisions in which his father specialized—whether, for example, to
entrust the bracelet to the "French boys" while they went looking for
a buyer. It turned out that his trust was not misplaced; after a long
wait, which made Tivadar increasingly anxious, George returned triumphant, money in hand. Perhaps this was an early initiation into
economic risk-taking, for which the future financier became so widely
renowned. Certainly, no risks were greater, and no decisions required
greater self-confidence, than those taken during the war.

But as the siege and bombardment of the city intensified, Tivadar
decided that going out on the street was becoming too dangerous;

and the next weeks were spent, together with his sons and his fellow conspirator Kozma, in the hiding place they had prepared in the earlier stages of the war. Even then, the Soros men didn't let themselves get dispirited. Stuck indoors, Tivadar and his sons played games involving geographical questions, and checking answers against large maps hanging on the wall. Not surprisingly, Tivadar kept winning these with great consistency, and at some point, George accused "Uncle Lexi" (referring to his father by his alias) of cheating. Tivadar, who clearly cared about his sons' opinions of him, took considerable umbrage at this, but allowed them to ask the questions from then on. After a few rounds of the game, Paul said there was an additional problem: Tivadar not only kept winning, but also "ate his winnings" by consuming tasty and hard to obtain cookies—and thus reduced the chances of the boys ever winning them back. This was followed by a serious debate on the rights and wrongs of the situation, in which George, in a clinching argument, told his father that for him and Paul this was "more a moral than a material question."

The refusal to be dispirited sustained the sequestered threesome through the deteriorating situation, the lack of food, the need to haul water from the outside, the broken windows that George tried to replace with cartons—thus risking being shot—and the inability to go down to the air raid shelter because Paul, who was clearly of draft age, might be recruited. But toward the end of the battle for Budapest, father and sons faced yet another, more serious moral test. While the fighting was going on, a young German soldier—he turned out to be seventeen years old and looked, in Tivadar's words, like "the very embodiment of that Aryanness whose fanatical adherents had sought to enslave people and exterminate races"[21]—accidentally made his way into the bathroom in their hiding place. Once he was discovered, the question, of course, was what to do with him. When the moment of decision arrived, "the eyes of 14-year-old George seemed filled with tears."[22] Tivadar offered the confused young man cigarettes and sent him out the way he came in. George's tears were clearly a response to an individual young man's plight; but perhaps, in that moment of great ambiguity, he was also influenced by Tivadar's principles and his refusal "to identify Hitler and what he stood for with the German spirit," or to blame a whole nation for what some, or even most, of its members had done.[23] Certainly, such principles were evident in much of George's later human rights work, which extended to many countries where factions of the population behaved inhumanely— but where others nevertheless needed and deserved protection.

The last encounter described in *Masquerade* announced the beginning of the war's endgame—although it did not immediately usher in anything resembling peace. On January 12, 1945, when the cry of "The Russians are coming!" was raised in the expectation of the oncoming German defeat, Tivadar found two Soviet officers outside their building and invited them in for tea. Thanks to his knowledge of Russian language and sensibility, acquired during his World War I adventure, he knew how to deal with his guests, and with problems that arose as the new victors took over and flaunted their power, sometimes in highly unpalatable ways. Wristwatches had to be surrendered on demand by anyone wearing them, and although Erzebet didn't talk about this at first, she was one of the many women who had the horrifying experience of being raped by Russian soldiers. George also remembered "perhaps the weirdest thirty-six hours" of his life, spent in a posh hotel where Erzebet's mother had been placed by Tivadar after she made her second escape from a hiding place and moved into one of the Yellow Star houses in the ghetto. In the hotel, they were tyrannized by a Russian soldier who refused to let them leave, accused Tivadar of being a spy because he spoke Russian, and alleged that George and Paul were parachutists because they didn't. The soldiers forced them to spend the night in a downstairs cellar with a strange collection of people, which included fascists and resistance fighters as well as a Russian who got very angry when he found in the morning that he overslept, and threatened to blow everyone up with a grenade.[24]

War is rarely over when its end is officially declared. The postwar period in Hungary, as elsewhere, had its share of chaos—and excitement. Hyperinflation reached levels unprecedented even during the Weimar period in Germany, and black market operations thrived. Tivadar, as usual, coped very well, and for a while worked as a translator for the Americans, who set up quarters at the Swiss embassy. Paul for a while traded sweaters for potatoes. George engaged in various more or less legitimate transactions, and gained early financial insights when he was asked by an acquaintance to exchange dollars for Hungarian currency and discovered that rates differed in various, hardly conventional venues (one of which was a market set up in a synagogue). He was therefore able to obtain a more advantageous rate for his client, and argued that in his role as broker, he deserved a higher cut. This, however, was refused, which provided another early lesson in the perils and advantages of various financial roles—although at this point in his development, George had no thoughts or fantasies of pursuing any of them.

What he did want to pursue was not yet at all clear. He had always been an avid reader, and his early ambitions involved politics, philosophy, journalism, and writing, although he apparently didn't think of studying any of them through formal education. Indeed, going back to school was not a happy experience. Some classmates were missing, and although segregation of Jewish students was no longer officially sanctioned, a group of non-Jewish students were quite aggressive. This was bigotry to which by then George would have been highly sensitized, and although he was clearly not of a pugilistic nature, he challenged one of his classmates to a boxing match—which he, rather satisfyingly, won.

Although George later remembered this period as one of continuing adventure, the accumulated tensions of the war (however well he was protected from its actual horrors) may have led to a buildup of internal anger. This was evident in a school newspaper (its one copy displayed on a wall), in which George was emulating the newspaper his father produced as a prisoner in Siberia—with the difference that his publication "attacked everybody. I attacked my history teacher. I accused him of corruption because he used to sell a magazine in class and everybody was expected to subscribe." When the teacher failed his unruly pupil, George retaliated by writing, "A good grade for a bank note. Only from Professor Takacs."[25]

It was perhaps experiences like these that, as he approached college age, prompted him to think about studying abroad—and his initial impulse was to go to the Soviet Union. This seemingly strange choice was propelled, he later told me, by his sense that "communism was very important" and he wanted to understand it. In this case, however, Tivadar decided to intervene. He had enough experiences of what had gone on in revolutionary Russia to know that this would be a dangerous step. George listened and decided to emigrate to Great Britain instead. This involved a very long wait for a passport and repeated letters to distant relatives who eventually agreed to take him in but gave him a very lukewarm welcome.

Altogether, after the drama of war and survival, life in London was weary, flat, stale, and unprofitable. He arrived there in the period of rations and bad coffee, without access to good universities or interesting people. His spoken English was not very proficient, and he kept being rejected by young women with whom he didn't know how to flirt. But the lessons of war and survival did not go unheeded: he had learned how to fend for himself, how to demand fair treatment when he was treated badly, and, occasionally, how to engage in small but advantageous financial transactions. He took jobs as a waiter (a role in which he was promised advancement to the position of assistant to head waiter if he worked hard enough!) and a swimming pool attendant, which not only brought him close to his favorite sport, but gave him ample time to read.

Throughout his time in London, George exchanged weekly letters with his family; here are some excerpts from one of the few available in English, in the Soros family archive:

Last week I thought that I would write a psychological letter. I did it: I wrote about you, although not with an overwhelming success. Yet I hope that my departure gave Pali [Paul] back his original position, that he had so much lacked since I had been born: the position of the only, if not the unique, child. And why could it not be that the difference between Pali and me was the cause of all the differences within the family? . . .

But what I planned to do last week did not concern you. I wanted to analyse myself. I needed it. I was discontent with something. I had to find out, with what? You know that hidden grievances are very dangerous: they disturb the whole countenance and are incurable as long they are hidden. The trouble with me was really not very serious. Yet, I do not like troubles with me, even in the small extent. . . . I am discontent, because I did not conquer England as I hoped. In all probability, I shall not conquer her. So I must resign myself to that.

I am discontent, because I have not found friends, I have not found a good company . . . but thousands of girls are running on the street and that makes my mouth water. I make great efforts but I am not attractive: I have no money, I do not speak English well enough, my interests are absolutely different from theirs. Moreover, I do not drive, I do not smoke and—I am afraid to dance . . . I am an austerity man. And I am astonished, because I never knew that before.

The letter is touching in its candor, and fascinating in its emphasis on internal states and the need for self-knowledge—as well as the trail of those early childhood conflicts.

While we now think of George Soros as a man of action, his intellectual as well as his inner life in this period was intense. After being enrolled in the "truly third-rate" Kentish Polytechnic, he managed to make his way (somewhat illicitly at first, as he wasn't officially admitted) to the London School of Economics, where, once he was officially accepted, he majored in economics, while nurturing his passion for philosophy and encountering such fascinating figures as Harold Laski and Karl Popper, who became his intellectual guiding light. Under Popper's influence, George wrote papers on "fallibility" and "reflexivity," which became his central philosophical concepts, but he was at that stage too shy to show these to his mentor. He also wrote a highly critical paper on Freud—perhaps to burnish his intellectual credentials—but was surprised when I mentioned it in our conversation. He said that he came to admire Freud's writings and ideas greatly, and eventually, during an anxious period, he entered into a short, modified psychoanalysis, which was apparently very successful. The specific reason for this, he told me, were problems with one of his own children, for which he took full responsibility. "I was too permissive," he said, adding that in this, too, he was trying to follow in Tivadar's footsteps.

In London, his practical situation gradually improved. He made friends and connected with a young woman who became his first girlfriend. Eventually, he got a job at a small, Hungarian-owned financial firm, where he started in a rather low-level position; but on that score, the rest is history.

In 1956, George emigrated to the United States, where Paul was already living; later that year, Tivadar and Erzebet, along with many others, made their risky escape from Hungary, following its tragically failed anti-communist uprising, and rejoined their sons in New York. There, they tried to establish themselves in ways that resembled their earlier life (attempting, for example, to set up a stand on the beach in Brooklyn selling coffee and pastries, as they did on Lupa Island). But Tivadar, for all his flexibility and ability to cope with new situations, found adjustment to American culture quite difficult. George recounts that during a job interview, his father was asked what he would like to accomplish at his potential place of employment. "I would like to start at the top and move to the bottom," Tivadar insouciantly responded, undoubtedly hoping to amuse. Instead, he failed to get the job. In late 1950s America, with its puritan ethic of hard work and upward striving, self-deprecating humor was not the way to get your foot in the corporate door.

Nevertheless, for George, Tivadar continued to be a lodestar. When I asked George whether he thought the idea of "fallibility" would have been useful for his father during the war—whether Tivadar could afford self-doubt as he had to make his life-or-death decisions—George replied simply that in addition to his sharp sense of judgment, Tivadar had "experience," and that made all the difference.

He was referring to the lessons of Tivadar's Russian experiences, which registered deeply in George's consciousness as well. This stood him in good stead when he decided to sponsor an Open Society Foundation in the Soviet Union—an undertaking, he told me, that he considers his "most important political involvement"—and which was the beginning of his own great adventure. In connection with this, he met the great Russian human rights activist Andrei Sakharov, who, on hearing about George's intentions, opined that his money "would soon line the KGB's coffers." In turn, George assured the famous dissident that he was "not an innocent American," and that he understood the Soviet Union better than most well-meaning but often very naive Western well-wishers. Indeed, he absorbed some of his own early lessons as well; it is amusing to see him (in a documentary film by Jesse Dylan about his international activities) offering his rather splendid watch to one of his Russian hosts, who had noticed it on George's wrist. Russian love of watches evidently survived many changes of regime.

The scope of George's pro-democracy work has been nothing short of mind-boggling, and his dedication to it unflagging. He is, of course, not unaware of the size of his achievements, but here too he pays tribute to Tivadar, saying that the Open Society Foundations are "a monument to my father" and to the principles he instilled in his sons early on. More than that, he thinks that his father's form of pragmatic altruism during the war was in a way more admirable than his own activities, because Tivadar "was more genuine in his contacts with people. I was operating on a level of abstraction." With a flicker of humor in his voice, he added, "My father dealt in retail, while I work in wholesale."

∽

THIS IS ENDEARINGLY self-deprecating; but if George values "retail" over "wholesale," that is because the personal is as important to him as the political—and he prefers the two to be closely interconnected. This, indeed, may have accounted at least in part for his startling change of direction in midlife. When I noted the rarity of his decision to stop engaging in financial activities, he said that being rich was "a liberation" because it gave him freedom to do what he wanted and to speak as he wished. Aside from finding the financial milieu frankly quite boring, he felt that working in it meant he had to be very careful about what he said. This was "a constraint" that he found highly discomfiting. "There is this big drive in me to speak freely," he told me—a statement that surely points to an impulse driving much of his work. Freedom of expression is a personal as well as a political principle.

But George added that if wealth can be a liberation, it also creates an obligation—to use it well and accomplish something meaningful. In his Open Society Foundations and many other humanitarian activities, he found a way to fulfill this obligation on a very grand scale and in ways that mattered to him most. And perhaps it was the intertwining of the personal and the political that made his efforts—in his own view—most successful in Central Europe. After all, he grew up there, and the sensibility, the modes of communication, and human relations in that region are familiar to him, making interpersonal understanding—on which so much depends—much easier. The place where he has been least successful in his own estimation is China—largely, he says, because "I didn't understand their culture." Culture, even in our globalized world, matters.

George and Paul were young enough when they emigrated to the United States to become completely acculturated there, but George, for one, has continued to value his Hungarian beginnings. When I noted that both Hungarian and Jewish cultures have contributed much more than their share of talented people to the world, George said, "Yes—and they are all of my generation." The wartime generation, in other words—whose experience of extremity was so informative about the human condition, and whose witnessing of destruction led to so much creativity. George also mused about an alternative scenario that might have come to fruition if Tivadar had his way before the war and sent Erzebet to the United States in 1939, promising to join her later. Erzebet refused to be separated, probably because she knew that Tivadar wanted her to leave in order to pursue a serious affair. But George is glad it didn't happen for a different reason—because then, he said, "I would have become a different person. And I am happy to be the person I am."

Origins matter, and the person George Soros has become is a multifaceted human being who has worked tirelessly to counter the worst tendencies in our collective life, whose consequences he witnessed firsthand in his childhood—and he is not ready to rest on his laurels yet.

The Financier

Sebastian Mallaby

GEORGE SOROS BECAME A FINANCIAL SPECULATOR at a time when finance and speculation barely existed. In the 1950s, the currency markets—scene of Soros's most memorable triumphs—were in a state of suspension: the value of the dollar was pegged to gold, and other currencies were pegged to the dollar. Most other speculative forums were similarly closed. Interest rates were regulated. Capital controls restrained traders from charging across borders. The markets for bonds and derivatives were shadows of their future selves. Even buying plain-vanilla shares in corporations could be a cumbersome business: an investor often had to find a willing counterparty and a mutually acceptable price "by appointment." And yet, in the course of half a century, Soros generated such vast speculative winnings that he could bestow billions on philanthropic causes. How this happened says much about the man and also about the era he embodied.

From the early part of his career, Soros developed three qualities that marked him out from his competitors. The first was an outlook that transcended national frontiers: he was a global figure long before the term "globalization" had entered the lexicon. His childhood in Hungary, his studies in the melting pot of the London School of Economics, his fluency in French and German: all taught him to see finance in cross-border terms, even when cross-border flows of capital were officially restricted. During his first years as a financial analyst, Soros grew wealthy by exploiting the distortions created by those capital controls. Later, he made a larger series of fortunes from the pressures arising from their removal.

Soros's second distinctive quality was a conviction that markets are inherently unstable. This set him apart from most financial thinkers of the period. In 1933 and 1944, Alfred Cowles, one of the founders of statistical economics, published two studies that laid the basis for the efficient market hypothesis, which posited that markets tend toward equilibrium. To be sure, market prices fluctuate as fresh information appears—word of an industrial breakthrough, a political crisis, a data release on the economy. But, according to the efficient market thinkers, markets respond to these bulletins by swiftly incorporating the new information into prices, which thus remain tethered to the fundamentals. After all, markets consist of experts whose job is to determine the fair value of assets. Rigorous objectivity keeps prices close to equilibrium.

Soros was ahead of his time in formulating sophisticated doubts about this consensus. His skepticism was rooted in his early exposure to Karl Popper, the Austrian philosopher who lectured at the London School of Economics after World War II. Popper's central contention was that human beings cannot fully apprehend the truth; the best they can do is to grope at it imperfectly. To someone of Soros's background, this notion had an obvious political appeal. It suggested that all dogmas were flawed: the Nazism and communism inflicted upon Soros's native Hungary each claimed an intellectual certainty to which neither was entitled. But Popper's insistence that reality is unknowable had implications for finance, too. The efficient market hypothesis presumes the existence of rational actors who drive prices to equilibrium. Soros had learned from Popper that no such heroes existed.

To Popper's emphasis on the limits to cognition, Soros added a further insight. Investors' actions change the behavior of the things they invest in. For example, enthusiasm about a company will drive its stock price up, allowing it to raise capital cheaply and thus perform better. Because of this self-fulfilling feedback loop, Soros realized, certainty was doubly elusive. First, financiers are incapable of perceiving reality clearly. Second, reality is itself affected by these unclear perceptions. Because of the interaction between these two forces, markets will sometimes swing far from equilibrium, completely losing touch with fundamental value. Soros dubbed this phenomenon "reflexivity," and his preoccupation with feedback loops led him to a view of markets that was radically at odds with the prevailing one.

Soros's third distinctive quality was related to the second. He had a feeling for risk: when to avoid it, when to embrace it. Stanley Druckenmiller, the trader who ran Soros's Quantum Fund from 1989 to 2000, regarded this sixth sense as Soros's most crucial skill: it was the quality that turned a good speculator into an outstanding one. Perhaps a bit surprisingly, successful financiers can be wrong about the direction of prices as often as they are right. Their profits come from weighting their winning trades more heavily than their losing ones. Because of his gift for risk assessment, Soros played with these weightings to an unusual degree. When he felt a powerful conviction about a particular trade, he aggressively increased its size; anticipating the insights later popularized by behavioral science, he overcame the natural instinct to cash in a winning bet early. Indeed, when he started to win, he often doubled down on a position.

Where did Soros's feeling for risk come from? Soros himself has pointed to the insecurity of his childhood: a Jewish boy growing up under Nazi occupation learned to live with the fear of losing everything. There is no doubt that this insecurity—the imperative of survival—helps to explain Soros's ambition and intense drive, but when it comes to his facility with risk-taking, another factor was at work as well. For Soros, speculation that would have felt terrifying to most people instead felt reasonable. In fact, in an intellectual sense, it could feel reassuring. Because of Soros's distinctive understanding of markets—his belief that they stray far from equilibrium until a shock forces a reversal—he was not afraid to bet that existing asset prices were radically out of whack. Where conventional thinkers might flinch, restrained by the belief that far-from-equilibrium situations should theoretically not occur, Soros greeted such situations as confirmation of his faith in reflexivity. Primed by his philosophy to expect dramatic market overshoots, he was psychologically prepared to extract every last dollar from them.

Thanks to these three qualities—a global outlook, a belief in market inefficiency, and a steely confidence in handling risk—Soros earned a remarkable fortune in a remarkable manner. Other tycoons amass billions by building institutions: think of Sam Walton of Walmart or Jeff Bezos of Amazon. Even within the world of money management, the great fortunes have generally been made by companies that achieve scale, such as BlackRock or PIMCO, or by companies that develop trading algorithms—that is, precise insights about patterns in markets that can be milked repeatedly. But Soros dispensed with all this paraphernalia. He built no company, developed no algorithm, possessed no intellectual property that could be bottled and sold. He made money—extraordinary amounts—from what he mysteriously called the "alchemy" of finance.

SOROS BEGAN HIS financial career at Singer & Friedlander, a Hungarian-owned brokerage in London. Hired in 1955 with the help of a family connection, he was a lowly and rather careless bookkeeper earning seven pounds per week, or about $230 in today's money.[1] But, from the start, Soros found himself among immigrants who took a global view. As his biographer, Michael T. Kaufman, tells us, one of Soros's first bosses at Singer was a gold specialist who tracked mining shares in Johannesburg, Brussels, Paris, and London, buying them wherever they were cheapest and selling them at a markup to clients in other countries. Singer & Friedlander applied the same principle of "international arbitrage" to oil stocks and industrial stocks, and Soros moved between departments, picking up trading tricks and contacts.

His first investment coup involved the initial public offering of shares in the Ford Motor Company. The company's bankers placed stock with investors in Europe as well as in the United States, but Soros spotted that demand in the home market was overwhelmingly higher. At his urging, Singer bought up Ford shares in London and sold them at a handsome markup in New York. Soros's seven pounds per week abruptly jumped to twelve pounds.

In September 1956, Soros left his job in London and set sail for America. He had fallen out with the senior partners at Singer, and a young American colleague had arranged for him to work at his father's small brokerage in New York, a firm called F.M. Mayer. In hiring Soros, Mayer's intention was to replicate Singer's success in international arbitrage, a business whose profitability was almost guaranteed by the post–World War II financial architecture. To protect the system of fixed exchange rates created at the Bretton Woods Conference in 1944, cross-border investment flows were restricted, and this segregation of national capital markets ensured that identical securities fetched different prices in different countries. For an enterprising broker with international connections, there were opportunities to buy low and sell high via discreet private arrangements.

When Soros arrived at F.M. Mayer, the big excitement was oil stocks. Egypt's government had seized control of the Suez Canal, a crucial link in the world's oil shipping routes. In October 1956, the British and French governments launched an ill-conceived attempt to take it back by military force. Oil prices fluctuated wildly, and Soros parlayed his international connections into profitable trading. Using his contacts from his time at Singer, he obtained commitments from brokers in London, which arrived as coded strings of letters, often via phone calls to Soros's apartment in the middle of the night. Then he circulated these offerings in New York, announcing them on the "pink sheets" that were distributed daily to brokerage firms. International arbitrage was beginning to earn Soros real money.

Sometimes the arbitrage involved ingenious improvisation. For example, the shares of a Canadian company, Northspan Uranium, were traded only in Canada. But Northspan had sold bonds to US investors, and these came packaged with warrants that conferred the right to acquire shares of Northspan at a set price in the future. Soros and a colleague at F.M. Mayer had the idea of detaching the warrants: they sold the bonds to a reputable broker that issued a "due bill," a promise to deliver Northspan shares once the warrants were exercised. Because the broker was a bond specialist with no interest in warrants, Soros got these due bills "for chicken crap," as one of his trading allies later put it.[2] Having thus effectively purchased Northspan shares at a deep discount and locked in a certain profit, Soros repeated the procedure with other companies that issued warrants. Because his firm lacked the capital to hold the resulting inventory of due bills, he cut deals with deep-pocketed investment houses, including Morgan Stanley in New York and S.G. Warburg in London. When the warrants matured, Soros and his collaborators reaped a fortune. The more successful Soros grew, the richer his network of connections.

In 1959, Soros quit Mayer in favor of the more exalted firm of Wertheim & Co. There he came up with another can't-lose trade, which was again predicated on his capacity to look at the world globally. Charged with researching European stocks, Soros traveled frequently across the Atlantic, where he put his connections and his language skills to work, and pretty soon he found that West Germany's listed firms harbored profitable secrets. Soros discovered that Dresdner Bank owned a portfolio of German industrial shares whose value exceeded Dresdner's own market capitalization. Effectively, Soros could buy $1 of Dresdner stock and get $2 worth of Germany Inc.—it was the closest thing to a sure bet you could dream of in the stock market. What's more, Dresdner was not an isolated case: Germany's insurers owned even larger portfolios of unnoticed assets. For example, the Munich-based insurance giant Allianz owned a hoard of German equities worth three times more than Allianz's own stock. Buying $1 of Allianz gave you fully $3 of Germany Inc.

Meanwhile Soros identified more bargains in Sweden. Here, the anomaly was that sleepy local investors treated stocks like bonds: they bought them purely to receive the dividends. By convention, both the dividends and the stock prices were fixed, no matter how profitable the companies. The result was that shares in thriving industrial empires could be had on the cheap—except that capital controls prevented foreign investors from buying them. Adapting the tricks he had learned at Singer & Friedlander, Soros came up with a way around this obstacle. In 1960, noticing that the Swedish telecommunications company Ericsson was listing its shares in London, Soros seized the opportunity to buy Ericsson stock in Britain and resell it in Sweden, thereby arming himself with a pot of Swedish krona. He then used the krona to buy shares in the ball-bearing manufacturer SKF, the most radically undervalued of Sweden's industrial companies. Because of SKF's size and profitability, Soros could place its shares with foreign clients at a 100 percent markup. Thanks to his worldly outlook and his language skills, he was generating almost risk-free profits.[3]

At the end of 1962, Soros shifted firms again, this time to Arnhold & S. Bleichroeder. It was another step up: the Bleichroeder side of the partnership had once served Imperial Germany's chancellor Otto von Bismarck. But before moving to his new employer, Soros negotiated a sabbatical: he wanted to work on his philosophy. All through his time at F.M. Mayer and Wertheim, he had labored privately over a sprawling and unpublished tract, and now he thought he had a chance to impose a publishable shape on it. To Soros's lasting frustration, this abstract endeavor never won him the recognition he craved. But his devotion would pay off in other ways. Having thus far flourished as a financier because of his international outlook, Soros was entering an era in which his philosophical training would become relevant.

ALL FINANCIERS HAVE to adapt if they are to succeed over a span of decades. The methods that work in one period won't work in the next, either because rivals get wise to your tricks and compete away your profits, or because something in the wider world disrupts your business. In the early 1960s, Soros experienced both kinds of setbacks. During his time at Wertheim, Soros had been one of just two or three brokers in America conducting firsthand equity research in Europe. But now international arbitrage became known to a wider circle of professionals; between 1960 and 1963, American holdings of foreign shares grew by more than a third. Then, in July 1963, the policy environment shifted. To dampen capital outflows, which had the effect of putting downward pressure on the dollar and threatening its peg to gold, President John F. Kennedy persuaded Congress to impose a levy on U.S. purchases of foreign securities. Soros's lucrative specialty was taxed out of existence. International arbitrage was over.

For the next three years, Soros made himself comfortable at Bleichroeder and did rather little. He sold some of his US clients' European holdings back to the Europeans. He continued to work on his philosophy, which he described as "the core of my being."[4] But in 1966, he emerged from his shell. Wall Street was in the midst of an inebriating boom, unlike any since the 1920s. *Fortune* reported on the invention of a new kind of financial outfit known as the "hedged fund," which doubled up its market bets by borrowing money. Finding himself at an impasse in his philosophical efforts, Soros resolved to join in the fun. He created what he called a model portfolio, comprising capital of $100,000 from Bleichroeder and an equal amount from Alberto Foglia, an enterprising Italian broker with whom he had worked on a lucrative deal a few years earlier. Then he divided the $200,000 into sixteen "slots" and hunted for investments to fill each of them.

In view of Soros's later methods, the model portfolio's design showed how much he didn't yet know. Creating sixteen equally sized slots was exactly what the mature Soros would avoid, since it discouraged weightier bets on the better ideas. In another sense, however, the model portfolio offered a flavor of what was to come. Soros was no longer exploiting his worldliness to buy blatantly undervalued Swedish equities, nor was he making can't-lose bets on Canadian warrants. Rather, his plan was to buy US securities in the midst of a stock market frenzy, shifting from the relative certainty of international arbitrage into the far riskier territory of Wall Street speculation. There was no lack of competition, and no obvious bargains to be found. But Soros would still perform spectacularly.

Thanks to Antonio Foglia, Alberto's son, some documents relating to the model portfolio have survived for posterity. A monthly update from Soros to his backers, dated November 1967, reports that the portfolio is up an astonishing 81 percent over the previous year, trouncing the 9 percent return from the Dow Jones Industrial Average. Almost as striking, the update offers a window onto Soros's intellectual methods, suggesting the eclectic, autodidactic, and self-certain tone that he also brought to his philosophy. In the opening passage of the update, Soros comments dizzyingly on inflation, the tax outlook, the budget deficit, monetary policy, and an expected clamp-down on speculative borrowing. He then shifts abruptly from big-picture economics to small-bore accounting, observing that McLean Trucking has reported a thirteen-cent decline in earnings per share in the third quarter, "but it seems to have escaped attention that $.10 of the drop was due to higher taxes in the absence of an investment credit."[5] Just as Soros's philosophy jumped digressively from modern art to Russian politics and from fallibility to Freud, so his financial thinking encompassed a full panorama. He was equally adept with the wide-angle and the close-up. If he had an advantage over his rivals, it evidently lay in the sheer sweep of his analysis.

The most extensive Foglia document is a report on the trucking industry.[6] Much of it is devoted to worthy equity analysis: in a section entitled "Current Outlook," Soros lays out how the industry is stuck between rising wages and falling tariffs, a grim pincer attack that had recently caused trucking stocks to fall by a third. But in other parts of the report, Soros displays an ability to construct an alternative, idealized vision, describing not what is actually happening, but rather what logically should happen. Like a philosopher piling syllogism upon syllogism, Soros builds his theory of the future. And although his style of expression is midcentury formal, a time traveler from the PowerPoint age might express his logic as follows:

Fact: *Trucking tariffs are regulated.*

Fact: *Regulators set tariffs so as to protect weak operators.*

Implication: *Regulators will set tariffs that are more than generous to efficient operators.*

Further implication: *Over time, efficient operators will accumulate enough earnings to buy out weak rivals.*

Conclusion: *The industry will consolidate and the winners will seek listings on the New York Stock Exchange.*

Investment thesis: *Large institutional investors will purchase the winners' shares and early speculators will be handsomely rewarded.*

Soros's ability to keep two pictures in his head—the real one and the idealized one—allowed him to form a powerful speculative conviction. His rivals were fixated on what was actually happening; Soros added his vision of what he thought should happen. Again, Soros's philosophy shaped his approach. He believed in his model of how things should work because he had trained himself relentlessly to inhabit such models.

Departing somewhat from the spirit of his sixteen-slot model portfolio, Soros expressed his conviction in his trucking thesis by devoting four of the slots to leading haulers. Initially their stocks declined: the pincer-attack part of Soros's report had been accurate. But, after a year or so, Soros's idealized logic also proved correct. In 1968, one of his trucking picks, Transcon, staged its debut on the New York Stock Exchange, exactly as Soros had predicted. And although the precise fate of the other three picks is lost to memory, Soros believes that all did well.[7] To adapt a phrase from Henry Kissinger, vision overcame reality.

The model portfolio's success provided Soros with a springboard for his next career jump. At the end of 1967, Bleichroeder invited clients to invest in a Soros-managed fund, which was dubbed First Eagle. Two years later, Bleichroeder followed up with a second, larger Soros fund called Double Eagle, which adopted the "hedged" structure described in the pages of *Fortune*. As well as allowing Soros to magnify his bets with borrowed money, the hedge fund format (the "d" at the end of "hedged" was by now forgotten) gave him immense trading freedom. He could buy the stocks of promising companies, just as he had always done, but he could also "short" the stocks of unpromising ones—that is, he could profit from their decline by borrowing their shares, selling them, and buying them back at a lower price later. The hedge fund structure also liberated Soros to bet on bonds or any other instruments that came along. The constrained financial climate of the postwar years was loosening up. It was a great time to be a speculator.

IN SOROS'S IMAGINED VISION of the trucking companies' future, one argument had been notable by its absence. Soros had failed to observe that the stronger operators, being perceived as stronger, would find it easy to raise capital, speeding their acquisition of weak rivals. This type of reasoning, emphasizing the way that perceptions influence reality, was already at the core of Soros's philosophy. But although Soros had benefited from his philosophic training by constructing abstract models of the future, he had yet to apply the substance of his philosophy to finance.

This changed in the late 1960s. Following the coup with the trucking industry, flawed perceptions—the limits to human cognition that Karl Popper had emphasized—became a central plank of Soros's investment method. He would latch onto an error of perception and probe its effects, searching for cases where the error led to a result that in turn led to further error, setting up a feedback loop. The first step in this analysis—the recognition of a flawed perception—was not especially distinctive; the same notion crops up repeatedly in the thinking of Soros's hedge fund contemporary Michael Steinhardt. It was the second step—the identification of feedback loops—that gave Soros an investment edge. "When I identified the makings of a self-reinforcing process, I could almost feel my mouth water like one of Pavlov's dogs," he later wrote.[8] "This is where the philosophy took on a practical application," he added.[9]

A boom-bust cycle in US conglomerates provided the first test of this new method. Soros began with the observation that investors assigned high price/earnings multiples to companies with rapidly growing earnings per share. For example, a star company with $10 million in earnings might have a price/earnings multiple of 20, and therefore a market capitalization of $200 million. Meanwhile, a stodgier company with the same $10 million in earnings might have a multiple of just 10, yielding a market capitalization of $100 million. So far, so logical: investors are supposed to anticipate the future, and the star company merits a high market capitalization because it will grow into it. But amid the merger boom of the late 1960s, Soros noticed an anomaly. If the star company bought the stodgy company, the star-stodge hybrid might be expected to justify a compromise multiple of 15, so that its merged earnings of $20 million would result in a market capitalization of $300 million—the same as the combined value of the two companies before the acquisition. But investors, excited to see the star's earnings double, tended to apply a multiple of at least 20 to the hybrid, meaning that the combined earnings of $20 million would generate a market capitalization of at least $400 million. Because of this error of perception, the merger would conjure $100 million in corporate value out of thin air.

Having diagnosed this alchemy, Soros proceeded to step two of his analysis. He observed that the merged company would use its inflated stock price as a sort of supercurrency with which to purchase more rivals. With each acquisition, the conglomerate's exalted price/earnings multiple would be applied to a larger quantum of earnings, resulting in a higher share price and hence an even greater ability to gobble up other companies. In this way, the initial flawed perception would set off a reflexive cycle. The conglomerate's market value would spiral upward. At some point, it would be so utterly divorced from fundamentals that it would crash back down again.

Soros's methodology mattered because of its implications for his speculative timing. A conventional investor, observing that the market was assigning an irrational price/earnings multiple to a conglomerate, might have immediately anticipated a fall in the value of its shares. Soros, observing that the market's flawed perception would reinforce itself, drew the opposite conclusion: at least for a while, a conglomerate's excessive valuation would drive up its value further. Equipped with this counterintuitive insight, Soros rode conglomerate stocks such as LTV Corporation and Teledyne as the bubble inflated, then profited a second time by shorting their shares as they crashed down again. The swings in both directions were wild. Between 1966 and 1968, LTV's share price rose roughly tenfold; between 1968 and 1970, it returned to its starting point. Soros recorded the vindication of his conceptual framework in *The Alchemy of Finance*, his dense attempt to explain his market philosophy, published in 1987. "Events followed the sequence described in my model," he wrote. "Multiples expanded and eventually reality could not sustain expectations."[10]

The beauty of Soros's conceptual framework was that it could be applied in multiple settings. In February 1970, hot on the heels of his success with the conglomerates, Soros published an investment note on a similar boom-bust dynamic in real estate investment trusts. The note is important because it provides an authentic, contemporaneous window on Soros's preoccupation with feedback loops, refuting skeptics who dismiss Soros's philosophizing as an after-the-fact rationalization of his speculative successes. "The conventional method of security analysis is to try and predict the future course of earnings and then to estimate the price that investors may be willing to pay for those earnings," Soros declared. "This method is inappropriate... because the price that investors are willing to pay for the shares is an important factor in determining the future course of earnings." The key to successful speculation in real estate trusts lies in the theory of reflexivity, Soros was saying: the value that investors perceive will drive the actual value that the trusts generate, which in turn will further affect investor perceptions. "We shall try to predict the future course of the entire self-reinforcing process," Soros promised.[11]

Following his usual approach, Soros began by pointing out an error of perception. Investors in real estate trusts assume that their performance is driven by the yield from the buildings they finance. But the truth is that the trusts' performance often reflects a Ponzi dynamic. When investors perceive the trusts to be performing well, the trusts can issue new shares at a premium, and the very act of doing so increases the per-share value for those who invested earlier. To illustrate: A trust might issue a hundred shares initially, charging $1 for each share and parking the proceeds of $100 in a bank account. Then, if investors grow enthusiastic, the trust will be able to issue another hundred shares, this time at $3 apiece; it will then have a total of 200 shares outstanding and $400 in its bank account. Without financing so much as a single building, the book value per share will have doubled from $1 to $2. Positive perceptions, and nothing else, will have handed the first round of investors a windfall profit.

Soros then proceeded to the next step in his analysis. As the trusts do well and attract additional investments, more capital will flow into the real estate sector. Initially, this will cause a boom in property values, adding further fuel to the boom phase of the reflexive cycle. In time, however, so much capital will crowd into the sector that marginal construction projects will be financed. The property market will be oversupplied. Eventually, a bust will follow.

As with the conglomerates, Soros's mental model had implications for his speculative timing. Even though he regarded the real estate trusts as bubble-prone and unstable, he was not going to steer clear of them, as conventional investors might. To the contrary, because he saw that flawed perceptions would initially be self-fulfilling, he bought trust shares aggressively. Sure enough, in the month or so after the investment note's publication, the shares almost doubled, and Soros notched up yet another killing. Later, after some missteps and hesitations, Soros shorted the trusts to profit from the down leg of the cycle.

By borrowing to magnify this second trade, he generated a profit that exceeded 100 percent of the capital committed to it.

∾

BY THE EARLY 1970s, Soros's three distinctive qualities were more or less established. He had a global outlook, a sophisticated diagnosis of market inefficiency, and an ability to assume risk. He had discovered the ideal vehicle for his talents: the hedge fund structure, which afforded unbounded freedom to apply his conceptual framework to any industrial sector or financial instrument. "There was no limit to what you could do," Soros recalled. "You could sell short, you could buy, you could leverage."[12]

There was only one cloud on the horizon. At Bleichroeder, Soros was advising brokerage clients at the same time as he was running his funds, which meant there was a potential conflict of interest. In the case of the real estate investment trusts, Bleichroeder distributed Soros's investment note to its customers, encouraging them to buy into the trusts even as the Soros funds already held them. Soros realized the note's impact when he received a call from a bank in Cleveland, asking for an additional copy because its original version had been rendered illegible by repeated photocopying. Soros was perilously close to infringing the regulations that prevented market operators from hyping their own books. He would have to make a choice: continue as a Bleichroeder broker or become a full-time hedge-funder.

In 1973, Soros reluctantly set up his own investment shop, Soros Fund Management. He rented an office a block away from his apartment on Central Park West, bringing along a lieutenant from Bleichroeder, an irascible, workaholic analyst named Jim Rogers. Some $13 million of the $20 million in the Bleichroeder Double Eagle fund followed Soros out the door, and for the next several years he racked up an extraordinary record.[13] With the exception of 1975, he outperformed the S&P 500 market index every year, and usually by a wide margin. In 1976, 1978, and 1979, his fund was up by more than 50 percent. In 1980 it was up by 102 percent. By the start of 1981, the Soros Fund, now renamed the Quantum Fund, had accumulated assets of $381 million, and Soros himself boasted a personal fortune of $100 million. Rivals expressed their admiration by echoing Ilie Nastase's tribute to Björn Borg: "We're playing tennis and he's playing something else." A profile in *Institutional Investor* called Soros "the world's greatest money manager."[14]

The key to Soros's extraordinary performance in these years lay in the third of his distinctive qualities, his willingness to take risk, which he deepened and expanded. Other parts of his investment method were more or less unchanged. Soros remained deliberately broad in his outlook: stocks, bonds, and commodities were all fair game, and the fund might take positions long or short. Likewise, Soros continued to seek out dynamic, far-from-equilibrium situations, homing in on areas where a dramatic correction appeared probable. But the novelty was that, when Soros found such a situation, he was now willing to bet the store. He was no longer operating out of someone else's firm, so there were no risk-management rules to restrain him. The success of the conglomerate and real estate trades had reinforced his faith in his investment judgment.

Judging from the scanty record of Soros Fund Management's first years, this faith was what converted a solid set of market insights into exceptional performance. For example, Soros spotted that traditionally inert bank stocks were poised to take off, partly because of financial deregulation and partly because of a rising cohort of bank executives who were far more ambitious than their predecessors. This was a smart but hardly dazzling insight; what distinguished Soros was the use he made of it. Other traders no doubt saw the same opportunity, established prudent positions, and grew their capital by 5 percent. Soros went all in and made 50 percent.[15] A similar pattern followed the Arab-Israeli War of 1973. Rogers pointed out to Soros that the Soviet weaponry used by Egypt had proved more formidable than expected; it followed that the Pentagon would embark on catch-up investments, rendering defense stocks attractive. Again, this was a solid insight, and Soros surely cannot have been the only speculator to see it. Rather, what distinguished Soros was that he plunged in hard, buying positions in multiple defense companies. In one especially gutsy move, he became the single-largest outside shareholder in the aerospace contractor Lockheed.

Underscoring the extent to which risk appetite could matter more than research, Soros was willing to place bets before taking the time to build the evidence that might support them. If he found an investment idea attractive on cursory examination, he figured that others would be seduced, too; as a student of reflexivity, he reasoned that superficial plausibility might be enough to render his bet profitable. One time, on a skiing vacation in Switzerland, Soros bought the *Financial Times* at the bottom of the chair lift, read about the British government's plan to bail out Rolls-Royce on the way up, and called his broker from the top of the mountain with an order to sell British government bonds. The remarkable fact was not that Soros saw the logic for doing this—presumably, any trader could see that a large corporate bailout implied increased government borrowing, which in turn implied higher interest rates and a bond-market sell-off. Rather, the remarkable fact was that Soros was willing to act on the spur of the moment—and from the side of a mountain. His motto was "Invest First, Investigate Later."[16]

If Soros's risk appetite held the key to his success, it eventually exhausted him. However much he believed in his approach to markets, there was no denying the psychological toll of putting his neck on the line repeatedly. In the old days, when he had engaged in international arbitrage and other can't-lose trades, it had not required much courage to go all-in. Now Soros was betting on his speculative perceptions about other people's speculative perceptions: going all-in required special reserves of conviction. The fear of a catastrophic trading loss sometimes made him paranoid. Then he felt paranoid that if he ceased to be paranoid his performance would suffer. His obsession with his trading took on a creepy, physical aspect: he saw himself as a sick person with a parasitic fund swelling inexorably inside his body, and if trouble was stirring in his portfolio, his back would seize up, driving him to take risk off the table. Throughout the 1960s, Soros had balanced his investment life with his writing, and in later years writing would resume its natural place near the center of his activities. But during the early years of Soros Fund Management, he had no time to breathe. "It was extremely preoccupying and very strenuous, and sometimes extremely painful," he would recall.[17]

At the start of the 1980s, Soros resolved that his pace was unsustainable. He paid off the irascible Rogers and began to look for new partners to whom he could delegate responsibility. The distraction of the search caused the collapse in performance he had feared: In 1981 the Quantum Fund was down 23 percent, its first loss ever. Several clients withdrew what was left of their money. A humiliated Soros took a break from the markets.

WHEN SOROS RETURNED to full-time investing in 1984, it was with a new sense of balance. During his midlife crisis, a psychoanalyst had helped him to slay some of his demons. He recognized his success and permitted himself to relax, knowing that doing so might kill the golden goose, but also knowing that not doing so would render success pointless. He compared this psychological transformation to a painful surgery he had endured to extract a hard ball of calcium from his salivary gland. Once the stone had been removed and exposed to the air, it crumbled to powder. "That is what happened to my hang-ups," Soros recalled. "Somehow, they dissolved when they were brought to light."[18]

With his life under control, Soros began to write again. Starting in August 1985, he kept a diary of his investment thinking, hoping it would help to hone his methods. The resulting "real-time experiment" is dense, repetitive, and filled with complex ruminations about scenarios that fail to materialize. But because it is free of the biases that afflict retrospective explanations of success, the diary is a true portrait of the speculator at work. Fortuitously, it also captures a key moment in Soros's trading life—a bet against the dollar that he described as "the killing of a lifetime."

The background to the dollar trade was the collapse of the controlled order that Soros had grown up in. The United States had abandoned the gold standard in 1971, and by the end of the decade the leading economies were dismantling the capital controls that inhibited cross-border trading. Coming on top of the invention of the hedge fund format, the resulting birth of the global currency markets transformed the possibilities for speculators. For the first time since World War II, money managers could bet on shifts in exchange rates, and other early hedge-funders such as Bruce Kovner of Caxton Associates were quick to exploit the opportunities. It is likely that Soros experimented in this new market in the 1970s, too; but partly because he had taken a break from writing, no record exists of such trading. (Asked whether he remembers speculating on currencies in the 1970s, Soros is apt to joke that he can only remember the future.) Whatever the case, the journal entries of 1985 show that by this point Soros was fascinated by exchange rates.

The fascination began with that tingling sense that he was out of step with the prevailing consensus. The standard view, as Soros wrote in his diary, was that currency markets, like equity markets, tend toward equilibrium. If the dollar is overvalued, US exports will suffer and US imports will be boosted. The resulting trade deficit will cause foreigners to need fewer dollars to buy American goods than vice versa. The relatively low demand for the dollar will drive its value down, cutting the trade deficit until the system is restored to balance. In the traditional view, moreover, speculators are in no position to disrupt this process. If they anticipate the currency's future path correctly, they will merely accelerate its arrival at the equilibrium point. If they judge wrong, they will slow its correction—but the delay will not persist because the speculators will lose money.

The way Soros saw things, this equilibrium theory failed to explain how currencies behaved in practice. Between 1982 and 1985, the United States had run a growing trade deficit, implying a weak demand for dollars; but over this period, the dollar had *strengthened*. Contrary to the prevailing argument, speculative flows of capital were fully capable of pushing the dollar up for a sustained period. The reason lay in reflexivity: a rise in the dollar tended to be self-reinforcing. Seeing the dollar appreciate, speculators would rush to buy it so as to profit from the trend; the trade fundamentals would not matter. Eventually, the dollar's prolonged strength would result in a trade deficit large enough to overwhelm the speculators' bias. The market would swivel 180 degrees, and a new trend of self-reinforcing dollar weakness would begin in earnest.

On August 16, 1985, when Soros began his real-time experiment, the challenge was how to judge the timing of this reversal. President Ronald Reagan had reshuffled his administration at the start of his second term, and the new team, led by Secretary of the Treasury James Baker, appeared determined to bring the dollar down to cut the US trade deficit. The fundamentals, insofar as they were relevant, reinforced these political signals: interest rates were falling, making it unrewarding for speculators to hold dollars. If the combination of political action and low interest rates could persuade even a few speculators to abandon the greenback, the upward trend in the currency could be broken. In the mature phase of a cycle, all the speculators who want to ride the trend have already climbed aboard. There are hardly any buyers left, so it takes only a few sellers to set off a market reversal.

Soros agonized about whether a dollar turn was imminent. If US growth accelerated, interest rates would rise, making a reversal less likely. On the other hand, US banks were in a parlous state following defaults in Latin America; if the banks entered a cycle of credit contraction, in which reduced lending and falling collateral values fed back on themselves, the drag on the economy would push interest rates down, making a dollar reversal more likely. Surveying these contradictory arguments, Soros seemed momentarily at a loss: "Who am I to judge?" he wondered to his journal. But then he answered his question: "The only competitive edge I have is the theory of reflexivity."[19] The theory encouraged him to assign particular importance to the risk of a self-reinforcing banking mess. With that, he resolved to bet against the dollar.

Despite the doubts that he expressed in his journal, Soros plunged decisively. As of August 16, Quantum owned $720 million worth of the main currencies against which the dollar would fall—the yen, the German mark, and sterling—an exposure that exceeded all the equity in the fund by a margin of $73 million. Gone were the days of the sixteen-slot model portfolio; his appetite for concentrated bets had become startling. "As a general rule, I try not to exceed 100 percent of the Fund's equity capital in any one market," he remarked breezily in his diary, "but I tend to adjust my definition of what constitutes a market to suit my current thinking."[20]

Three weeks later, on September 9, Soros's second diary entry reported that his experiment had begun badly. A batch of bullish US economic indicators had increased the chances that the Fed might raise interest rates; this had buoyed the dollar, and Quantum's bearish bet had cost the fund $20 million. Soros duly embarked on another bout of soul-searching, now adding a further dimension to his analysis. Putting himself in the shoes of Fed policy makers, he argued that interest rates were likely to stay low even if the economy strengthened. Normally, a strong economy threatened inflation, leading the Fed to push rates up. But given the backdrop of Latin American defaults, the Fed would hold off on raising interest rates because of its responsibility as a bank regulator—the last thing that wobbly lenders needed was more expensive capital. Soros added that the Fed would have room not to raise interest rates because Reagan's reshuffled administration was determined to rein in the budget deficit, relieving inflationary pressure. All this added up to an investment view. Soros would stick with his gutsy currency bet, though he resolved to abandon half of it if he continued to lose money.[21]

If Soros had blinked after his initial loss, his life story might have turned out differently. But Soros did not blink—and the prize arrived quickly. Less than two weeks after the second diary entry, on September 22, 1985, Secretary Baker assembled his counterparts from France, West Germany, Japan, and Britain at the Plaza Hotel in New York. Together the five powers promised coordinated intervention in currency markets to push the dollar downward. Naturally, the markets responded. The news of the Plaza Accord delivered Soros an immediate profit of $30 million.

This, however, was merely the beginning. The Plaza Hotel meeting ended on a Sunday, when US dealers were enjoying their weekends. Soros immediately called brokers in Hong Kong, where it was already Monday morning, with orders to buy additional yen for his portfolio. He continued to build his bet against the dollar for the rest of the week: by Friday he had added $209 million to his holdings of yen and German marks, and had established an extra $107 million worth of short positions in the dollar.[22] Everything Soros knew about reflexive feedback loops argued that the dollar would keep falling once it reversed. Rather than cashing in his bet, Soros piled on harder.

Needless to say, there was a risk in this aggression. The Plaza communiqué was thin on actionable detail; it depended on the uncertain commitment of governments to follow up with concrete measures.[23] But more than any other New York fund manager, Soros had a web of political contacts in Washington and abroad: not for the first time, his global outlook came in useful. His contacts in Japan and Europe encouraged him to believe that Plaza's signatories were serious, and besides, there was a further consideration. The dollar presented what speculators call an asymmetric bet: even if you thought that the probabilities of the dollar rising or falling were balanced, the *size* of any rise would be modest, whereas a fall could be dramatic. After all, the dollar was already overvalued—both politics and the fundamentals argued for a fall—and the main thing propping it up was self-fulfilling speculation. If the prevailing bias among speculators had been reversed by the Plaza Accord, the dollar might fall a long way. If the prevailing bias had not been dislodged, the dollar might hold firm; but there was not much room for it to appreciate. It followed that a bet against the dollar could earn Soros a fortune or lose him a negligible amount. It would be like betting on a 50-50 coin flip, except that a correct bet would be rewarded by a five-to-one payout.

His nerves steeled by this insight, Soros added another $500 million worth of yen and German marks and almost $300 million of additional bets against the dollar.[24] "I have assumed maximum market exposure in all directions," he recorded in his diary.[25] By leveraging his bets with borrowed money, Soros had effectively wagered three times his total capital on one trading conviction.

Soros's next journal entry, in December 1985, reviewed a dramatic four-month period. It had begun with a hypothesis that the dollar was ripe for reversal; it culminated with the theory's confirmation. His repeated conjectures about a crisis in the banking system had turned out to be a red herring. "The outstanding feature of my predictions is that I keep on expecting developments that do not materialize," he admitted.[26] But the errors had been dwarfed by one central success. Soros had understood that nothing more substantial than slippery perceptions had driven up the dollar, and therefore that a trigger could set off a reversal. Because he had grasped the system's instability, he had understood the Plaza Accord's meaning faster than others. A political jolt had kick-started a new trend, which would now feed on itself and become self-sustaining. In the four months from August, the value of Soros's fund jumped by 35 percent, a gain of $230 million. Convinced that the act of writing his diary had contributed to his performance, Soros joked that his profit represented the highest honorarium ever received by an author.[27]

The Plaza Accord triumph reflected all three of Soros's distinctive qualities. Currency trading was by its nature global, and Soros had been a global thinker before most New York money managers could point out Tokyo on a map. Currency trading was also the perfect proving ground for Soros's theories of reflexivity: he was correct that currencies overshoot fundamentals, and in time academic economists would come around to this conclusion as well.[28] Finally, currency trading rewarded speculators with a keen feeling for risk. Soros's bet against the dollar had shown that an individual with a tiny team of traders could earn as much as a large company. But doing so required the guts to assume "maximum market exposure."[29]

There was something else about the Plaza trade that proved durably significant. It showed how Soros, having profited from international arbitrage in the days of capital controls, could now profit from the tensions caused by the removal of those controls. In the new world of floating exchange rates and free capital flows, currencies could be driven far from equilibrium, disrupting the business models of exporters and importers, stoking resentments among nations, and inflaming protectionist passions. Governments would therefore be drawn into various forms of market intervention; Plaza was just one example. For a speculator like Soros, these government interventions would create a special category of opportunity. Normally, traders pit their wits against other traders: if one believes the market is going up and the other believes it is going down, both have plausible reasons for their view and the question is finely balanced. But trading against a government is not like that. When the government intervenes in the currency market, it is not acting on its sense of market logic. Rather, it is trying to change that logic: it is conducting policy, not maximizing profits. For a speculator, trading against an adversary who is willing to lose money can be a gift. By understanding governments, and by judging whether their interventions were likely to succeed, Soros would pull off the investment coups for which he is most reviled and celebrated.

IN 1989 SOROS handed over the reins of the Quantum Fund to Stanley Druckenmiller, a trading prodigy and close student of Soros's investment methods. Freed of his responsibility, Soros moved his family to London with the idea of focusing on philanthropy: it was one of those times when he wanted to step back from the markets. The fall of the Berlin Wall and the collapse of communism in Eastern Europe made the timing ideal, and the challenge of fostering open societies in former autocracies preoccupied Soros at least as much as finance. At Druckenmiller's insistence, Soros restricted his role at Quantum to that of non-executive chairman, weighing in with questions and advice but not second-guessing Druckenmiller's trading decisions. To satisfy his periodic speculative urges, Soros maintained a small sub-fund of his own. Only when an especially big opportunity arose did Soros and Druckenmiller confer intensively.

Seven years after the Plaza trade, in 1992, one such opportunity presented itself. As Soros could see clearly from his vantage point in London, there were tensions in Europe's exchange-rate mechanism. This system had been set up in 1979 to dampen currency fluctuations within Europe: it was a prime example of the way that the global regime of floating exchange rates harbored major exceptions. Under the rules of the mechanism, participating currencies were allowed to move against one another within a narrow band, and if that flexibility was not enough, a country could negotiate devaluation. The goal was to achieve a compromise between exchange-rate stability, which would facilitate cross-border trade and investment, and interest-rate flexibility, which would facilitate member states' efforts to smooth economic cycles. Full currency union, of the sort that Europe adopted later with the euro, would involve a single central bank and a single set of interest rates across the entire bloc. It would abolish the ability of one country to cut interest rates to fight a recession.

Europe's compromise worked well until the start of the 1990s, when German unification strained it. The vast cost of integrating Germany's poor East created inflationary pressure, pushing the Deutsche Bundesbank to raise interest rates. Higher German interest rates came at a time when other European economies were experiencing a recession that called for lower interest rates. The high rates in Germany coupled with low rates elsewhere induced capital to flow into marks; as a result, the weaker European currencies, notably the Italian lira and the British pound, fell to the bottom of the permitted band—and threatened to break out of it. This presented Europe's governments with two options. Either Germany could cut interest rates in order to attract less capital, while the Italians and British did the opposite, or central banks could intervene in the currency markets, selling marks and buying lire and pounds. If both interest-rate adjustment and currency intervention failed, Italy and Britain would be forced into devaluation.

As they studied this chessboard, Druckenmiller and Soros saw that both alternatives—interest-rate adjustments and currency intervention—stood a good chance of failing. Germany's central bankers might be reluctant to cut interest rates for the sake of European cohesion: for them, the fight against domestic inflation was paramount. The central banks of Italy and Britain were caught in the opposite bind: they would resist raising interest rates because their economies were in recession. Meanwhile central-bank intervention in the currency markets seemed unlikely to work. In the years since the Plaza trade, cross-border flows of money had tripled and currency speculators had amassed formidable war chests. A single hedge fund, employing fewer than fifty people, might muster financial firepower comparable to a government's.

In August 1992 Druckenmiller began to position Quantum for a currency realignment. He was especially focused on the fragility of Britain, because Quantum maintained an office there. The London-based analyst Scott Bessent pointed out that British homeowners had floating-rate mortgages, so interest-rate hikes would hit them immediately. As a result, the Bank of England would be especially averse to raising rates to shore up the currency. On top of these considerations, Britain's commitment to European monetary collaboration was fragile. If Britain could not defend sterling, it might prefer to crash out of the system rather than negotiate a devaluation. Druckenmiller duly bought marks and sold pounds, investing $1.5 billion in this position.

Quantum's next move came directly from Soros. On September 8 he attended a speech by Helmut Schlesinger, the Bundesbank president. Far from hinting that Germany might cut interest rates to help the exchange-rate mechanism's weak economies, Schlesinger declared that he could not promise to do so. He had little confidence in the fixed relationships among European currencies, he said. To underline the point, he alluded particularly to the unsoundness of the Italian lira.

Soros approached Schlesinger after the speech. To make sure he had heard correctly, he asked him what he thought of the ECU, the notional European currency that preceded the euro. Schlesinger replied that he liked the concept of a European currency, but would have preferred to call it the mark.

To Soros, Schlesinger's message was unmistakable. The Bundesbank president was open to the idea of European solidarity, but he wanted it to be on German terms: he was not going to compromise the Bundesbank's tradition of fighting inflation. In a state of some excitement, Soros called Druckenmiller in New York and told him the Italian currency was heading for a fall. Druckenmiller quickly added a bet against the lira to his existing bet against sterling.

Soros flew to New York and invited a currency expert named Robert Johnson to visit him and Druckenmiller. The three men huddled together at Soros's midtown office.[30] Soros asked Johnson to describe the risks in betting against sterling. He wanted to understand the downside.

"Well, sterling is liquid, so you can always exit losing positions," Johnson responded. "The most you could lose is half a percent or so."

"What could you gain on the trade?" Druckenmiller asked.

"If this thing busts out, you'd probably make fifteen or twenty percent," Johnson answered. He was suggesting a reward-to-risk ratio of thirty to one. The asymmetry was extraordinary.

"How much would you do in your own fund?" Soros asked, referring to a portfolio that Johnson ran for Bankers Trust.

Johnson indicated that he would leverage himself up to take advantage of this trade. He might bet three to five times his fund's capital.

"Oh my God," Druckenmiller said quickly. His $1.5 billion bet against sterling represented less than half of Quantum's capital. Johnson was saying he should do much more. This would be the Plaza trade on steroids.

On Friday, September 11, the lira broke through the bottom of its permitted band, and over the weekend Italy negotiated a 7 percent devaluation. Soros and Druckenmiller booked a profit, but their main focus remained on Britain. The conventional wisdom held that sterling would not follow the lira—at least not immediately. After all, Italy had long been Europe's most shambolic rich country; in contrast, Britain was run by the Conservative Party, which had transformed the country's economic performance. Further, the Bank of England had recently announced that it was borrowing $14 billion of foreign exchange to expand its ability to intervene in the markets in support of sterling. On the Monday following the lira's fall, sterling actually rose slightly.

On Tuesday the pound was down again. That evening, Bundesbank president Schlesinger used a press interview to reiterate that Europe's weaker economies should not expect Germany to come to their rescue. Druckenmiller read the comments on the news wires in New York and decided it was time to move. He walked into Soros's office and announced that he would steadily increase his bet against sterling.

Soros listened and looked puzzled. "That doesn't make sense," he objected.

"What do you mean?" Druckenmiller asked.

Well, Soros responded, if Schlesinger's view had been reported accurately and there was almost no downside, why just build steadily? Why not sell as much sterling as possible? "Go for the jugular," Soros advised him.

Druckenmiller could see that Soros was right: indeed, this was the man's genius. Druckenmiller had done the analysis and seen the trigger for the trade, but Soros was the one who knew when to go nuclear.[31]

For the rest of that Tuesday, Druckenmiller and Soros sold sterling to anyone prepared to buy from them. Under the rules of the exchange-rate mechanism, the Bank of England was obliged to accept offers to sell sterling at the fixed rate of 2.7780 marks, the lowest level permissible in the band, but this requirement only held during the trading day in London. With the Bank of England closed for business, it was a scramble to find buyers, particularly once word got around that Soros and Druckenmiller were selling crazily.

Late that day, a hedge-funder named Louis Bacon called Stan Druckenmiller. The two talked about how the drama might play out, and Bacon said he was still finding ways to dump sterling.

"Really?" Druckenmiller blurted out. He told Bacon to wait, and a few seconds later Soros joined the call.

"Where did you get the market?" Soros demanded furiously.[32]

After going home for a few hours, Druckenmiller returned to the office at 2 A.M. He wanted to be at his desk when London trading reopened and the Bank of England would be forced to resume purchases of sterling. Scott Bessent, the portfolio manager who was based in London but was working out of New York this week, arrived shortly after Druckenmiller. He could see the hulking outline of the boss standing in his dark office, the nighttime Manhattan skyline stretched out behind him. The only light in his office came from the telephone: Soros was on the line, and Druckenmiller had hit the speaker button.

A disembodied Eastern European accent filled the dark room. Soros was urging Druckenmiller to leverage himself up and redouble his selling. At moments like this, only one thing mattered. As Soros had put it in his journal seven years before, you had to assume "maximum market exposure."

When the markets opened in London, the Bank of England attempted to fight back against the speculators. It intervened twice before 8:30 A.M., each time buying £300 million worth of sterling. But the buying had absolutely no effect. Soros Fund Management was clamoring to sell sterling by the *billion*, and its clamor was driving legions of imitators to sell also. By 8:40 A.M. the bank had purchased a total of £1 billion, but sterling still refused to budge. Ten minutes later, the chancellor of the exchequer, Norman Lamont, told Prime Minister John Major that intervention was failing.

Britain could have devalued then and cut its losses. But to Lamont's frustration, the prime minister refused to do so. He had been responsible for taking Britain into the exchange-rate mechanism, and he feared that devaluation might trigger a challenge to his leadership from one of his lieutenants. Before he let sterling go, he wanted other members of his cabinet to share in the decision. And so, for the rest of the trading day, the Bank of England continued to follow the rules of the exchange-rate mechanism, buying sterling even though it knew full well that it would soon be devalued. On the other side of the trade, Quantum sold the currency by the truckload, increasing the value of its bet to about $10 billion. With each passing hour, the wealth of British taxpayers flowed into the coffers of currency traders. It was the perfect illustration of the fortune to be made from betting against governments.

That evening, at 7:30 P.M. London time, Britain announced its exit from Europe's exchange-rate mechanism. The markets had won, and the government had at last admitted it.

∾

SOROS AND DRUCKENMILLER made over $1 billion from the sterling trade, roughly four times more than the second biggest winner, Bruce Kovner of Caxton, and about five or six times more than Soros's Plaza winnings. The news reached the public after Gianni Agnelli, the Italian industrial magnate, let slip to journalists that his investment in Quantum would earn him more that year than his takings from Fiat, his car company. When Soros opened his front door the next morning, he was met by a throng of reporters, and over the next months the press drooled over his winnings. Soros was said to have enlarged his personal fortune by $650 million that year, and one magazine observed that it took Soros five minutes to earn what the median American family could expect for a full year of labor. But the profits of the Soros funds were considerably larger than outsiders imagined. Druckenmiller had made a further killing on a series of ancillary bets—including a correct call that France, unlike Italy and Britain, would successfully withstand the attacks on its currency. The fund also shorted the Swedish krona before its devaluation in November 1992, again pocketing upward of $1 billion. Having learned a lesson from the publicity following the sterling trade, Soros and Druckenmiller made sure that nobody told the press about Sweden.

The currency trades of 1992 marked the high point for Quantum. The fund was up 69 percent that year and a further 63 percent in 1993, the latter reflecting the winnings from the resiliency of France and other sequels to the crisis. Soros's global outlook and his search for market disequilibria helped explain this success, but by now these characteristics were shared by a small industry of "macro traders"—Druckenmiller foremost among them. What still distinguished Soros, as the sterling trade had shown, was the third of his original strengths: his feeling for risk, his timing. At the crucial moment, it was he who told Druckenmiller to go for the jugular. Without that prompting, Quantum would doubtless have made large profits, just as other traders did. But it would not have multiplied its exposure roughly fivefold in a single day. The jugular advice was worth several hundred million dollars.

Over the next years, Soros and Quantum never quite matched this moment of dominance. It was partly because governments caught up. During the 2000s, the compromise (or "soft") currency pegs that had proved so lucrative to traders in Europe were gradually abandoned: either currencies were allowed to float, making profitable dislocations rare, or nations opted for full currency union, as in the case of the euro. Where soft pegs still existed, governments grew better at ambushing speculators with emergency capital controls, bans on bank lending to hedge funds, and other regulatory clamps: they were less easily bullied. But the other transformation that took place was in Soros himself. The speculator was giving way to the international statesman.

Even in 1992, these dual and dueling personas were already evident. As a speculator, Soros could see the financial pressures in Europe and extract profit from them. As a philanthropist and public intellectual, he could see those same pressures and lament their consequences. "Speculation can be very harmful," Soros told an interviewer after the devaluation of sterling; a single European currency "would put speculators like me out of business, but I would be delighted to make that sacrifice."[33] Around the same time, Soros met with Jean-Claude Trichet, the governor of the French central bank, and told him that, out of concern for the destabilizing effects of his own trading, he would not attack the franc. The claim to magnanimity was disingenuous, since Quantum was soon to make a killing on its view that the franc would hold firm. But the comment nevertheless captured Soros's split-personality syndrome. The world's greatest speculator was unwilling to defend speculation.

Five years later, the split had only deepened. In the summer of 1997, Druckenmiller and the Quantum team made a $750 million profit on the devaluation of the Thai baht, effectively rerunning the playbook that had worked with sterling. But rather than celebrating this win, Soros denounced speculation. "The main enemy to the open society, I believe, is no longer the communist but the capitalist threat," he declared publicly, despite his capitalist fortune. "The laissez-faire idea that markets should be left to their own devices remains very influential," he went on. "I consider it a dangerous idea."[34] A few months later, Quantum's Asia team identified another winning trade, this time involving the impending fall of South Korea's currency. But despite the huge attractions of this speculative opportunity—over the next six weeks, the South Korean won would collapse by fully 60 percent—Soros earned precisely nothing from it. For reasons that almost certainly included Soros's reluctance to play the role of predator, Quantum sat on the sidelines during Korea's currency turmoil. Instead, Soros visited Korea to hobnob with its new president and to offer benign advice on navigating stormy markets. He went not as a speculator but as a statesman and philanthropist.

The struggle between Soros's two personas was most acute in Russia. For years Soros had maintained a rule that he would not invest in Russia: his only involvement there was philanthropic. But in 1997 he crossed his red line. Going over the heads of Druckenmiller and his Quantum colleagues, he committed almost $1 billion to a consortium that bought 25 percent of Svyazinvest, Russia's sprawling, state-owned telephone utility. The bet was reckless on its face. Every speculator knew that Russian investments would be in trouble if the politics turned bad, and a lumpy stake in a state company was not something one could exit in a hurry. But Soros's gamble was all the crazier given his privileged knowledge of Russia. Just at the time when Soros the speculator was bidding for Svyazinvest, Soros the philanthropist was extending a secret loan of several hundred million dollars to prop up Russia's reformist government. The speculator was risking $1 billion on the theory that Russia was stable. The philanthropist had inside knowledge to the effect that the government was close to falling. In its speculation against sterling, the Soros team had used its insights into the government's weak position to stage a profitable attack. In Russia, Soros was privy to the government's frailties, yet he invested as though he had never thought about them. The following year, when Russia devalued and defaulted, Soros Fund Management lost 15 percent of its capital on its Russian exposures, or roughly $1.5 billion.

What was Soros thinking? The answer involves a tragedy of Shakespearean proportions. Soros's ego, which had driven him to try to be a great philosopher, and which had paid enormous dividends for most of his investing life, now turned out to be the flaw that cost him billions. Earlier in his career, he had been capable of stunning vanity, redeemed only by his willingness to confess to it. "I fancied myself as some kind of god or an economic reformer like Keynes (each with his General Theory)," he wrote. "Or, even better, a scientist like Einstein (reflexivity sounds like relativity)."[35] But by the late 1990s, intoxicated by wealth and fame, Soros had developed a full-blown messiah complex. He began to imagine himself as nothing less than a savior. Explaining his decision to cross the line from philanthropy to speculation in Russia, he wrote:

> To be a selfless benefactor was just a little too good to be true. It fed my self-image as a godlike creature, above the fray, doing good and fighting evil. I have talked about my messianic fantasies; I am not ashamed of them. . . . I could see, particularly in Russia, that people simply could not understand what I was all about. . . . It seemed to me that to appear as a robber capitalist who is concerned with cultural and political values was more credible than to be a disembodied intellect arguing for the merits of an open society. . . . By entering the fray as an investor, I descended from Mount Olympus and became a flesh and blood human being.[36]

Soros came down from Mount Olympus like a messiah to save sinners. With a loss of more than $1 billion, he suffered his own cross.

❧

WHAT TO MAKE of this epic career, spanning almost half a century of trading? Despite his vanity and errors, Soros was one of the great investors of his generation—possibly *the* greatest. In 2010, a study by the Edmond de Rothschild Group ranked hedge funds according to the dollar winnings paid out to investors: Quantum came out at the top. Quantum and its predecessor, Double Eagle, averaged annual returns of 36 percent between 1969 and 1989, the period of Soros's direct control, and 33 percent if you add in the Druckenmiller era, running to 2000. This outclassed the great hedge fund rivals of the period: Julian Robertson's celebrated Tiger Management racked up an average return of 27 percent in its two-decade run, starting in 1980; Michael Steinhardt, who traded actively between 1967 and 1995, averaged 26 percent. Even Warren Buffett's storied Berkshire Hathaway was a whisker behind Soros. Between 1969 and 2000, the period considered for Quantum, Berkshire's annual return averaged 32 percent.[37]

Beyond this achievement, a boon to his investors and philanthropy, Soros embodied and occasionally shaped the era he inhabited. His early trading exploited capital controls and the distortions they created, and the difficulty of bottling money up behind borders helped to persuade governments to abandon the controls from the late 1970s. Soros's later triumphs accelerated the growth in cross-border money flows, showing first how traders could amplify government policy, as in the Plaza trade, and later how they could overturn it, as in Europe's 1992 crisis. The costs to taxpayers and citizens could be grievous, as Soros was the first to say. But the costs were at least partly of the governments' own making. By committing themselves to unsustainable currency pegs, politicians were giving up their ability to cut interest rates to fight recessions, thereby condemning their people to hardship; in attacking these pegs, speculators were compelling governments to recognize their error. The British press dubbed the day of Soros's victory over sterling "Black Wednesday." But Druckenmiller proposed a better name. The devaluation had restored Britain's monetary freedom. It was "White Wednesday."

Perhaps Soros's greatest legacy lies in the minds of the speculators who succeeded him. He stood for an oddly antiquated, Renaissance ideal: that one thinker—worldly, multilingual, curious about politics, psychology, philosophy, and economics—can wrap his mind around the world, blending gossip from the corridors of power with statistics about companies. Like most great traders, Soros inspired others, and his ideas about boom-bust cycles, feedback loops, and asymmetric bets have become pervasive among speculators. In an economy that is increasingly specialized and computerized, perhaps none of Soros's successors will match the master's extravagant triumphs. But so long as there are markets in the world, there will be traders trying to beat them.

Philanthropy
with a Vision

Darren Walker

GEORGE SOROS DIDN'T JUST WAKE UP in the middle of a midlife crisis and invent modern philanthropy. He's part of a long line of enormously wealthy Americans who have chosen to take their wealth and do good in the world. Yet Soros's way of giving is different from the path taken by his predecessors, and along the way he has reenvisioned what philanthropy can accomplish.

Philanthropy is a vastly important and often misunderstood element of how the United States functions. Often viewed as acts of charity, philanthropy at its best is about using money to advance social goals, education, equity, justice, science, health, and culture.

George Soros became a philanthropist in middle age because he had a great deal of money and a philosophical and strategic sense that the world could benefit from his willingness to support reforms and democratic values. He started with a focus on South Africa but gradually, as his wealth grew and the Soviet empire collapsed, his range and impact expanded to dozens of nations. Eventually Soros recognized that his global philanthropy should also have a US component, nationally and on specific issues such as crime, justice, and drug policy.

Soros is often compared to such great figures in philanthropy as Andrew Carnegie, John D. Rockefeller, the heirs of Henry Ford, and more recently Bill and Melinda Gates. Carnegie of course built thousands of libraries, and he literally wrote the book on modern giving. In *The Gospel of Wealth*, published in 1889, he laid out his view that men got rich through hard work and God's will, and thus it was their duty to put their extra money carefully and responsibly toward benevolent causes. No squandering money or handing it out willy-nilly for workers to squander.

Whereas Carnegie focused his efforts principally in America and the United Kingdom, Rockefeller's footprint was truly global. He built the first modern Western hospital in China and founded Peking Union Medical College. The world public health system was a creation of his: he laid the groundwork for the World Health Organization. Rockefeller also promoted global food security. The food-research institutes he established around the world ultimately helped propagate the Green Revolution and feed a billion people. The Ford and Gates foundations have followed similar paths, seeking large-scale solutions to the overarching problems that humanity faces.

George Soros has given away money on a scale comparable to Rockefeller.[1] But for a different ideal. As industrialists, Rockefeller, Carnegie, and others had an absolute belief that Americans like themselves, with science and industry, could solve the world's problems. They could look past social injustice because ultimately science would address that, too. But Soros's focus on open society is broader than scientific or developmental progress. His vision is of a world and a nation where the open society principles, human rights, and equity are the objectives. And so he could never look away. His philanthropy has been shaped by his own lived experience, growing up in Hungary, surviving the Nazis, and then watching the Iron Curtain descend on Eastern Europe. Seeing democracy destroyed there had a profound impact on him that lasts to this day. It gives him a sense of urgency. He knows what happens when democracy and democratic institutions are harmed.

Soros was forty-nine years old when he decided to try philanthropy. It was a time of unease for him, despite his success in the world of finance. He was insecure. Driven. A workaholic. Self-critical and even self-torturing. Depressed. Though he was a brilliant researcher who cultivated hundreds of useful contacts in markets around the world, in private life he longed to find meaningful interests and expand his limited circle of friends.[2]

Of course he was adept at making money—by then he'd built a personal fortune of $25 million[3]—but he had little interest in the status symbols or luxuries that wealth can buy. Around that time his marriage unraveled and he and a business partner parted ways. And the unrelenting, often round-the-clock pressure of global high-risk trading wore on him. When a dinner companion asked when he first realized that he liked making money, he told her, "I don't like it. I'm just good at it."

His true lifelong passion was philosophy, and that gave him another reason to be depressed. He'd spent years working on a book called *The Burden of Consciousness* that he dreamed was going to be his ticket to the pantheon of great thinkers of humanity. But he could never get this magnum opus to work and finally set it aside. So now, instead of making his mark as a philosopher, here he was, traveling ceaselessly on business and longing for a change.

Starting out in philanthropy, he had only a vague notion what he wanted to do. He called his foundation the Open Society Fund, after a main tenet of his philosophy that he was hoping to test in the real world. But the immediate motivation was less noble: to reduce his taxes. The Open Society was a so-called charitable lead trust designed ultimately to let his children inherit his wealth tax-free as long as he gave away up to $3 million a year for twenty years.[4]

For a man of Soros's growing wealth, this was a modest and commonsensical start. But he gradually awoke to the possibility that by applying his philosophy to real-world problems he could do great good. He'd adopted the idea of the open society from the philosopher Karl Popper, his mentor at the London School of Economics. It was a clear and compelling vision of democracy; asked to define it in the mid-1990s Soros said:

Concepts shouldn't be defined; they should be explained. . . .
Open society is based on the recognition that we all act on the
basis of imperfect understanding. Nobody is in possession of the
ultimate truth. Therefore, we need a critical mode of thinking;
we need institutions and rules that allow people with different
opinions and interests to live together in peace; we need a democratic form of government that ensures the orderly transfer of
power; we need a market economy that provides feedback and
allows mistakes to be corrected; we need to protect minorities and
respect minority opinions. Above all, we need the rule of law.
Ideologies like fascism or communism give rise to a closed society
in which the individual is subjugated to the collective, society is
dominated by the state, and the state is in the service of a dogma
that claims to embody the ultimate truth. In such a society, there
is no freedom.[5]

This open society concept was pioneering, trailblazing, radical,
and courageous because Soros took it to places where such ideas were
far from the norm. In 1979, a friend of his named Herbert Vilakazi,
a university lecturer in Connecticut and a member of the Zulu nation, returned to his native South Africa to teach in one of the Black
"homelands" established under the apartheid system. When Soros
went to visit the following year, Vilakazi showed him a South Africa
that few whites, even South Africans, ever got to see.[6] Vilakazi guided
Soros through Soweto township, where police had brutally crushed
riots a few years before, and introduced him to lawyers and activists
associated with Nelson Mandela, who was then serving a life sentence
on Robben Island for conspiring to overthrow the apartheid state.
Soros saw a challenge. "Here was a closed society with all the institutions of a first world country, but they were off limits to the majority
of the population on racial grounds," he wrote. "Where could I find
a better opportunity for opening up a closed society?"[7]

Soros decided to try working for change within the system. He
started with an institution, the University of Cape Town, that had

begun to accept a small number of Black students on scholarship. The school was paying most of the costs, but as an inducement to expand the program more quickly, Soros offered to add a stipend for each student. "My thinking was that I would pay their lodgings, their supplemental costs," he wrote. "In this way I would be using the mechanism of a generally oppressive state to subvert it, to expand a small area of interracial activity. At the same time I would be helping to build a black elite."[8] University authorities assured him that the number of Black students would soon increase, and Soros wrote a check.

A year later, meeting with the scholarship students on a follow-up visit, Soros found them angry and disillusioned. It turned out the program wasn't expanding at all; the administration had used Soros's donation to reduce the university's own financial commitment. Soros made sure the students got paid as promised but canceled his plan. Evidently identifying a closed society was one thing; opening it, quite another. "Instead of me taking advantage of the apartheid state, the apartheid state was taking advantage of me," he wrote.[9]

Soros didn't let his failed bet in Cape Town faze him. "I was experimenting," he said, "exploring ways to use my money."[10] Remember, he was a trader; he was famous on Wall Street for being able to take a loss, even a staggering loss, learn from it, and bounce right back. Indeed, the South Africa experience shaped his understanding in significant ways. Most important, it opened his eyes to racism, solidifying his sensitivity to race and anti-Blackness. The venture also reinforced his faith in philanthropy through scholarships. The students had impressed him, and he became further convinced that university education was the best way to prepare young people for participating in open societies.

South Africa wasn't the only closed society in which cracks were starting to show. Despite the Soviet Union's grip on its satellites in Eastern Europe in the early 1980s, Soros had started giving grants— money for Polish and Hungarian intellectuals and dissidents, a dozen at a time—to make trips abroad. These exchanges encouraged the spread of critical thinking and were personally interesting for Soros, who got to know some of the grant recipients and familiarized himself with the troubles of the region.

The West's attention in those days was on Poland, where the anticommunist Solidarity movement drew millions of members and survived the 1981 imposition of martial law. Soros was an early supporter of Solidarity, but he focused more of his energy on Hungary, his native land. Though still traumatized from the events of 1956, when a reform movement was suppressed by Red Army tanks, Hungary was again trying to liberalize. In hopes of increasing trade with the West, Communist Party leaders had relaxed their grip on the economy slightly, letting a second economy of mom-and-pop businesses operate on the side. The Hungarians nicknamed this slight opening "Goulash Communism."[11]

In his visits to Budapest, Soros quietly let it be known that he had millions of dollars to commit to the cause of opening Hungarian society. He proposed to start an independent foundation that would advance Hungarian art and culture. Private foundations were forbidden in Hungary, of course, but the presence of a Hungarian American willing to write big checks was too much for all but the staunchest ideologues to resist. High-level apparatchiks invited Soros to make a proposal, the start of negotiations that went on, sometimes heatedly, for weeks. Soros was determined not to cede control of the money, as he had done in South Africa. On this point tempers got so hot that the Hungarians gave in only when Soros was at the door of the conference room, threatening to leave.[12] Finally, in May 1984 the Hungarian government and the American private citizen agreed. Soros would be permitted to fund a quasi-independent foundation operating in conjunction with Hungary's august Academy of Sciences. Soros wanted to call it the Open Society, but the name was judged too provocative. The two sides settled on the Hungarian Academy of Sciences / George Soros Foundation.[13]

The state-owned media barely took note, but no fanfare was needed. As a lawyer working with Soros later said, "It marked the first time that Communist authorities anywhere had met with people from the private sector and negotiated on matters of social and cultural significance. They offered guarantees of independence and accepted the participation of so-called forbidden people. It was simply unprecedented."[14]

Soros guarded the foundation's independence by hiring one such forbidden person as his board chairman and personal representative: Miklos Vasarhelyi, a sixty-seven-year-old survivor of the Soviet crackdown. Vasarhelyi had been press secretary to Prime Minister Imre Nagy in 1956 and had barely escaped with his life when Nagy was hanged. He'd served four years in prison and for years had been permitted to work only menial jobs. But he still knew the levers of power in the government—how far to push them and when to back off—and Soros trusted him to help spot opportunities and set strategy.

One of the first projects Soros and Vasarhelyi pursued involved copying machines. The flow of information in Hungary was strictly controlled, as it is in all closed societies. The Communist Party owned the printing presses and the airwaves; copying machines were few and out of reach, some literally under lock and key. If your workplace even had one and you wanted something copied, you'd have to submit your document with a request form and then wait, sometimes for days, to get it approved.

But through its affiliation with the Academy of Sciences, Soros's new foundation had connections with libraries and schools and institutes all over the country. He and Vasarhelyi ordered two hundred state-of-the-art Xerox machines from the West, complete with three-year service contracts, and offered them to institutions at heavily subsidized prices.[15] As soon as the first batch was snapped up, they ordered another two hundred machines and then another two hundred.

The more copiers became available, the more people started using them freely. The state tried to tighten the regulations but with so many machines in service, it could not enforce them. Instead the party began to lose control of information. Within a few years, in intellectual settings at least, access to copiers became the norm in Hungary, and information, bottled up for the previous forty years, began to flow freely. Soros later said proudly, "We achieved a tremendous amount with very little money. And we felt good, fighting evil."[16] Hard-liners in the bureaucracy were suspicious, of course, but the foundation took pains to mollify them. "We carefully balanced projects that would annoy the ideologues in the Party with other projects that they couldn't help but approve, and we made sure that there was always a positive balance," Soros said.[17] Thus he found himself supporting not only dissidents but also rural dairy associations. Overall the project succeeded brilliantly.

Soros worked diligently to identify and fund new experiments, and within a few years his giving met and then exceeded the $3 million annual rate targeted in his original estate plan. By 1989, when the Berlin Wall fell, Soros had already opened Open Society foundations in Poland, Ukraine, the Soviet Union, and China, giving away almost $8 million per year.

Then came the collapse of the Soviet Union itself in 1991, co-incident with a period of dazzling profits at the Quantum Fund that included Soros's bet against the British pound in 1992. Suddenly the coffers overflowed, and as he drily put it, the sums of money he had available to donate exceeded the capacity of the existing foundations to spend it well.[18]

The amount of personal wealth he could afford to give soared into the tens and then hundreds of millions of dollars per year, and give Soros did. He moved fast. By 1993 he had extended the Open Society network across almost all of the former Soviet empire, with twenty-five foundations in Albania, the Baltic States, the Czech Republic, Kazakhstan, Kyrgyzstan, Moldova, Romania, and Slovakia, among other places. He also opened twenty art centers across Eastern Europe that exhibited contemporary art.

Soros saw the collapse of communism as a moment of historic transformation. The world was entering a new era, ripe with promise for true democracy and open societies in places that had not experienced them in half a century. And before long, the Open Society had so many networked offices, so many programs, that it resembled the Rockefeller foundations that spread throughout Asia in the 1920s, from China to India and everywhere in between.

Soros was exhilarated. His single largest investment was the funding of Central European University, an international school focused on disciplines that had been forbidden or curtailed during the communist era—social sciences, humanities, business, and public policy. This was exactly the knowledge people would need to privatize and liberalize formerly Iron Curtain states.[19] "I recognized the need for an institution that would reinforce the idea behind the revolution of 1989," Soros said, "the idea of an open, pluralistic, democratic, market-oriented form of social organization."[20] In its very presence the new university embodied the open society ideal of transformation—one of the buildings of its Budapest campus was the former headquarters of the Hungarian secret police.[21]

When asked how this sprawling charity network would be able to foster democracy and openness in societies that had spent generations under totalitarian rule, Soros had a complex answer:

> It is impossible to say. The transformation of a closed society into an open one is a systemic transformation. Practically everything has to change and there is no blueprint. What the foundations have done is to mobilize the energies of the people in the countries concerned. In each country I identified a group of people—some leading personalities, others less well known—who shared my belief in an open society and I entrusted them with the task of establishing the priorities. I had an overall vision and, with the passage of time, I learned from the experience of individual foundations. I reinforced the initiatives that were successful and abandoned the ones that were not. I tried to transfer the successful programs from one country to the others. . . . But I did not impose

anything from the outside. I gave the foundations autonomy and exercised control only through the amount of additional money I made available.

Open society is meant to be a self-organizing system and I wanted the foundations not only to help build an open society but also to serve as a prototype. We started in a chaotic fashion and order emerged out of chaos gradually. The scope for the foundations was practically unlimited. We tried to choose projects that made a real difference. . . . The priorities were rapidly shifting. For instance, travel grants were usually effective in the early days but they are less so today. Our main priorities are education, civil society, law, the media, culture, libraries and the Internet. But these categories do not describe adequately the scope of our activities. The activities came first and the categories afterwards. Nobody knew everything we were doing, and I liked it that way.[22]

Soros took delight in happening upon projects sponsored by his foundations unbeknownst to him—a treatment program for recovering alcoholics in Polish prisons, a weeklong international conference of teachers on a new approach to health education. At the Open Society art centers, he didn't like most of the art on display, but happily admitted, "I am not competent to judge. [And] in my view, it is an essential feature of an open society that not everything should be to my liking. If I tried to control the content of every program, I would not be creating an open society. And I could certainly not have expanded the foundation network as fast as I did."[23]

The bursts of innovation from the foundations affected Soros deeply, giving him a sense of satisfaction that he had never known as a solitary philosopher: "Things were happening that I did not think of, indeed, could not think of, because often they were beyond my comprehension. It gave me a sense of liberation. Finally, I broke out of my isolation and connected with the real world."[24]

Soros's philanthropy evolved rapidly in the early 1990s. He still didn't want his name on buildings, but he very much did want a broader impact on the world—an ambition made urgent by the gnawing awareness that wherever in the world the idea of democracy resonated, it was under threat.

All this was on Soros's mind when in 1993 he sat down to dinner in Manhattan with the great social activist Aryeh Neier, a fellow émigré from Hitler's Europe who had escaped the Third Reich as a toddler with his family. During the Vietnam War, Neier had been a leader of Students for a Democratic Society. He had gone on to head the American Civil Liberties Union, and then he had cofounded Human Rights Watch and built it into a global network.

Soros and Neier had gotten to know each other not only through Human Rights Watch meetings (Soros was a donor) but also because of their shared involvement in South Africa. Even as he concentrated on the Soviet bloc, Soros had never lost sight of the place where his giving had begun. Following the release of Nelson Mandela from prison in 1990, South Africa was in the midst of a transition from the closed horror of apartheid to a new multiracial democracy. A new constitution would take effect in 1994, but the intervening years were chaotic and often bloody. Soros funded fellowships for Black journalists and poured money into public-interest lawyering, legal education, networks of Black lawyers, and the establishment of a constitutional court—all going back to his fundamental belief in the rule of law. Much of that money flowed through Human Rights Watch programs.

Over dinner, Neier told Soros that he was tired of the constant fundraising he had to do to keep Human Rights Watch afloat. Soros said that, for his part, he was at a point where he could no longer run the Open Society network by himself. What was more, there was growth to think about—a practically endless list of high-potential projects that Soros knew were out there to fund. As Neier later recalled, the two quickly came to terms: "I told him I'd be interested in working globally. We agreed I'd become president and we'd expand the writ of the foundations to take in other parts of the world."[25] For Neier that evening, the numbers Soros mentioned were practically surreal. He was giving Open Society about $180 million a year, and his goal for the coming year was to give $300 million. Toward dessert he added that he was in a position to spend twice that amount if they found worthy causes.

Soros's philanthropy was about to enter a new phase, as his boldness, his courage, and his willingness to do what is unpopular were amplified by Neier's vision, especially his global scope. It's important to remember that Soros was not a full-time philanthropist. He'd never stopped working at his day job—and all that money he now planned to give away wasn't going to make itself.[26] He wasn't like Bill Gates, who at age fifty could say, "I'm sorry, Microsoft. I'm out of here. I'm not going to write another program." Instead, Soros was more like Rockefeller and Carnegie, who kept running their huge enterprises later in life. He depended on Neier in much the same way that Rockefeller relied on his principal business and philanthropy adviser Frederick Taylor Gates in building the University of Chicago and Rockefeller University and the international networks, and that Carnegie counted on his secretary, James Bertram, in building his thousands of libraries and Carnegie Hall.

When Neier started work, he discovered there was no road map to the Open Society network. Soros had hired dozens of staff people in New York to administer the philanthropies, award grants, and send out checks, but they were like the blind men and the elephant—nobody understood the whole beast. This was part of Soros's creativity-out-of-chaos philosophy. But the foundation network had grown too big, and it was Neier's job to add order and coherence. First he had to identify all the legal entities and tax practices behind Open Society projects—a task that took many months. "In my first year there was hardly a day that I didn't learn about some significant program that I was not aware of previously," Neier later said.[27] Eventually he was able to wrap almost all of the foundations into one overarching Open Society Institute, with an annual report and a budget of sorts.

Soros meanwhile charged ahead, seeking new, high-impact projects, some on a scale so large that normally only a fiscally healthy government would consider taking them up. For example, he bank-rolled a $100 million project to revive preschool education across the entire former Soviet Union and Eastern Europe. He staked another $100 million to sustain the work of thousands of Russian scientists whose government paychecks had dried up, and another $100 million to connect the former Soviet Union's regional universities to the Internet.[28]

He turned yet again to South Africa, whose new egalitarian con-stitution was now in place, and where public institutions that had served only whites were now called upon to serve everyone. Soros contributed more than $150 million over the next twenty-five years to support reconciliation, legal reform, education, public health, and independent media. The foundation also addressed the acute hous-ing shortage that arose as Black families left homelands and slums for towns and city neighborhoods that had previously been off-limits. Soros pledged another $50 million to help finance low-income hous-ing and construction.

South Africa also served Soros as a beachhead as Open Society foundations expanded across the continent. Today they form a net-work even more extensive than that of the Ford Foundation at the peak of its engagement in Africa during the 1960s. While Ford, like most other Western foundations, focused on promoting moderniza-tion and economic growth, Open Society was radically different: it emerged as the most consistent and robust funder of human rights, doing pioneering work on the empowerment of women in African societies, on economic justice, on public access to health care, on ac-countability and transparency in governance, and much more.

Very few Americans knew anything of these efforts, because until the mid-1990s almost all of Soros's giving was on other continents. The lack of personal acclaim didn't matter to Soros, who is radical as a philanthropist. Impact, not approbation, was what he wanted. He has never sought to be loved; he knows that what he is seeking in the world makes him hated in some quarters and puts him at risk. Programs and causes he funds make him the enemy of authoritarian

regimes and despots in closed societies, and of fascists and nativists
in open ones.

Arguably the strongest imperative to emerge from Open Society's
burgeoning growth in the 1990s was its initiative against corruption.
The effort started small, with the funding of two fledgling advocacy
groups. The first, Global Witness, was formed by three young people
in London who'd worked for Greenpeace. Fighting to save the hard-
wood forests of Cambodia, they had come to recognize corruption
as the underlying threat. The forests were being destroyed by surviving groups of the Khmer Rouge who financed themselves by selling
timber on the world market through crooked elements of the Thai
military.

The second organization, Transparency International, was
founded in Berlin as an independent monitor of corruption among
the world's governments. Its Corruption Perception Index, ranking
countries by their perceived misuse of public power for private gain,
soon became an important touchstone in diplomacy and commerce.
Not only did Open Society help provide TI's inaugural funding, but
also, as the organization gained influence, Aryeh Neier persuaded
its leaders to create another listing, the Bribe Payers Index, of the
countries and companies that were doing the bribing. "The public
needed to know the Western governments and businesses that were
paying off corrupt officials around the world," Neier explained. Naming names—particularly calling out the corporations exploiting vulnerable nations—is hardly conventional philanthropic practice, but
Open Society often went where others wouldn't.[29]

Soros and Neier were particularly concerned about the impover-
ishment of countries with abundant natural resources. When Open
Society funded a program in Angola in 1998,[30] Soros confronted
what he called the greatest disparity he'd ever seen in a single country
between immense wealth from oil and incredible poverty. José Edu-
ardo dos Santos, who had been president for two decades, was amass-
ing a $20 billion fortune in a strife-ridden land where the average
worker earned less than two dollars a day. Human rights abuses often

followed from such corruption, as governments persecuted those trying to expose it. In Suharto's Indonesia, for example, where Open Society was also active, journalists and independent judges were imprisoned by the regime.

Before long Soros's concern about corruption became sweeping and far-sighted. With the ascent of capitalism and the expansion of global markets following the end of the Cold War, he thought, corruption now figured among civilization's greatest threats. In 2000, he wrote:

> Around the world, democracy is on the march. Totalitarian and authoritarian regimes have been swept away. Popular resentment against the remaining ones is growing. But it is too early to declare victory. For although capitalism is triumphant, we cannot speak of the triumph of democracy.
>
> The connection between capitalism and democracy is far from automatic. Repressive regimes do not willingly abdicate power and are often abetted by business interests, both foreign and domestic, particularly in countries where resources such as oil and diamonds are at stake. Perhaps today's greatest threat to freedom comes from an unholy alliance between government and business, such as in Peru under President Alberto Fujimori, Zimbabwe under President Robert Mugabe, Malaysia under Prime Minister Mahathir bin Mohamad, and Russia under the oligarchs. In these cases, the appearances of a democratic process are often observed, but state powers are diverted to benefit private interests.[31]

As he gained experience as a philanthropist, Soros became bolder and more outspoken.

Expanding Open Society into the United States in the mid-1990s, Soros had a very specific rationale. For fifteen years he had devoted his philanthropy to opening closed societies. The opportunities presented by the collapse of communism and the abolition of apartheid had been vast and impossible to ignore. But he understood that to validate his beliefs, Open Society needed to address the flaws of open societies as well.

To test this thinking, he convened an eclectic group of deep thinkers and radical practitioners to his home near New York in February 1996. They included the moral philosophers Tim Scanlon and Bernard Williams; Seyla Benhabib, a philosopher of feminism and migration; Leon Botstein, the president of Bard College; Ethan Nadelmann, a drug-policy reformer; David Rothman, a medicine and human rights expert; the political theorist Alan Ryan; and Aryeh Neier. From the weekend they spent together emerged the rudiments of a plan to found an Open Society Institute in New York that would funnel money to services and advocacy groups across the country focused on prison reform, youth development and afterschool programs, professional standards and ethics in law, medicine, politics, and other fields, and more.

Quite presciently, Soros judged that the most blatant threat to American democracy was the Clinton administration's crackdown on crime. The Violent Crime Control and Law Enforcement Act of 1994 was the biggest anti-crime bill in US history, a major escalation of the war on drugs that had started under Richard Nixon. It put tens of thousands more police officers on the streets, established special drug courts, and established the so-called three strikes law, which mandated life imprisonment for anyone convicted of a violent felony after two or more prior convictions. The bill was widely popular—it broadcast the message that America was tough on crime. But Soros, having experienced totalitarianism, looked at the new law and saw hallmarks of an authoritarian state: more cops, more rigid rules, more punishment. He wanted to fund a powerful, symbolic project to remind Americans of democracy's superior appeal.

The decision to expand his giving to America brought Soros into contact with Herb Sturz, a behind-the-scenes genius of social justice work who was America's first serial social entrepreneur, a transformational force in the arc of social justice. He created so many successful social ventures that if he were a venture capitalist he'd be a billionaire. He founded the Vera Institute of Justice and the Center for Court Innovation, both of which Open Society would later support in a big way; he influenced federal legislation that expanded after-school programs for children and youth across the country, and he pioneered the After-School Corporation, which became a national model. It exists to this day. At one point Sturz was a deputy mayor of New York City. He headed the City Planning Commission. He wrote op-eds in *The New York Times*. He did it all.

It was Sturz who suggested to Soros that a way to make a particularly effective statement against President Clinton's crackdown on crime was to focus on improving an American city that had been left for dead. This made a lot of sense to Soros. Places like St. Louis and Chicago and Detroit were regarded as symbols of all of America's ills. Cities were where the war against drugs was primarily being waged. To address urban woes in a more democratic way would send a powerful countermessage. Soros saw the connection immediately and liked the idea.

Various factors converged to make Baltimore the city of choice for the Open Society to plant its flag. Baltimore is situated between New York, where Soros had his base, and Washington, where he hoped to get the attention of policy makers. Also, Soros had gotten to know the city's mayor, Kurt Schmoke, who took the then-radical view that drug addiction is best addressed with medical help, not prison—making Baltimore the only American city that saw drug abuse as a public health issue.[32] With no corporate headquarters and few other possible sources of philanthropic support, the city welcomed the initiative. What was more, Diana Morris, a respected former project director at the Ford Foundation, had recently moved to the city and was eager to take the project on.

A major seaport and industrial center, Baltimore had once been a place people moved to. But then had come suburbanization and white flight, supported by redlining policies by which the federal government and banks withheld mortgages from Black aspiring homeowners.[33] Then followed the familiar cascade of evils and ills—disinvestment, lack of wealth creation among Black people, low income, a shrinking tax base. With insufficient revenue to support them, the schools spiraled downward. Poverty bred despair. Baltimore became ground zero for drugs, with the highest per-capita number of intravenous heroin users in the United States. And the war on drugs made it all worse.

Open Society came to town in 1997 without fanfare but with a raft of innovative projects. In the words of a reporter, its programs focused on "three interlocking problems: untreated drug addiction, the criminal justice system's overreliance on incarceration, and the obstacles impeding Baltimore's inner-city youth from succeeding inside and outside the classroom."[34]

The list of projects was astounding. There was a pioneering "harm minimization" treatment program for people with drug dependency, built in part around drop-in centers with counseling and a newly approved drug that when placed under the tongue lessened withdrawal symptoms and reduced heroin cravings.[35] In the education system there were programs to shift the emphasis from discipline to learning and to make elementary schools and high schools inviting, safe, and supportive. There was an after-school debate league that rose to national prominence even as it improved attendance and performance during the school day. Open Society worked with the courts and police to keep young teenagers from being thrown into adult jails. Its parole reform effort stressed lowering recidivism in part by finding jobs and connection in the community for ex-prisoners; it heightened the importance of "reentry" in the vocabulary of the justice system.

There was an Open Society Baltimore fellowship program to provide funding to individuals, young and old, who had ideas for improving the community. There was a venture fund for community-minded entrepreneurs. There were workforce development programs that helped people prepare for the job market by teaching them interview skills and anger management techniques and how to meet social expectations in the workplace. There were programs that tracked people into apprenticeships and starter jobs, including one that brought together the city's major hospitals to define career ladders for low-skilled workers in billing, blood testing, and other departments.

The foundation encouraged its program directors to pounce on opportunities as they emerged. A program on school absenteeism, for instance, uncovered the fact that some twenty-three thousand of the city's eighty thousand high schoolers in a given year—mostly boys of color—were being suspended or expelled; the project changed course to work with teachers, administrators, and the Maryland Board of Education on reforming the code of conduct.

To help make sure its projects stayed timely and relevant, the foundation relied on a board made up of local leaders and advocates recruited to reflect the population. At the time, Open Society Baltimore was one of very few independent charitable foundations among America's eighty thousand whose board was majority Black.

The bar Soros set for the foundation was incredibly high: he wanted it not only to solve some of Baltimore's problems and generate lessons that would apply to other cities, but also to energize national discussions about America's urban woes. He gave the organizers a budget of $8 million a year, and the checkbook was always open to seize unexpected opportunities or compelling ideas.

As you would expect, some of these initiatives succeeded and some failed. What was most clear at the end of five years was that the Open Society not only had done good but also had woven itself into the social fabric of the city. While Open Society today funds more than $250 million a year in programs and grants across the United States, Baltimore remains its flagship urban foundation.

Compared to older, more traditional philanthropic organizations like the Ford and Rockefeller foundations, Soros and the Open Society Foundations were charting a course that was far more progressive and radical. Rockefeller in particular was rooted in development economics and science—alleviating poverty through health, food security, and so on. The Rockefeller Foundation had a modest legacy commitment to a group of civil rights organizations, and the Ford

Foundation funded human rights and racial justice organizations. Yet neither foundation possessed what is needed most to advance radical change in a democracy: a living donor prepared to spend millions on public persuasion in the context of elections and ballot measures.

Soros was indifferent to conventional thinking, and Open Society not infrequently took big, spontaneous risks. Gara LaMarche, chosen by Soros and Neier to launch Open Society's operations in the United States, discovered this fact soon after accepting the assignment. A veteran of Human Rights Watch and the ACLU but a self-described novice at running a philanthropy, LaMarche carefully refined the set of core issues on which Open Society US would focus its quarter-billion-dollar budget: criminal justice, drug policy, reproductive rights, money in politics.

But within a few months Soros became intensely concerned about the rights of immigrants. President Clinton had signed a welfare reform bill that among its harsher provisions took away social-safety-net protections from green-card holders—legal immigrants who were permanent residents. Soros told LaMarche that he wanted to set up a fund of $50 million to blunt the impact of the new law. "I was pretty new at philanthropy, and that seemed like an awful lot of money to me," LaMarche later wrote. "Not only did we not have a plan for it, we had never previously considered immigration as a focus area for the new U.S. programs."[36]

Nevertheless he and Neier scrambled, and within three weeks the Emma Lazarus Fund took shape. It would focus on services like language classes and legal assistance, as well as advocacy to change the law. Within a few years the money was spent and Open Society had become the largest funder of immigrant rights work; eventually the law was repealed and nearly all the benefits restored. "A pretty good return on our investment. None of it was planned," wrote LaMarche, who would run Open Society's US operations for more than a decade.

Under LaMarche's leadership, Open Society did pioneering work in social justice, funding many remarkable initiatives. Among the rising leaders whose work it supported was Bryan Stevenson, who created the Equal Justice Initiative to defend prisoners on death row and who would later found the National Memorial for Peace and Justice, commemorating the more than four thousand African Americans who were lynched in the United States.[37] Open Society also funded the work of the civil rights lawyer Michelle Alexander, who on her 2005 fellowship wrote her landmark book *The New Jim Crow*, which shined a light on mass incarceration and was the first book to popularize the idea of ending it. Through its fellowships and programs, Open Society brought credence to the idea that America had created a prison system that was race- and class-based, that the United States was the most over-incarcerated country in the world.

Open Society also did impressive work on LGBTQ rights—no other large foundation fastened onto this issue as aggressively. It didn't take up the movement in a major way, but by funding it at all, Open Society legitimized the aspiration and helped elevate the cause among the set of issues that progressive philanthropists talked about.

In these ways Soros redefined how philanthropy in a democracy can work—by bending society steadily, patiently toward justice, and by fostering the flow of issues and ideas. An open society requires patience and constant nurturing. At the Gates Foundation, when you're working on a vaccine, or at Rockefeller, when you're working on a new seed, every experiment may not yield a discovery, but it usually yields knowledge. It doesn't take you back. It accretes. But by its nature an open society is always contested, so the work of the philanthropist has to be a very different kind of work, at a different pace. Success is incremental and can be reversed. As we've seen recently in the United States, a handful of bad years can undo all the progress of a generation. In a democracy, from a social justice perspective, progress doesn't necessarily accrete.

Take the work Open Society does on voting. In a democracy, there are often powerful interests seeking to deprive marginalized groups of the vote—women, Black people, those without property, immigrants. The idea of participation by all citizens is perennially challenged. A major barrier to social justice in America has been barring or discouraging African Americans from voting. In the 1960s, the NAACP Legal Defense and Educational Fund was the preeminent institution that helped advance the Voting Rights Act.[38] It brought suits against states like Mississippi, Alabama, and Georgia to open up the polls. Nearly six decades later, in the run-up to the 2020 election, Mississippi, Alabama, Georgia, and other states were closing polling stations, requiring voters to produce driver's licenses, putting up all sorts of barriers that were clearly intended to suppress the Black vote. And once again on the front line, suing those states, was the Legal Defense Fund.

Of course the LDF, like the American Civil Liberties Union and other key institutions, was deeply engaged in this good work long before George Soros turned to philanthropy. But because he has always understood the centrality of race, Open Society has pitched in to support them to the tune of many millions of dollars a year. Typically the support takes the form of endowments and unrestricted institutional funding, which have nurtured their ability to survive long-term and keep up the fight. Soros has invested in them the way a venture capitalist invests in the companies in their portfolio: by finding the best talent and the best ideas, giving them operating capital, and believing that those who run the organization are best positioned to know how to deploy that capital.

Unfortunately, this kind of investing is a rarity in philanthropy. In 2019 the Ford Foundation commissioned a report from the Center for Effective Philanthropy on the state of unrestricted multiyear funding. The numbers were abysmal—only about 12 percent of all philanthropic giving fell into this category.[39] What holds it back is the "egos and logos" challenge. Philanthropists want their names on things. For the kinds of infrastructure support Soros provides, there aren't naming opportunities. You could say that not claiming credit is his signature; Central European University is not called George Soros University.

Unburdened by the egos and logos problem, Soros has been a pioneer on issues he thinks are significant. He is never afraid to jump first. The result is that Open Society has done more than any other philanthropy to take overlooked democratic concerns and move them from the margin to the mainstream of awareness and debate. As an example, the first program he funded in the United States on a national scale was the Project on Death in America, in 1994. It grew out of his personal experience. His mother had died not long before, at the age of eighty-nine. He was struck by the fact that because he could afford it, she was able to die at home with excellent care. He had conversations with her in the process of her dying that were very meaningful to him. So he became concerned that other families, who did not have his resources, would be unable to arrange a good death. Over the course of nine years and with $45 million in grants, the project set out to transform the experience of dying in the United States.[40] It promoted the reduction of suffering and emphasized the ability of people to live out their lives in dignity and comfort. It persuaded modern medicine to embrace palliative care and hospice, to make death less clinical and more humane.

Open Society did similarly pathbreaking work on disability rights in the 2000s. Before Soros, American foundations had viewed disability through a paternalistic, telethon, pity-these-poor-people lens, and not as an issue of justice. But starting with small grants in 2007 and working on a large scale by 2010, Open Society laid the groundwork for a disability rights movement that has reverberated not just in the United States but around the world.

Open Society has set the standard for boldness. Except for Soros, there weren't major philanthropists speaking out on marriage equality, marijuana legalization, or discrimination against Muslims. He has been swift to call out political leaders who are moving their democracies toward absolutism. After 9/11, he denounced George W. Bush's war on terror as an "erosion of the moral authority of the United States."[41] The Open Society opened a policy branch in Washington to counter the impact of the Patriot Act on immigration, civil liberties, privacy, due process, and religious tolerance.

And in 2013 when the Black Lives Matter movement grew out of protests over the death of Trayvon Martin and started working to raise awareness of the reality of white supremacy in America, there was no support from the large established foundations. In the 2016 presidential campaign, Hillary Clinton and Bernie Sanders would say the words "all lives matter" because "Black lives matter" made white voters uncomfortable.

Characteristically, Open Society fully embraced the Black Lives Matter movement, working closely with smaller foundations and family offices. So that in 2020, when the murders of George Floyd, Ahmaud Arbery, Breonna Taylor, and others brought home to all Americans the reality of racial injustice, more and more white people were ready to say that Black lives did matter. That reckoning was shaped by the framework Open Society helped build.

When you look for how Soros's work is informing a new generation, you need look no further than the philanthropy of MacKenzie Scott or Laurene Powell Jobs or Jon Stryker. These are billionaires who have followed in the steps of his radical social-justice grant making and system of beliefs. But I sometimes despair that there are too many new billionaires who are libertarians and as arrogant as Ayn Rand. In a recent panel discussion, a tech executive said that to address a major social problem, "we should just put a bunch of programmers in a room and they could solve this." This is how many in a new generation of wealth think about social issues.

George Soros's legacy is a challenge to this kind of thinking, a repudiation of philanthropy driven by technocratic ideas and a recognition that the root causes of social problems are in fact the things he identified at the very beginning of his journey. Open societies and democratic institutions need attending to. Racism, patriarchy, ableism, classism, and other forms of prejudice and bias underlie many of the world's problems. Philanthropy needs to resist the ideology of certitude and dedicate itself to curiosity, openness, equality, dignity, and justice.

Politics with a Purpose

Gara LaMarche

How did George Soros become a major figure in US politics and the target of the far right's nativist and anti-Semitic rage? The story goes back nearly twenty years.

On Tuesday, November 2, 2004, a steady stream of guests poured into George Soros's elegant Fifth Avenue apartment: financiers and executives, philanthropists and labor leaders, writers and actors, politicians and pundits. As canapes and drinks were passed around, most guests hovered around television sets tuned to CNN's coverage of the US presidential election. The mood in the room early in the evening was almost giddy; all day long, leaks of exit poll data seemed to indicate that the Democratic challenger, Senator John Kerry, would oust President George W. Bush from the Oval Office after a single term.

Of course that didn't happen, and as the night wore on, the mood turned glum. But that it came close to happening at all had much to do with the man hosting the party. During the previous two years, George Soros had invested heavily in Democratic politics, becoming one of the first "megadonors" after the McCain-Feingold campaign finance reforms drove large contributions from political parties into so-called independent expenditures. With an initial $20 million pledge, Soros organized other wealthy progressives to join him in creating America Coming Together, a massive, independent, direct-voter-contact operation. At the same time, he helped launch other institutions that would endure well past the 2004 contest, changing the shape of progressive politics and laying the groundwork for the Democrats to win a majority in Congress in 2006 and the White House in 2008. Over the years, Soros would play an important role in the rise of a new generation of political talent, from Barack Obama and Stacey Abrams to a host of progressive prosecutors around the country who are transforming criminal justice policy by rethinking the "tough on crime" approach that has been the predominant mindset since the 1970s.

It's a remarkable story, all the more so because Soros does not particularly like politics and thinks that fortunes like his should not give the men, women, and families who hold them outsized weight in policy and government. Indeed, through the work of his foundation, Soros has been one of the most prominent funders working to reduce the impact of money on politics. It's one of the many ironies and contradictions about a man long active in finance, global statecraft, and philanthropy, who was first drawn somewhat reluctantly to meaningful political engagement primarily by his concern about the Bush administration's policies (particularly the war on terror and its assaults on civil liberties and human rights), but who stuck with it to become one of the biggest forces in US progressive politics in the twenty-first century.

GEORGE SOROS HAD not been one of those rich people obsessed with politics. He was regularly approached for political contributions and occasionally gave them, usually to Democrats, including a $100,000 gift to the Democratic National Committee as early as 1992. But if pushed to describe his politics, Soros might have called himself a Rockefeller Republican, in the tradition of Nelson Rockefeller, the longtime governor of New York who was a leader of the liberal wing of the Republican Party in the 1950s and 1960s. As many as a dozen US senators still fit that description into the late 1970s.

To the extent Soros had a public image, at least to an informed public, it was as a wizard of shrewd investments—particularly after he "broke" the Bank of England in 1992—and, with his role in the collapse of communism in Eastern Europe and the former Soviet Union, as a promoter of democracy in formerly totalitarian and authoritarian regimes. Through the growth and boldness of his US philanthropy, which took on drug policy, immigrants' rights, and mass incarceration, Soros soon became controversial among Republicans before ultimately serving, in a gross distortion of his actual views, as a poster child for the radical left. But he has had continued cordial and productive dealings with George Pataki, the Republican governor of New York and a fellow person of Hungarian ancestry. Also around that time, Soros was invited to join a dinner in Washington with six US senators—three Republicans and three Democrats—who met once a month for a home-cooked meal and had a practice of inviting a guest to join them for conversation. Though Soros was disappointed by the dinner-table discussion—all the senators wanted to do was ask him about the markets, while Soros preferred to talk philosophy and global affairs—he was treated with respect.

At that time Soros's political giving was not particularly notable and almost completely reactive, as much political giving is. He gave because someone asked, or because a friend or colleague was hosting a fundraiser. While he sometimes consulted his children—his son Robert had a strong interest in New York State politics, and his son Jonathan was a regular host of candidate fundraisers—he had no political adviser or strategy.

This began to change when Hamilton Fish V, the scion of an old New York political family—his father and grandfather had served in Congress as Republicans, and Fish had run unsuccessfully for Congress as a Democrat—was hired in 1999 as a consultant to organize Soros's political contributions. Fish began to group requests from US House and Senate candidates into categories, like "toss-up" and "long shot," and attempted to align Soros's giving with his issue interests as manifested by his foundation's priorities, like immigration, criminal justice, and reproductive rights. For incumbents, he looked at voting records, and challengers were asked to fill out a questionnaire.

That's not rocket science, but it made Soros's giving a bit more focused. According to Fish, Soros appreciated the guidance but was largely uninterested in the horse-race aspect of politics. He did not see the work as "game-changing."

When Morton Halperin, a former State Department official and chief lobbyist for the American Civil Liberties Union in Washington, went to work for Soros in 2002 to build a larger DC policy presence, Soros bought out some of his time to advise on political contributions, and in addition to aligning them with Soros's substantive interests, Halperin involved Soros a bit more in legislative leadership battles, like the contest between Nancy Pelosi and Steny Hoyer for who would become Democratic leader in the US House. Soros quietly aided Pelosi, forging a long-lasting partnership. In the early 2000s, as Soros became increasingly exercised about the administration of George W. Bush—telling Halperin that "Bush is going to destroy the country, we have to do something about it"—and as he grew interested in learning how right-wing donors influenced elections, he turned to Halperin to take some initial steps in exploring a larger political role.

And at the same time, Soros was exploring how to have an impact in a more direct way—by supporting ballot initiatives to reform state drug laws.

◌◌

WHEN SOROS TURNED his philanthropic attention to the United States in the mid-1990s, after a decade of focusing primarily on Eastern Europe and the former Soviet Union, he started with two issues that epitomized for him American failures of open society, each representing a taboo in public discussion and academic research and practice. One, strongly influenced by his experiences with the death of his parents, was the Project on Death in America, devoted to improving care at the end of life, particularly pain relief. The other, originally called the Lindesmith Center (after the late Alfred Lindesmith, a prominent scholar of addiction), was a think tank devoted to drug policy, a field where ever since the Nixon-era and Reagan-era wars on drugs it was virtually impossible to obtain funding for any research that did not reflect the dominant prohibitionist view. The center originally had no articulated policy agenda, and Soros was careful to say he did not have definite views about drug legalization. But it soon became a critical center for research, discussion, and debate.

To lead the Lindesmith Center, Soros hired Ethan Nadelmann, a Princeton University scholar who had written extensively on drug policy. An energetic evangelist for a different approach to drugs who formed alliances with libertarians and conservatives as well as progressives, Nadelmann came to enjoy Soros's confidence and soon began to suggest ways that Soros could fund efforts to chip away at weak links in the war on drugs.

The opening wedge was the use of marijuana for medicinal purposes. There was significant evidence that the active chemicals in marijuana have a positive effect in stemming anxiety, controlling nausea, and relieving pain. A number of patients around the country had become aware of this and were using marijuana to deal with one or more of these symptoms—often from cancer or its treatments, multiple sclerosis, or Alzheimer's disease—but they ran the risk of arrest and prosecution, as did those helping them, and obtaining marijuana illegally was not always easy. If a state removed penalties for the use of marijuana for healing, it would not only help patients but also open up thinking about the other injustices and inconsistencies of drug prohibition.

Twenty-five state constitutions authorized the use of ballot initiatives or referenda to enact or repeal laws. This approach to legislating required the first step of collecting a significant number of voter signatures to place the measure on the ballot—as a practical matter, considerably more than the law required, in order to withstand the inevitable legal challenges—and in some cases a supermajority vote was required in order for a new law to pass. The rules varied considerably from state to state.

Until the late 1990s ballot initiatives were used most regularly in California, and almost always to advance policies favored by the right, such as two that were voted on in 1978: Proposition 13, which limited property taxes and made it more difficult to raise them in the future, and the so-called Briggs Initiative, which sought to bar gays and lesbians from teaching in schools. Proposition 13 won and the Briggs Initiative failed, but experiences like these had left some liberals skeptical about the popular democracy that ballot initiatives facilitated; in any case, they had rarely made use of these mechanisms.

Despite this, Nadelmann saw this path as a way to break through the political logjam that had so many officeholders cowed by fears of being seen as "soft" on drugs. Whether voters were ready for full marijuana decriminalization—Nadelmann's ultimate goal, but one Soros was far from ready for in 1995—they might be persuaded that denying pain relief was unnecessarily harsh. Nadelmann consulted with Bill Zimmerman, a California strategist knowledgeable about initiative campaigns, and Chuck Blitz, a Santa Barbara philanthropist. They engaged the pollster Celinda Lake to assess public opinion and determined that such a measure could pass if they got it on the ballot for the 1996 election. Zimmerman estimated the campaign would cost about $3.5 million.

When Nadelmann laid out the strategy to Soros, he didn't reject it, but he was reluctant to act without funding partners. Soros had recently met Peter B. Lewis, the chairman of the Cleveland-based Progressive Insurance Company, who had himself relied on marijuana for pain relief and who was strongly interested. Nadelmann practiced shuttle diplomacy between the two men, who were just getting to know each other. Soon thereafter, a third donor came into the mix: George Zimmer, the founder of the Men's Wearhouse chain, whom Nadelmann had met at the World Economic Forum in Davos. By early 1996 the three men had agreed to work together and finance the initiative campaign—by that time it had a number, Proposition 215—with Soros providing an initial donation of $500,000.

A fourth donor, John Sperling, preferred to focus on his home state of Arizona. A former union organizer who had made his fortune through the for-profit University of Phoenix, Sperling was backing a treatment versus incarceration initiative in Arizona that year.

In November the California initiative passed with a 55 percent majority, and the Arizona measure with an even larger margin, 65 percent, with both campaigns tapping into unusual political coalitions and alliances that scrambled the standard right-left divides. In Arizona, for instance, former senator and 1964 Republican presidential candidate Barry Goldwater served as the campaign's chairman.

The success of the two initiatives caught public attention and ushered in a wave of attacks from voices like *New York Times* columnist A. M. Rosenthal and former secretary of health, education and welfare Joseph Califano, who headed a Columbia University center for the study of addiction and called Soros "the Daddy Warbucks of drug legalization."[1] The media connected the dots, and Soros, whose US philanthropy was just getting started and who had always had a low political profile, was suddenly thrust into the spotlight, accused as a stealth drug legalizer. This was the first manifestation of what in time would become a right-wing obsession with demonizing Soros.

At the same time, Nadelmann and his allies were encouraged by the strong political showing and scanned the country for other opportunities where there would be public support to chip away at the war on drugs, such as favoring treatment over incarceration or reforming asset-forfeiture laws. Drawing up a campaign budget of about $9 million for the multistate effort, Nadelmann approached Soros for additional support, and he agreed to put up a third of the money if Peter Lewis and John Sperling would do the same. According to Nadelmann, Lewis and Sperling said yes within twenty-four hours of being asked. All six ballot measures passed, with an additional three related measures enacted into law by the voters in Arizona.

In 2000, the three men—who had only met twice as a group as they spent a total of $30 million together—teamed up for a broader drug initiative in California, Proposition 36, which mandated that eligible nonviolent drug offenders be sent to treatment programs instead of to jail or prison. It passed with 61 percent of the vote. In the same year, however, medicinal marijuana ballot measures were defeated in Massachusetts, Colorado, and Nevada, ushering in a bad patch for the direct-democracy approach. Two years later, in the post-9/11 climate of fear and insecurity, medical marijuana campaigns also lost in Ohio and Michigan.

This period, largely preceding George Soros's entry into national politics on a wider scale, proved to be a harbinger of several tendencies that would mark Soros's political work. First, he relied heavily on experts—in this case, Nadelmann and the team around him—for advice on the most strategic opportunities. He took a strong interest but never micromanaged. Second, as in his philanthropy, while he did not seek controversy, he did not shy from it, either. Third, he liked having partners, leveraging his donations with those of others and at times agreeing to be leveraged by them.

These ballot initiatives changed the law, and consequently millions of lives. They also shook up the public debate over drug policy and incarceration, creating a climate for more political boldness and attracting a new generation of activists who saw criminal justice policy as a set of injustices in dire need of reckoning. In many ways, at least in the United States, this may be the greatest legacy of Soros's political and philanthropic involvement.

∾

As THE NEW century dawned, Soros had not been particularly alarmed by the prospect of a George W. Bush presidency, because Bush had run on a platform of "compassionate conservatism." Indeed, one of Bush's key education advisers in Texas, Uri Treisman, had also worked closely with Soros's foundation, helping to evaluate the considerable investment the foundation had made in the Mississippi-based Algebra Project, founded by the civil rights activist Robert Parris Moses.

Despite his involvement in state ballot initiatives on drug policy, Soros remained largely unengaged with candidates and political parties, but at his urging the Open Society Foundations had been quite active in funding research and advocacy in support of campaign finance reform. The foundations supported groups like the Brennan Center for Justice and Public Campaign, a new effort to promote the public financing of elections, in which Soros joined forces with the Schumann Foundation, of which Bill Moyers was president. And in 2002 Congress passed the McCain-Feingold law, named after its two Senate sponsors; it was the first piece of significant campaign finance reform legislation since the post-Watergate reforms in 1974. McCain-Feingold regulated the flow of "soft money" into party committees, seeking to limit the power of corporations, unions, and wealthy donors in the political process.

Even as he decried the influence of money on politics, Soros remained aware that any reform of the system would inevitably be "gamed," as money would always find a way. Indeed, that's what happened with McCain-Feingold: large donations from institutions like businesses and labor (accepting for a moment the false equation of the two, since labor donations represent the small-dollar dues of working people) did not cease but were channeled into "independent" and even less adequately regulated vehicles. This accelerated even more after the Supreme Court's 2010 decision in *Citizens United v. FEC*, which equated corporate spending with speech and removed all limitations on it.

One of the many ironies about Soros's engagement in politics is that the unintended consequence of a reform he backed was to open up new avenues for his role in the political process. As Mark Schmitt, a former aide to Senator Bill Bradley who was hired by the Open Society Foundations to advise on money in politics and other democracy reforms, put it, before McCain-Feingold, donors were "passive investors" in established party committees. But afterward, they could "take command" of alternative fundraising vehicles and "actively move the chess pieces."

~

SOROS IS AT his core a globalist, and in the first term of the George W. Bush administration, he concluded that US leadership had become a "threat to the world order." Soros opposed the war in Iraq and deplored the falsehoods and misrepresentations that the administration promoted in order to manipulate the country into war, but his deepest objection was sparked by Bush's declaration of a "war on terror" after the attacks of September 11, 2001. Soros agreed that the terrorist attacks were despicable and had to be dealt with, but the incursions on human rights and civil liberties undertaken in the name of the war on terror were unforgivable and would be hard to roll back. These included the roundups of Muslims and South Asians across America for questioning, as if ethnicity and religion were themselves a cause for suspicion; the rash passage of the Patriot Act, which expanded the definition of support for terrorism and expanded government surveillance powers; the indefinite detention of suspects at the Guantanamo Bay detention camp; and the practice of torture by US agents there as well as at the notorious Abu Ghraib prison in Iraq.

Of particular concern to Soros was Bush's view that in the war against terror, "either you're with us or you're with the terrorists"[2]—effectively equating dissent with treason. Such was the climate of intimidation and fear in the weeks after the 9/11 attacks that it was hard to obtain public agreement even on an anodyne statement declaring that dissent is patriotic, as Soros learned to his dismay when an effort to collect the signatures of prominent Americans—writers, university and foundation presidents, religious leaders, and others—for such a declaration failed to attract a critical mass. Soros ended up signing it himself with his US foundation board leadership and taking out an ad in the *New York Times*.

For all those reasons, as Soros wrote in *The Age of Fallibility*, he concluded that "nothing else I could do would benefit the world as much as helping to limit President Bush to one term."[3]

With this goal in mind, Soros engaged two consultants, Tom Novick and Mark Steitz, to solicit their separate views on how increased spending in the 2004 election cycle could be put to best use. (It was not unusual for Soros to ask two people to take on the same task, as a hedge and to keep control.) Novick and Steitz came up with similar recommendations: They proposed a grassroots mobilization effort starting in key battleground states and expanding to other states that might be put into play. They also identified opportunities for the critical period in the late spring and early summer, following the conclusion of the Democratic primary season, when the presumptive nominee would likely be out of money until public financing funds were released after the Democratic convention.

At the same time, and independent of Soros's inquiries, a number of political strategists working with large advocacy institutions and labor unions had been thinking along similar lines. The prime mover in these efforts was Gina Glantz, a top aide to Andrew Stern, the new president of the Service Employees International Union, and a former campaign manager for Walter Mondale in 1984 and campaign manager for Bill Bradley's 2000 challenge to Al Gore for the Democratic presidential nomination. Glantz was struck that a number of the friends she had made in politics and labor did not seem to know one another, so she invited a group of them to a dinner in the spring of 2003. Her guests included Ellen Malcolm, the founder and president of Emily's List, which worked to elect pro-choice female Democratic candidates; Harold Ickes, a former Clinton administration deputy chief of staff; SEIU president Andy Stern; Steve Rosenthal, the former political director for the AFL-CIO; and Carl Pope, the president of the Sierra Club.

Although each of these individuals and their affiliated organizations were powerful political players, they'd never worked closely together on an election. Having studied the provisions of the new

McCain-Feingold law, Glantz and Malcolm suggested that they could come together as an independent political organization under Section 527 of the Internal Revenue Code, observing its prohibitions against directly advocating the election or defeat of a particular candidate and steering clear of any collaboration with the candidates or political parties. Over coffee, after the proposal for joint activity had been discussed for a while, Glantz remembers Carl Pope picking up a sugar packet and tossing it into the center of the table, declaring, "I'm in." Soon the others were as well.

No one in this group had met George Soros, but they had heard that he was interested in backing a plan to beat Bush, so they made contact.

By all accounts the pivotal event was a gathering in July 2003 at Soros's summer home in the Hamptons. Malcolm, Pope, Ickes, and Rosenthal were invited for the weekend to lay out their plan, and Soros, eager to have partners in any effort that would emerge, invited Peter Lewis, his collaborator on drug policy ballot initiatives, and a number of other progressive political donors. These included Rob Glaser, a former Microsoft executive active in the support of progressive media (including Air America, the short-lived liberal radio network); Anne Bartley, a former Clinton aide and stepdaughter of the former Arkansas governor Winthrop Rockefeller; Patricia Bauman, a longtime leader of civic engagement efforts in the philanthropic world; Rob McKay, an heir to the Taco Bell fortune and later board chair of the Democracy Alliance; and Dorothy and Lewis Cullman, New York philanthropists and political donors.

Over the course of an afternoon, the political strategists made their pitch for an independent political organization, America Coming Together (ACT), that would make sophisticated use of new data techniques to identify possible supporters, hire field organizers in key states, knock on doors in the early months to register voters, and follow up as the election neared to make sure they turned out to vote. A parallel effort, the Media Fund, would create hard-hitting ad content, separate from the communications for the eventual candidate. They then retired to a nearby motel for the evening while the donors met among themselves.

When the strategists returned the next morning, Soros told them that he and Peter Lewis were willing to put in $10 million each, and he asked Steve Rosenthal to call Andy Stern to encourage SEIU to put in $20 million, though he was concerned that the effort not be perceived as a labor union initiative that he'd just tagged onto. Ellen Malcolm, screwing up her courage, suggested to Soros that if he wanted to avoid that impression, he should give the same amount he was asking SEIU to put up, $20 million. Soros said yes, as did Lewis. The other donors at the gathering, many of whom lacked the capacity for an eight-figure donation, pledged $3 million among them. Malcolm, an experienced fundraiser, was flabbergasted at what had been accomplished in a weekend, recalling, "It was more than Emily's List had ever raised to that point."

Steve Rosenthal was hired to run ACT, and Harold Ickes oversaw fundraising and the operations of the Media Fund.

In the 2004 election cycle, ACT raised $146 million and put on an impressive show of "boots on the ground" that hadn't been seen in many years. ACT employed forty-five thousand paid canvassers in battleground states, with eighty-six offices, four thousand staff, and twenty-five thousand volunteers. On the media side, a typical example was a health-care ad that ran in seventeen states. It never mentioned John Kerry, but as a woman on screen lamented her mounting health-care bills, an off-screen narrator intoned, "Health-care costs are soaring. Under President Bush, millions more Americans are uninsured. And those who have coverage are paying more out of pocket."

Along with ACT and the Media Fund, Soros was an early backer that year of another advocacy organization, America Votes, a national collaboration of issue organizations working together at the state and national level to increase voter turnout and support progressive policy initiatives. Headed originally by Cecile Richards, an experienced organizer from Texas (where her mother, Ann Richards, had been governor) who had worked as an aide to Nancy Pelosi and later became president of Planned Parenthood, America Votes for the first time brought together in coalition labor, civil rights, environmental, religious, and other organizations unused to working together and seeing beyond their particular issues or constituencies. Some of the groups had significant electoral capacity, some relied on America Votes to provide it, but all coordinated their strategies through the coalition.

Soros's other significant electoral contribution in 2004 was a donation of $2.5 million to MoveOn.org, the progressive membership organization that came into being during the impeachment of President Bill Clinton (from which it had urged Congress and the country to "move on") and had most recently grown substantially as a hub of popular opposition to the Iraq war. Soros paired his contribution with one of equal size by Peter Lewis, with the funds set aside to match small-dollar donors to the organization.

After the 2004 election, Rosenthal and the other ACT leaders were eager to continue it as a permanent organization, since despite falling short of victory, it had built capacity on the ground across the country. Keeping it going at a modest level in off years, and ramping up to full capacity in election years, would break the boom-and-bust cycle of civic engagement that had bedeviled progressives for decades. But while Soros had been relatively pleased with the work he supported, he and Lewis decided against continuing their financial support.

As the columnist Thomas Edsall observed in *The Washington Post*, "By all measures but one, ACT and the Media Fund were a great success, helping to turn out record numbers of new voters. But that one measure was the one that counted," since Bush was reelected and Republicans made gains in both the House and the Senate.[4] That measure—the bottom line of victory—was obviously important, and the nation faced two more years of consolidated Republican rule. But it was far from the only measure of ACT's impact. In Carl Pope's view, echoed by many others, Soros's role in supporting a collaboration among progressive groups that had rarely worked together before "catalyzed the creation of a multi-issue left." Gina Glantz believed

that while Soros fell short of victory, he "created a class of organizers in the states who have gone on to be the backbone of the progressive movement" and of many subsequent victories. She credited
Soros and his fellow donors with "fostering a culture of innovation"
and even, given the enormous scale of the effort, making it possible for field organizers to be better paid. Patrick Gaspard, an ACT
official who later served as Barack Obama's White House political
director, US ambassador to South Africa, and president of Soros's
Open Society Foundations, pointed out that everywhere ACT was on
the ground, John Kerry overperformed at the polls relative to other
states. Mark Steitz, one of the two consultants whose opinion Soros
solicited early on in his effort to defeat Bush, observed that the tools
ACT developed in 2004 played a substantial role in Barack Obama's
victory four years later.

WHILE SOROS DECIDED against continuing his support of ACT after
the 2004 presidential election, he did not lose interest in building a
stronger political infrastructure for the center left. Indeed, his sense
of strengths and weaknesses in the ecosystem of progressive organizations was deepened by his 2004 experience.

A number of efforts had been made in the past to persuade Soros
to counter the right, but because Soros had always resisted political
labels and did not approach his philanthropy in ideological terms,
he'd always been resistant. In the late 1990s, for instance, Bill Moyers
came to an Open Society board dinner at Soros's house in Bedford,
New York, armed with a recent report from the National Committee for Responsive Philanthropy (NCRP) called *Moving a Public Policy
Agenda: The Strategic Philanthropy of Conservative Foundations.*[5] The report
argued that progressive donors should follow the example set by the
conservative movement, particularly its corporate base, in the years
following the enactment of Lyndon Johnson's popular Great Society
programs. The corporate lawyer Lewis F. Powell, a future Supreme

Court justice, laid out the stakes in a now legendary 1971 memo to the
US Chamber of Commerce, arguing that business had been compla-
cent in the undermining of capitalism on college campuses and in
the media, and that conservative US foundations ought to invest in
new conservative institutions to turn this picture around. The Bradley, Scaife, and Olin foundations took up this challenge and funded
conservative think tanks, media, and leadership programs, most notably the Heritage Foundation and the Federalist Society, the latter of
which promoted conservative and "originalist" jurisprudence in opposition to the "rights revolution" that had emerged from the Warren
Court's rulings in the 1960s. By the early 2000s, progressives could see
that conservative ideas and policies dominated the terms of American political debate, even when center-left Democrats like Carter and
Clinton made it to the White House.

Moyers went away empty-handed from that dinner at Soros's
home, but he may have made an impression. Soros was eager to continue working with Peter Lewis and Andy Stern, and the three donors
began to explore what they could do together, joined by the California philanthropists and bankers Marion and Herbert Sandler, who
relied on advice from John Podesta, the former Clinton White House
chief of staff and the head of the Center for American Progress, a
new progressive think tank. Under discussion was the creation of a
$300 million fund that would identify and finance coordinated invest-
ments in progressive infrastructure.

In time, though, the quartet of donors could not agree on a common plan, but Soros, Lewis, and Stern soon grew interested in another,
broader collaboration that was taking shape, this one spearheaded
by a former Commerce Department official named Rob Stein. Stein
had spent some months pulling together data on the scale of right-
wing institutions in media, ideas, law, leadership training, and civic
engagement, and displayed it side by side with what he could find
that was comparable on the progressive side. Not surprisingly, as with
the NCRP report a few years earlier, it showed progressives badly
outgunned.

Soros's son Jonathan had attended one of Stein's presentations and was impressed. He encouraged his father to attend a confidential breakfast at the office of Alan Patricof, a New York Democratic donor, and Soros attended, along with Peter Lewis. They were impressed by the data, but even more by what Stein proposed to do with it: create an alliance—a kind of donor "club" —composed of people who would agree in advance to underwrite the investments in building new organizations and strengthening existing ones. As Stein made his presentation to groups of donors around the country—in Los Angeles, San Francisco, Boston, Washington, and elsewhere— interest built, and by early 2005 he and his colleagues were ready to convene all the interested donors in one place.

At a posh resort outside Scottsdale, Arizona, about fifty donors and a handful of their advisers assembled in April 2005. Stein gave opening remarks; Soros was interviewed by Bill Moyers; the donors got to know one another; the results of further research were presented; and a series of high-tech instant polls took the attendees' temperature on a variety of issues and approaches. Some, long frustrated with the Democratic Party and its various arms, were eager to cut to the chase, and at one point the voice of the actor and director Rob Reiner boomed from the back of the room: "Where's the strategy?"

That would have to wait for a second meeting in the fall, by which time the group—now called the Democracy Alliance—had arrived at a business model and a strategy. From the second weekend gathering emerged decisions to collectively commit roughly $30 million to relatively new groups like the Center for American Progress; Media Matters for America, which tracked right-wing talk radio, Fox News, and similar outlets to expose bigotry, falsehoods, and hypocrisy; and the American Constitution Society, which proposed to do for progressive jurisprudence and academic and judicial leadership development what the Federalist Society had achieved on the right.

The next year, with Soros in the lead, the Alliance would invest heavily in building capacity for the progressive movement. Central to this effort was Catalist, a data warehouse for voter information. The science and practice of using various kinds of data to predict voter behavior was developing substantially in these years, following the advances made by George W. Bush's top political adviser Karl Rove, who identified niche audiences—like NASCAR fans or Cracker Barrel customers—that correlated heavily with conservative political sympathies. Progressives were eager to catch up and avoid squandering their ad spending or door knocking on voters who would never vote for a Democrat. Catalist was set up as a nonprofit organization separate from the Democratic Party, as a movement resource and utility that would be available only for civic engagement efforts.

The members of the Democracy Alliance paid a stiff entry fee along with annual dues of $30,000, and they pledged to give at least $200,000 a year to causes recommended by the Alliance's staff and board. (According to Rob Stein, Peter Lewis had offered to guarantee the entire operating budget, but Stein turned him down, believing that it would harm the new organization to be overly reliant on any one donor.) While over the years the Alliance would become a significant force in progressive politics, two decisions made at the outset—both of which Soros strongly urged—could be said to have limited its impact, relative to what emerged as its counterpart on the right, the network funded and led by the Koch brothers. The first was not to create a pooled fund, from which a central strategy could be funded as needed, but to leave the question of which organizations to support to individual donor option, as long as they met the $200,000 minimum and funded groups on the recommended list. This made funding somewhat more of a popularity contest, with an edge to charismatic leaders who were good at schmoozing the donors, a skill that was not always correlated with impact. The second was to keep the size of the Alliance's staff fairly small, which limited its capacity for research, assessment, and evaluation. Soros and some of the other donors felt that sufficient capacity existed within their own organizations and that the Alliance did not need to duplicate it.

Nevertheless, the Alliance, which in time grew to more than one hundred members, including a number of labor unions along with the high-net-worth donors, has steered more than a billion dollars to progressive groups in its first sixteen years. As part of this effort, the Alliance also helped existing anchors of the progressive infrastructure like the Center on Budget and Policy Priorities, the Brennan Center for Justice, and the Center for Community Change, which had been primarily dependent on foundations, diversify their support with significant contributions by individual donors.

Soros remained active in the Democracy Alliance, and always had an employee represent him on the organization's board. According to Rob Stein, quite apart from his financial contributions, Soros "validated" the Democracy Alliance. He participated regularly, though he was by far the richest and most generous of the donors, and many other members joined or stayed in the Alliance because they wanted to be around him.

More broadly, Stein believes, "Soros has been a North Star for the development of a more confident progressive capacity. He gave us the gift of imagination—of hope in ourselves."

As Soros became more involved in US politics, he began to take more of an interest in emerging leaders with political talent, as he had done for decades in other parts of the world, building working relationships with many heads of state, key ministers, and leaders of intergovernmental organizations.

According to Michael Vachon, Soros's one-person political staff since 2001, Barack Obama was one of the first politicians in whom Soros took an interest. Soros first met him in Chicago in 2003 (during a trip barnstorming and fundraising for ACT), when Obama, then an Illinois state senator, was thinking of running for the US Senate. The two men had breakfast at the Four Seasons Hotel, where Soros expressed his admiration for Obama's memoir, *Dreams from My Father*, and afterward Vachon, who had joined Soros at the breakfast, remarked, "I think we may have met the first Black president." For his part, Soros thought that the fact that Obama had spent part of his childhood abroad augured well for his global consciousness.

Soros went on to hold the first big New York fundraiser for Obama's senate campaign, with Vernon Jordan as the featured speaker, and he and his family members hosted additional fundraisers over the next year.

In December 2006, with Obama now in the US Senate and contemplating a presidential run in 2008, Obama came to see Soros at his office in New York. By then he had published a second book, less autobiographical and more policy-focused, called *The Audacity of Hope*.

"Your first book was really good," Soros told Obama after they were seated in his office. "The second one is a bit empty." Yet Soros was enthusiastic about the prospect of Obama's candidacy and agreed to back him. By this time Soros was a significant Democratic donor and was known to have a good relationship with Senator Hillary Clinton, Obama's principal opponent for the nomination, and so Soros's endorsement made news and was widely viewed as a big boost for Obama. (While an admirer of Hillary Clinton, whom he worked with on poverty and women's rights issues in Haiti, Soros had not been a fan of Bill Clinton, believing he had wasted opportunities to rebuild democracy in the former Soviet sphere after the collapse of communism and seeing him as a transactional political operator.)

Before agreeing to make his preference publicly known, Soros called Hillary Clinton to deliver the news himself, arguing that it would strengthen the ultimate nominee to have a vigorous primary process. "Thank you for telling me," she responded. "I look forward to your support in the general election."

Despite, or perhaps especially because of, his early and ardent backing of Obama's candidacy, Soros was extremely disappointed by Obama's presidency. According to his son Alex, he had expected to play the kind of role for Obama that Bernard Baruch, an earlier financier and statesman, had played for both Woodrow Wilson and Franklin Roosevelt—a kind of outside adviser on economics and global relations.

An early sign that this was not to be was Obama's failure to take Soros's advice on how to deal with the worst financial crisis since the Great Depression. As Soros put it in a 2011 essay, "I published a series of articles in the *Financial Times* but got little response from the Obama administration. I had many more discussions with Larry Summers before he became the President's economic adviser than after. My greatest disappointment is that I was unable to establish any kind of personal contact with Obama himself."[6]

More was at stake for Soros than just access, since he was a man accustomed to being sought out by a steady stream of heads of state when they came to New York each year for the UN General Assembly. He feared the policy choices Obama and his team were making would not make maximum use of the crisis. As he and the economist Rob Johnson later wrote in an article titled "A Better Bailout Was Possible": "We believe a critical opportunity was missed when the balance of the burden of adjustment was tilted heavily in favor of creditors relative to debtors in the response to the crisis and that this contributed to the prolonged stagnation that followed the crisis."[7] Soros had urged Summers to inject equity into fragile banks and write down mortgages to help the economy recover, but Summers rejected the advice out of fear that it would mean nationalizing banks.

While giving Obama some credit for managing an extremely difficult economic situation, Soros also felt the way the president handled it, both in terms of the public relations of the administration's actions and Obama's tendency to accommodate the Republicans, were politically costly. He wrote: "The electorate showed no appreciation of Obama for moderating the recession because it was not aware of what he had done. By avoiding conflict Obama handed the initiative to the opposition, and the opposition had no incentive to cooperate. The Republican propaganda machine was able to convince people that the financial crisis was due to government failure, not market failure."[8]

Soros was unable to arrange a meeting with the president until September 2010, when Obama was in New York for the annual UN General Assembly meeting. The administration was eager to keep

Soros on board and spending on behalf of Democratic candidates in the critical midterm elections that year. The meeting did not go well. Each proud man misread the other, Soros arriving with a list of actions he thought Obama should take and Obama irked that Soros thought he had not already considered these actions. The two men only met in person once more.

Guided by Vachon's eye and by the recommendations of his foundation officials, Soros has arguably had more influence at the state and local level. He was an early patron of two young Black political stars who came within a hairsbreadth of becoming governors of their states, Andrew Gillum of Florida and Stacey Abrams of Georgia.

Gillum, elected at age twenty-three to the Tallahassee City Commission, first came to Soros's attention in 2002 through his foundation's support of the Young Elected Leaders project of People for the American Way. Stacey Abrams's longstanding effort to register Black voters through her New Georgia Project, long a favorite of Soros, so successfully expanded the electorate in the state that it voted Democratic in the 2020 presidential election, for the first time in almost thirty years, and in January 2021 elected two Democrats to the US Senate, creating a Democratic majority for the first time in ten years and providing a critical margin for President Joe Biden's governing agenda. Many believe that Abrams lost her gubernatorial bid in 2018 only because of widespread voter suppression (overseen by her opponent Brian Kemp, then Georgia's secretary of state); when she formed a new organization, Fair Fight, to protect and expand voting rights in Georgia and across the country, Soros was an early and generous backer.

Soros has also dabbled a bit in New York City politics, as an early backer of what first seemed like a longshot candidacy by Bill de Blasio, who was elected to the first of two terms as mayor in 2013. In the 2021 mayoral race, his family lent support to Maya Wiley, a first-time candidate who had once worked for Soros's foundation as a racial equity specialist and an adviser on criminal justice programs in South Africa.

∾

GEORGE SOROS BECAME involved significantly in US politics when he saw George W. Bush as threatening the international order, as a means to protect the values he'd spent billions of dollars trying to advance through his foundation. So it makes sense that he would come around to using the tools of politics to take on one of his signature issues: criminal justice reform.

From the very earliest days of Soros's US philanthropy, he put a strong focus on the criminal justice system as one of the starkest manifestations of the shortcomings of open society in America: mass incarceration, long before that was a widely used term of art sparking a social movement; policing abuses; indigent defense; and the death penalty. In his philanthropy and through parallel lobbying efforts from his Open Society Policy Center, Soros funded hundreds of fellowships for writers and activists. One of the first went to Michelle Alexander, a scholar who used the support to write *The New Jim Crow*, which galvanized a generation of activists. Another went to Vanita Gupta, a young lawyer with the NAACP Legal Defense Fund who took on a case of rampant prosecutorial abuse in Tulia, Texas, where half the town's Black population was rounded up in a drug sting operation. Gupta went on to head the Civil Rights Division in the Justice Department under President Obama and returned to government as associate attorney general under President Biden. Many other grants went to formerly imprisoned persons and their family members, an early recognition that those most affected by the justice system should be in the vanguard of efforts to reform it. It is increasingly hard to find the leader of a criminal justice reform effort working today at the state or federal level who has not been the beneficiary of a Soros Justice Fellowship.

Soros and Open Society were at times the leading funder of the movement to ban stop-and-frisk policing, and have underwritten much of the considerable progress in rolling back the death penalty, which had long seemed intractable, by shifting the focus of reform to questions of innocence and error. In the twenty years or so since Soros took on the issue, executions have declined to their lowest point in decades (despite an appalling spate of federal executions in the last days of the Trump administration), and public support for capital punishment has sunk below 50 percent.

One element of the decline in executions is that many fewer prosecutors seek to impose the death penalty, particularly in traditional high-execution states like Texas and Florida. Veteran prosecutors have begun to realize, apart from the moral considerations, that the death penalty is expensive and time-consuming without any proven impact on public safety. But it's also the case that in many jurisdictions, the prosecutors in place are new ones, a striking set of changes in which Soros's political giving has played a key role.

There are 2,300 elected prosecutors in the United States. Most are men, most are white, and most have enjoyed effective lifetime tenure, often cruising to reelection every four years without opposition. (In the nearly eighty years from 1942 to 2021, only five men served as Manhattan district attorney, and two of them, Frank Hogan and Robert Morgenthau, held the office for a combined sixty-seven years; Henry Wade, whose name is attached to the landmark abortion rights case, was district attorney in Dallas for thirty-six years.) The shape of criminal justice in their jurisdictions—who is tried and how they are sentenced—is powerfully determined by prosecutors.

In 2004, around the time that Soros became active on the national political scene, he was persuaded by Ethan Nadelmann to make a foray, backed by the Working Families Party, into a prosecutor's race in Albany County, the seat of New York's state government. David Soares, a Black immigrant from Cape Verde, challenged and beat the incumbent, pulling off a stunning political upset after a campaign based primarily on opposition to the draconian Rockefeller drug laws.

Soros didn't engage in another district attorney race for a number of years, but in 2015 he created a pilot project to oust prosecutors in Mississippi and Louisiana. The initiative, which became the Justice and Public Safety PAC, has since helped to elect more than thirty new prosecutors, with wins far outnumbering losses. Led by Whitney Tymas, an African American woman and former Virginia prosecutor who started her career as a public defender in West Harlem, Justice and Public Safety did not just sit back and wait for candidates to approach it for assistance. Aided by research from the political consulting firm BerlinRosen, it undertook analyses of which communities were most in need of a shift in prosecutorial priorities, conducted messaging research, identified and recruited promising candidates (most of them women and men of color), and created winning campaign plans using television, radio, digital advertising, mail, and field operations.

The payoff has been enormous, not only in victories, but in the changes these prosecutors have made once in office. Scott Colom, the African American prosecutor for four Mississippi counties, was able in just a year to double the number of defendants diverted to alternative sentencing programs. In Chicago, Kim Foxx enacted significant bail reforms. James Stewart, the Caddo Parish attorney in Louisiana, advocated for unanimous jury verdicts to strengthen defendants' rights. Aramis Ayala, the state attorney for the Ninth Judicial Circuit in Florida, vowed not to seek the death penalty. Stephanie Morales, the commonwealth attorney in Portsmouth, Virginia, dropped most misdemeanor marijuana cases. John Creuzot, the Dallas County district attorney, successfully pressed for the conviction of a police officer who shot an innocent Black man. Parisa Dehghani-Tafti, the commonwealth attorney for Arlington County, Virginia, stopped prosecuting low-level marijuana cases. Kim Gardner, the St. Louis district attorney, reduced the jail population to stem the spread of COVID. Perhaps the most well-known of the reform district attorneys, Larry Krasner of Philadelphia, has been a center of resistance to Trump administration justice policies.

And in the course of electing reform candidates, the project has ended the careers of some notorious prosecutors, like the Chicago incumbent involved in the cover-up of the killing of Laquan McDonald and the bigoted sheriff Joe Arpaio in Maricopa County, Arizona.

Predictably, there has been a strong backlash. Soros is one of the right's leading bogeymen, and once the "law and order" establishment got wind of his engagement in these races—as Whitney Tymas puts it, "when they know he is coming, they get ready"—right-wing voices like Newt Gingrich and Tucker Carlson have systematically sought to make him, and not the injustices of the system, the issue. Of more concern, since these attacks in most cases do not seem to have had much of an effect on the electoral contests themselves, the new prosecutors have been subjected to sustained and vicious attacks from the law enforcement establishment. In many cases, particularly for those who are women of color, the attacks have come in the form of misogyny, hate mail, and racist threats directed specifically at the Black women leaders. After Aramis Ayala announced her bold stance on the death penalty, Florida's governor, Rick Scott, transferred her cases to another state attorney. She sued him, but the governor prevailed in court. She chose not to seek reelection, and the Justice and Safety PAC backed her chosen successor, who won.

If all Soros did was act alone to usher in a new generation of prosecutors committed to justice and smart on crime, it would have been a great achievement. But as in his other political and philanthropic activities, he created a "market" that did not exist before. How many national donors knew or cared about who was running for district attorney in some southern county? The success of the Justice and Safety PAC soon attracted other donors, sometimes working on the same races as Soros, and often taking on races in other jurisdictions.

Soros was first drawn to deeper engagement in US politics by his concerns about the global impact of the Bush administration, and so it is natural that he would also concern himself with politics outside the United States as well—and that his high-profile role in opposition to George W. Bush would have ramifications in other parts of the world.

At times, this involved trying to topple a dictator, as in Soros's support for the "No" campaign, the 1990 plebiscite in Chile seeking to end the regime of General Augusto Pinochet. At other times, it has involved promoting human rights reformers, like Corazon Aquino in the Philippines, who ran for president in 1986, two and a half years after the assassination of her husband, Senator Benigno Aquino, an outspoken opponent of the autocratic president, Ferdinand Marcos.

More complicated have been situations where Soros became active politically—or was perceived, not always accurately, to be active—in places where his foundations were also prominent players. Sometimes, as in China, his already limited ability to operate was further restrained by the regime's awareness of his opposition to Bush. Societies already distrustful of independent activity tend to see as unwelcome a donor who is also capable—albeit through his private funding, not his foundation—of seeking regime change.

This pattern was repeated throughout the former Soviet sphere. Even in those countries where Soros was not politically active—to the extent that distinction is meaningful in parts of the world where the lines are much more blurred than they have traditionally been in the United States—he was accused of funding the opposition. As Leonard Benardo, vice president of the Open Society Foundations, put it, Soros's image steadily shifted from being the "darling of subsidizing textbooks, giving travel grants and supporting health systems and Internet resources" to a figure of menace.

AT THIS POINT in Soros's life in philanthropy and politics, it is sometimes hard to separate the man himself, and what he actually does, from the backlash to him. The manufacturing of outrage against Soros—painted as a "radical left puppet master," falsely accused of collaboration with the Nazis (as a child, no less), denounced as a nemesis of public safety, religion, and American culture—is a lucrative engine for right-wing fundraising, both through direct contributions and in advertising on conservative media. It is also, as David Brock, the founder of Media Matters for America, points out, a "convenient way to stigmatize the groups that Soros supports," which is the ultimate goal for Soros's adversaries.

For many, he exists primarily as a symbol. Progressives admire a man who took on George W. Bush and Donald Trump and champions immigrants and prisoners, who in 2020 alone committed more than $100 million in rapid-response grants to low-wage workers affected by COVID and $300 million to frontline Black organizations following the death of George Floyd at the hands of the Minneapolis Police Department. They also love him for his enemies, like Fox News, Newt Gingrich, and Rudolph Giuliani.

At times it seems those enemies, and the rest of the vast right-wing media empire, from talk radio to Newsmax and the further digital reaches of conspiracy theorists, wouldn't know what to do without Soros, who is (or at least their caricature of him is) a tremendous asset to them in stoking their base to stay tuned in or online and to donate money. (An insufficiently examined aspect of the extreme polarization of the US electorate is that, particularly on the right, it has made a lot of media figures and institutions rich.) While there has always been a strong anti-Semitic strand in the opposition to Soros, particularly in Europe, it has been more pronounced in the last few years.

Soros has said that he doesn't take the attacks personally: "On the contrary, they have stimulated me to fight harder. I'm proud of my enemies—much less of my friends." By which he means not only his disappointments in leaders like Bill Clinton and Barack Obama, but his discomfort with some of the orthodoxies of the left, which in their most intense form amount to what some call cancel culture, in which the acceptable zone for discussion of controversial ideas is severely restricted. In this respect, if they actually paid attention to Soros and the depth of his commitment to Karl Popper's principles of an open society, his right-wing critics might find more in common with Soros than they realize.

❧

THERE IS NO QUESTION that the vast majority of attacks on George Soros and his role in politics are false, designed to create fear and raise money, and far too many traffic in nefarious anti-Semitic tropes. But none of that means his political activities should be free from criticism. Are there valid ones to be made?

As is so often the case with Soros, who holds himself to the high standards of scrutiny he demands of others, some of the soundest critiques emanate from the man himself. He readily concedes that he mishandled his early opposition to George W. Bush, taking out newspaper ads and barnstorming the country with anti-Bush speeches, making himself the issue and possibly feeding his own ego in a way that hurt his cause.

As he wrote in his book *Soros on Soros*, "There has been too much attention paid to me as a person. . . . But this preoccupation with myself is beginning to have some harmful side effects. I became a public personality in order to promote certain ideas."[9]

There is also a belief that Soros doesn't spend *enough* money on politics. While the $27 million he spent in the 2004 election was a high-water mark at the time, he has often been eclipsed in recent years by donors like Donald Sussman, Dustin Moskovitz, Reid Hoffman, and, since he became a Democrat, Michael Bloomberg.

Somewhat surprisingly, the conservative anti-tax organizer Grover Norquist is a grudging admirer of Soros, for his work on Eastern Europe and on drug policy (which to Norquist has a welcome libertarian cast). He once even invited Soros to speak at one of his famous Wednesday morning breakfasts for conservative activists. (Soros was impressed with and envious of the glimpse it gave him of the coordination on the right.) But Norquist told John Cassidy of *The New Yorker* in 2005 that Soros "tried to buy the Presidency on the cheap," spending only $27 million in 2004 when "he should have been in for two and a half billion dollars, for crying out loud."[10]

In particular, at the time of the 2010 US midterm elections—when the Democrats lost control of the Congress in the Tea Party wave—Soros resisted efforts to get him to spend heavily to stem the tide. In part this was because of his disillusionment with the first two years of the Obama administration, but in part it was his instincts as an investor coming to the fore: "I learned not to step in front of an avalanche."

Some say that Soros, in his political giving as well as his philanthropy, is at times too captivated by charismatic personalities and less drawn to efforts where leadership is distributed with no dominant spokesperson—that he understands Georgia, where Stacey Abrams is the face of a movement, more than Arizona or Texas, whose political ecosystems feature quietly effective but less celebrated leaders. If this is true, it is a tendency Soros has in common with many political givers and philanthropic leaders, however much they may talk about strategic impact. The cult of personality in movements and organizations remains strong, and Soros has not been immune to it.

Apart from that observation, and from questions about the amounts of money he contributes, given the scale of the Koch network efforts and the huge donations made to Republicans by the late Sheldon Adelson, it's hard to find many complaints about Soros from his own side of the political spectrum. He is widely regarded as someone who keeps his eye on the larger political and social context, asks good and often tough questions, welcomes being challenged, and eschews micromanagement of his political investments. In his philanthropy, Soros often talks of his desire to have a "selfless foundation," where the emphasis is on the causes being supported and the leadership of those on the front lines, not on the foundation or its staff. This ethos permeates his political giving as well.

A key factor in maintaining this approach is his one-man political team, Michael Vachon, who has studiously avoided the limelight and the kind of self-aggrandizement that is all too common among political strategists and advisers. Even so, anyone who has dealt with or watched Soros in the political sphere finds it difficult to imagine

Soros—famously a big-picture person—without Vachon, who represents him in all matters political and commands wide respect. Yet Vachon is the first to deprecate his own role and that of all political advisers: "If you win, you're a genius; if you don't, it's someone else's fault."

Contradictions are easier to identify. Soros thinks money has too much influence in politics, but he is using the system he decries as a tool to change it. He would make the distinction that while most on the right, like the Kochs, spend money on politics to advance their bottom-line interests—to protect their oil and gas investments and to limit taxes and regulations that constrain their wealth and their business practices—his giving aims to bring about political changes that run counter to his narrow self-interest on a personal and business level.

Soros came into politics to oppose Republican politics and policies, and thinks the party has been captured since 2015 by a "confidence trickster," but he believes to this day, even more strongly than in the past, that the United States would benefit from a revitalized and responsible Republican Party. Soros is proud of his support for the McCain Institute, and his longstanding relationship with the late Arizona senator. He's surely right that a more diverse and tolerant Republican Party would be a boost for democracy. But given his toxicity on the right, Soros is perhaps the last person in America who is capable of bringing this about.

THE MOST IMPORTANT thing about George Soros as a leading donor and activist in US politics is that it is a role he has come to reluctantly. That in his adopted country, this man of many talents—as an investor, thinker, strategist, and philanthropist—is now best known, and at times reviled, for his involvement in politics is one of the great ironies of Soros's ninety-plus years.

And yet he has made some very large marks on politics. He was in many ways the first "megadonor" after the campaign finance rules changed in the early 2000s. He has been followed by many others, on the left and on the right, and hasn't been the biggest for some time. But Soros paved the way, whatever one thinks of that development, and as with all his other undertakings, he has been more shrewd and strategic, over many years, than almost any other. Other Democratic donors at his scale, like Tom Steyer and Michael Bloomberg, have created their own entities and often run field programs with staff accountable to them. Soros has worked, by contrast, to react to others' good plans and ideas—as in the beginning with America Coming Together—and to empower existing organizations, building permanent capacity that he does not seek to control.

As David Brock put it, "The way that giving worked on the left was very different before Soros. There were a lot of 'pop-up' organizations. He changed the mindset." Leonard Benardo adds, "He has been smart and valuable about the need for patient capital, understanding that the left has been plagued by funding streams that are too short term." Cecile Richards, who first met Soros when he decided to fund America Votes, appreciated Soros's approach when she took over Planned Parenthood a few years later: "George was steadily helpful in building us into a political force," whereas for years, despite the organization's broad base of support, it lacked any apparatus for politics.

Soros was the first significant donor to understand the importance of data—of a more scientific approach to politics, if you will—and has steadily supported the maintenance of a capacity to collect, analyze, and offer access to high-quality political data free of profit and marketing considerations. At the same time, by his leadership in backing ACT in the 2004 election, he revitalized largely dormant voter contact operations, and his investment in field organizing laid the groundwork for Obama's electoral victory and (when adopted by the broad nationwide coalition Health Care for America Now!) the passage of the Affordable Care Act, Obama's signature achievement.

Soros understood that the disparate and disconnected nature of the progressive movement at the outset of this century—issue and constituency groups working on parallel tracks, with poor communication and little sharing of strategies and plans—was a huge impediment to electoral and policy success. Virtually every investment Soros has made in the political sphere sought to change this dynamic, overcoming these divisions and silos through collaborative vehicles and campaigns: America Coming Together, America Votes, the Democracy Alliance, and more recently Win Justice, a field-based partnership of Community Change Action, Planned Parenthood Votes, Color of Change PAC, and the Service Employees International Union. While it is far from the case that the progressive world moves seamlessly and without divisions, duplications, and rivalries, it has developed habits of collaboration that funders like Soros have encouraged and rewarded.

As a financial investor Soros was closely watched, and he helped to move and shape markets by the steps he took. In the political sphere he was also keenly aware of being watched as a person who took risks that often made it safer for others to follow. As Andy Stern observed, Soros "also understood the theater of it—he believed in reflexivity and knew that his entry would create its own momentum." He was the first donor to see the potential in state and local efforts, like ballot initiatives to reform drug policy or uncontested city and county prosecutor races, where he could make an impact. Over time he was able to change the terms of the debate, enact policy, and elect new leadership that made a real difference for millions caught up in the overcriminalization of America.

While Soros has fostered these deeper trends and made investments in structures and collaborations that outlast campaign cycles in a political world famously addicted to short-termism, he has also played an outsized role in the political careers of younger leaders of color like Barack Obama and Stacey Abrams, who have changed the face of American politics.

Soros has played a leading role in the transformation of progressive politics, and in the transitions to democracy of numerous countries on virtually every continent. And yet in his tenth decade the world remains by most measures a pretty disturbing place. While preserving the forms of democracy, too many countries—the United States included—have been drawn to authoritarian rulers and right-wing populist movements that persecute minority racial, ethnic, and religious groups and seek to dismantle the collaborative institutions to which Soros has devoted his life. In his native Hungary, despite Soros's considerable role in helping the country move past Soviet-era repression, Viktor Orbán's relentless and anti-Semitic attacks on Soros drove his Central European University out of the country, and it is not safe for Soros to spend time in his beloved Budapest.

Most fundamentally, the core tenets of open society are challenged as never before. Political and ideological differences can be fought out, as parties and philosophies have their times in and out of power. In Andy Stern's formulation, Soros wants a system that functions, but is skeptical when one side has too much power. But those cycles of "normal" politics depend on a shared belief in underlying democratic systems and norms, and on a common understanding of the facts—a transpartisan belief that the truth matters. As Soros wrote in *The Age of Fallibility*, "Underlying the political debate there must be some agreement on the principles governing the critical process that is at the heart of an open society. Foremost among those principles is that the truth matters. Absent agreement on that principle the political contest deteriorates into a shameless manipulation of the truth."[11]

It's hard to argue that in the United States (despite coming to the brink and stepping back from it when the 2020 presidential election was concluded) this scenario has not come to pass, with every election now cast in apocalyptic terms, with not just public policies on the line but the very existence of our democracy at stake. As long as he is around—and given his deep investments in institutions and movements that will long outlast him, beyond that—George Soros will be in this fight, the nemesis of those who shamelessly manipulate the truth. For as Laura Quinn of Catalist noted, "Soros is an emblem of a society which values institutions and norms—the exact embodiment of the enlightenment values they are trying to kill."

An Eastern
European Mind

Ivan Krastev

Aß AN OLD SOVIET JOKE GOES, three men are sitting in a cell in
the KGB prison in Moscow. The first is there because he crit-
icized the Bolshevik political leader Karl Radek (later murdered by
Stalin). The second is there because he spoke out in favor of Radek.
The third man is Karl Radek. Now take a TV studio or a parliamentary hall instead of prison, and replace the name "Karl Radek" with
"George Soros" and you will get a sense of the role George Soros
plays in Eastern Europe today. But while it is relatively easy to be a
critic or admirer of Soros, in a political and intellectual environment
in which George Soros is the major dividing line, the one impossible
position is to be George Soros.

In writing this essay, I was continuously reminded of the iconic scene from Woody
Allen's film *Annie Hall* in which an effete professor tries to impress a young lady
by rambling on about the intellectual theories of Marshall McLuhan, only to be
interrupted by the sudden appearance of McLuhan himself, who tells the professor
to shut up, because he has gotten all his ideas wrong. If it were not for the ongoing
conversations with my friend Lenny Benardo, in my view the most interesting interpreter of George Soros's thinking (and the unnamed coauthor of this piece), I would
have never dared to write this essay, out of the fear of sharing the fate of the effete
professor from Allen's movie.

Soros is an Eastern European for whom the ideal of open society has been a guiding philosophy, not only in his private thinking but also in his public actions. He came to this belief in large part because of his experiences as an Eastern European, but when the post-Soviet era failed to bring open society to the region, Soros came to be seen more as a problem than an asset.

To tell the story of George Soros and Eastern Europe requires us to start at the beginning.

ON DECEMBER 23, 1939, a guest arrived at the editorial offices of the Budapest newspaper *8 Orai ujsag* (*8 O'Clock News*). The next day, a short article bearing the headline "George Soros Brings a Donation" was published. It dutifully reported:

> He enters the room and skillfully shuts the door behind him. Standing on tiptoes, he reaches up to the high doorknob and turns it comfortably. Hatless but with a leather bag flung over his shoulders, our smiling guest is a ray of sunshine in the office.
>
> "My name is George Soros," he says, clicking his heels. We admit that it is not every day that we have dealings with young gentlemen from the fourth grade of elementary school.
>
> "I just dropped in after school," says George and slides open the wooden dual-compartment pencil case clutched in his palm. From an assortment of erasers and pen wipers he digs out two pieces of paper the size of a standard postage stamp. Two tiny hands start unfolding the pieces and place two ten-pengö notes on the counter. "There you go!"
>
> "George," I address him sternly. "What is this supposed to mean? What do you intend to do with all this money?"
>
> With his angelically mischievous blue eyes sparkling, he turns to me. "I brought this money for the Finnish people. There is a war in Finland at the moment, Daddy told me."[1]

Most probably this was George Soros's first ever political contribution. And if you ignore the size of the donation (twenty pengö, about $74 in today's money), you find in it all the core characteristics of his later political philanthropy—moral clarity, acute sense of timing, and a firm belief that his contribution can make history. The charitable act was made in the midst of an existential crisis for the young Finnish state, a small distant country that few could point to on a map.

Soros's first political donation also captures well the Eastern European sources of his future philanthropy. Being born in post-Habsburg Eastern Europe means that you are inevitably residing in a small nation-state—one whose independence is perilous and contingent. Anxiety and insecurity are a constant frame of mind. The Czech writer Milan Kundera captures this sense of insecurity by defining a small nation as "one whose very existence may be put into question at any moment." Kundera makes clear that a citizen of a large country fails to ponder his country's survival, as "his anthems speak only of grandeur and eternity." By mordant contrast, he writes that "the Polish anthem . . . starts with the verse: 'Poland has not yet perished.'"[2]

In 1946 the Hungarian intellectual István Bibó offered a similar perspective. Historical trauma, he suggests, makes Eastern European societies fear and resent external powers; it also produces a belief that "the advance of freedom threatens the national cause."[3] Eastern Europeans have learned to be suspicious of any cosmopolitan ideology that traverses their borders, whether it be the universalism of the Catholic Church, the liberalism of the late Habsburg empire, or Marxist internationalism.

George Soros's intellectual sensibility is a product of these circumstances. He is a cosmopolitan reared in an environment suspicious of cosmopolitanism. He is also a product of the 1940s, a turbulent and often dizzying decade that inspired a reading of history as emblematic of revolutionary waves. "My experience with revolutionary moments started when Nazi Germany occupied Hungary in 1944," Soros once wrote. "I was not yet fourteen years old. By some measures, it started even earlier, when I used to join my father in the swimming pool after school and he would regale me with tales of his adventures in Siberia during the Russian revolution of 1917. If I add my father's reminiscences to my own experiences, I can claim to have a memory going back a hundred years."[4] An assimilated Jew reared in a society in which people are prized for having roots rather than legs, Soros has an elective affinity for history and ideas that clashed with the social strictures imposed around him.

The stark contrast that Soros makes between open society and closed society derives from two almost polar opposite ways to understand the world and two distinct regimes of solidarity. "What do we owe each other?" asks the moral philosopher Tim Scanlon in his important book of the same name. Do we owe our support to the most vulnerable in our community, or to the most vulnerable people in the world? Soros's answer, almost instinctual, is that humankind is our natural community.

Soros's father, Tivadar, the truest of cosmopolitans, learned Esperanto while in the trenches of World War I; it was his way to keep faith with the ideals of a liberal universalism so badly scarred after that conflict. For George Soros, the discourse of human rights and open society become the language through which he communicates with the world.

Eastern Europe, with its often ill-defined geographic borders—in the best Habsburg tradition, he would always call the region Central Europe—has at least three distinct meanings for George Soros. It is the place of his upbringing and where his philosophy was shaped. It is also the setting upon which Soros's global influence was forged. But Eastern Europe is also where the most ardent anti-Soros conspiracy theories originated. Soros, in this sense, can never be decoupled from his native region. His very political identity was fashioned through the promulgation of false identity documents on the black market in Nazi-occupied Budapest. And although his foundations have supported the identity aspirations of different ethnic and political groups, for him the most valuable identity was always the one that saves human lives and human dignity.

A focus on human dignity, not only human rights, was central to Soros's conceptual framework. It was this preservation of human dignity that he revered in the hard-fought struggles of Eastern European dissidents. The anti-politics of dissidents—the primacy placed on moral conduct over alignment with established political institutions—was the landscape into which Soros threw himself in the 1970s and 1980s. The sovereignty of the individual and the autonomous power of civil society were the parameters for Soros's new thinking on how to effect change.

Soros's decision to invite Aryeh Neier to become the first president of his Open Society Foundations set the stage. Neier was not simply one of the legendary figures of America's civil rights movement. He was also one of the founders of Helsinki Watch (what would eventually merge into Human Rights Watch) and a bridge between Eastern European dissidents and the American human rights community. Neier was no stranger to the intellectual and physical plight of dissidents in both domains.

Neier's galvanizing of the human rights movement coincides with the period the Yale intellectual historian Samuel Moyn provocatively calls "the last utopia."[5] Moyn posits that human rights do not represent the culmination of humane, enlightened Western thought; nor, as is customarily thought, was the human rights movement a reaction to the carnage and genocide of the Second World War. For him, it is only in the 1970s (and not following 1789, 1848, 1918, or 1945) that human rights emerged as a force of its own. The present ideological form of international human rights is not some progressive evolution of Enlightenment precepts, but largely a reaction to (and an attempt to regroup after) the exhaustion of the utopian social visions of the postwar period, especially anti-colonialism and Marxism. Human rights by the 1970s represent a *retreat* to an individualistic ethic of rights against states.

This new ideological formation can be illustrated by the 1975 Helsinki Accords, which turned out to be a rotten bargain for communist regimes. What the Soviet Union gained in Helsinki was the recognition of its post–World War II borders. The cost, however, was a recognition of the primacy of individual rights irrespective of the position of the state. This defense of individual rights swiftly became a core ideological component in the East-West confrontation, and in the struggle of Eastern European and Soviet dissidents against communist regimes.

George Soros's political philanthropy became a striking expression of the autonomous power of the human rights movement. Soros and Neier contributed to a process whereby the human rights movement after the Cold War affirmatively embraced internationalism as the preferred vehicle for its own "utopian" vision, alongside an ever more expansive, progressive, and substantive human rights corpus of international law. In this dynamic, the Open Society Foundations would become among the most powerful and effective advocates for institutions like the International Criminal Court and the International Criminal Tribunal for the Former Yugoslavia. Soros's vision of the open society envisioned not only the transfer of power from nondemocratic to democratic governments but also the supplanting of the nation-state by international institutions.

Soros's detractors have maligned him for advocating some form of global government. This is a distortion of his actual views. Soros has long championed global governance—never government—namely, the empowerment of international law and norms of cooperation as features of a functioning international order. His commitment to international justice and global solutions to global problems emerge directly from these convictions.

For Soros, post-communist Eastern Europe was not simply the place where his philosophy originates, but the dreamland where the open society would find its most fervent advocates. Soros's personal experience living in a closed society led him to embrace the ideal of an open society; so, too, did the fact that Soros is an Eastern European, and in his words, "People in Eastern Europe care much more about poetry and philosophy."[6] Some could rightly argue that his romantic vision of the region as one in love with poetry and ideas was rooted in the fact that when Soros arrived there in the 1970s and 1980s, he encountered two types of people: anti-communist dissidents and communist spies—and both belonged to the intelligentsia.

∾

SOROS HAS OFTEN remarked that *The Open Society and Its Enemies*, the magnum opus of his intellectual mentor, Karl Popper, "struck me with the force of revelation." But his revelation in reading Popper calls to mind the epiphany of Molière's character Monsieur Jourdain, who discovered that all his life he was speaking prose without knowing it. Popper's open society philosophy resonated with Soros because it best articulated in philosophical terms what Soros had learned on the ground in Hungary from 1944 to 1947. Facing, in turn, the Nazis followed by the Soviets, Soros was particularly drawn to the notion that those who make claims on ultimate truth put their societies on the road to dictatorship. Popper just made this point more forcefully than anybody else.

Open society was never a doctrine or a simple institutional arrangement; it was a way of thinking. It is realizing the fallibility of your own positions; the readiness to change your views when the facts change. John Maynard Keynes's famous crack, "When the facts change I change my mind. What do you do?," is redolent of Soros's own judgment. "If there is anything really original in my thinking," he writes, "it is this emphasis on misconceptions."[7]

Already a successful investor in the late 1970s, George Soros steeled himself after trading hours to finish his decades-long philosophical study *The Burden of Consciousness*, a project he had started while a student at the London School of Economics thirty years earlier. He would eventually send the manuscript to Popper, who "did not remember me but responded enthusiastically." Soros traveled to see him in London and upon introducing himself received an unanticipated response: "I am so disappointed." "When I received your manuscript," Popper noted, "I thought you are an American who understood what I was talking about when I described the dangers of totalitarian society. But you are Hungarian; you experienced them at first hand."[8]

Both Popper and Soros are rationalists who reject a deterministic view of history and believe in the power of reality to bite. Both are cosmopolitans. Yet in one vital sense, Popper's view of the world differs significantly from Soros's. Popper left Eastern Europe when the 1920s and 1930s were still considered "postwar." For George Soros, by contrast, the 1930s were his prewar years. *The Open Society and Its Enemies* is written by a Habsburg intellectual who bore witness to the horrors of Europe's self-destruction from the leafy precincts of the University of Canterbury in New Zealand. By contrast, Soros was a survivor of these regimes. Soros's theory of reflexivity was tested repeatedly in 1944 as he watched how people's expectations, more than anything else, became the motor of history and how deadly wrong these expectations could be. The conviction that a single individual can change the course of history was an insight that Popper lacked.

"1944 was the formative experience of my life," Soros has written more than once. It was in this crucial year during the war that he first experienced what he would later define as a "far-from-equilibrium situation." "Nazi persecution, Soviet occupation and being penniless in London," he asserts, "all qualify as far-from-equilibrium situations."[9]

Soros credits his father's and his own experiences in Nazi-occupied Hungary for his particular aptitude in contending with "far-from-equilibrium situations" or "revolutionary situations." His father impressed upon him "that there are times when the normal rules do not apply, and if you obey the rules at those times you are liable to perish." "My father," he explains, "who had lived through the revolution of 1917, had told me that in revolutionary times anything is possible and I was guided by his advice."[10]

Soros's success in the market was the most convincing evidence that his father was right. Yet Soros's political philosophy is focused on the idea that revolutions are never the answer to the problems of the world, and that the only way to improve the human condition is by piecemeal social engineering, one of Popper's core concepts.

∾

BEING A PERSECUTED minority is an intrinsic element of Soros's Eastern European experience. And he is historically sensitive to the fact that persecuted minorities often become the scapegoats of revolution. His unwavering commitment to the Roma community in Europe is the best expression of this sensibility. What all Eastern Europeans have learned from history is that relying on the nation-state to defend you is a fool's errand. Jews in particular have learned the hard way that the state can become your worst enemy. In the interwar period Eastern Europe was haunted by the specter of betrayal. For Jews, it was a double betrayal: nationalist elites accused Jews of disloyalty, while Jews were betrayed by the nation-states of which they were citizens.

A groaning bookshelf documents the complex and variegated experiences of the assimilated Jews of Central Europe. Their sin was not that they refused to integrate into the culture of the newly born nation-states, but that they did it so well. It was the success of their integration rather than its failure that was the real "Jewish problem" in places like Budapest. As the historian Amos Elon demonstrated in the case of Germany, the successful assimilation of the Jews posed a troubling question for the cultural majority: If non-Germans can embody German culture better than Germans, what precisely does it mean to be German? Does German genius even exist anymore?

Sympathy with the fate of small nations and identification with persecuted minorities—those who can easily become stateless persons—are an integral part of Soros's Eastern European inheritance. But while many Jews who survived the Holocaust were ready to blame universalism and cosmopolitanism as the utopia that cost them dearly, George Soros escaped the horror of the Holocaust recommitted to these same universal values. "I don't think that you can ever overcome anti-Semitism if you behave as a tribe," he has written. "The only way to overcome it is if you give up the tribalness."[11] Fittingly, it is here that the philosopher Henri Bergson, from whom Karl Popper borrows the concept of open society, comes into play.

Bergson's polarity of tribal and universal resonated for Popper, and, in turn, Soros, who saw the tribal as dissonant and inconsistent with the imperatives of modern society.

Soros's conceptual framework and political beliefs are rooted in the philosophy of liberal universalism born in the last decades of the Austro-Hungarian Empire. His worldview is shaped by what the anthropologist Ernest Gellner defines as the "Habsburg dilemma"—the tension between individualist liberals, often Jews, defending the idea of a pluralistic, tolerant, patchwork empire, and nationalist intellectuals offering the alternative of a "closed, localized culture, idiosyncratic and glorifying its idiosyncrasy, and promising emotional and aesthetic fulfillment and satisfaction of its members."[12] For Soros, Soviet communism and the interwar nationalistic regimes in Eastern Europe were no more than different articulations of the ideal of a closed society.

IN 1989—THE *annus mirabilis* that saw Germans rejoicing on the rubble of the Berlin Wall—Francis Fukuyama, a US State Department official, neatly captured the spirit of the time in an influential essay. With the end of the Cold War, he argued, all major ideological conflicts had been resolved. The contest was over, and history had produced a winner: Western-style liberal democracy. Taking a page from the philosophy of Hegel, Fukuyama presented the West's victory in the Cold War as a favorable verdict delivered by history itself. The overthrow of communism was the most marvelous of all revolutions not only because it was liberal and peaceful but also because it was a revolution of the mind. "The state that emerges at the end of history is liberal," Fukuyama insisted, "insofar as it recognizes and protects through a system of law man's universal right to freedom, and democratic insofar as it exists only with the consent of the governed."[13]

Soros was never a devotee of the "end of history" consensus. He never was a triumphalist. While many in the West were busy celebrating the free world's victory in the Cold War, Soros was worried that the West risked wasting a rare historical moment.

What made Soros's conception of the events of 1989 different from most other participants and observers was his understanding that the end of communism meant not only the remaking of the communist world but the remaking of the world itself. Soros never signed on to the delusion that 1989 could remake the East while the West stayed as it was. Soros always perceived the dynamic and dialectical element in human development, as reflected in his doctrine of reflexivity.

In understanding Soros's quest to support political reform in Eastern Europe, it is important to remember that even though he left Eastern Europe in 1947, he never evolved into the archetype of an Eastern European political émigré. Unlike, say, Zbigniew Brzezinski or Madeleine Albright, Soros did not spend the Cold War years preoccupied by the fate of Eastern Europe and the struggle against communism. Certainly, Soros still had friends in these countries, but he wanted to be considered American. What attracted him to the United States was principally the universalism of its worldview, and he sought to embody it in his own self-presentation. Unsurprisingly, then, Soros's first act of political philanthropy started not in Eastern Europe but in South Africa, in 1979. He may have hoped for the West's triumph in the Cold War, but he was not a classic Cold Warrior.

Most political émigrés from Eastern Europe in the 1980s were suspicious of Mikhail Gorbachev and his grand plans for reform. That skepticism was born of previous attempts at change that lasted only for intermittent periods, such as Hungary in 1956 or Czechoslovakia in 1968, and were later suppressed. Soros, by contrast, was attracted to the Soviet leader's sincerity and advocated supporting him despite being unsure about his chances of success. It didn't hurt that Soros saw some of himself in the great communist reformer.

"Just as a man created God in his image," Soros wrote in 1990, "I shall do the same with Gorbachev. I believe that Gorbachev's view of the world is not very different than mine."[14] Along with the German poet and essayist Hans Magnus Enzensberger, Soros shared a fascination with "heroes of retreat." "It was Clausewitz," Enzensberger wrote, "the doyen of strategic thinking, who showed that retreat is the most difficult of all operations. That applies in politics as well. The *ne plus ultra* in the art of the possible consists of withdrawing from an untenable position. But if the stature of the hero is proportional to the difficulty of the task before him, then it follows that our concept of the heroic needs not only to be revised, but to be stood on its head. Any cretin can throw a bomb. It is 1,000 times more difficult to defuse one."[15] This is an apposite description for how Soros saw Eastern Europe and the role of Gorbachev in the late 1980s.

Even so, Soros's admiration for Gorbachev's undertaking never made him a wholesale enthusiast about the Soviet leader's enterprise. In 1989 he stated that he had "decided to go all out with my foundations in 1990, exactly because I am so pessimistic."[16] As is clear from Soros's words, he would never be capable of following in lockstep with Gorbachev—or, frankly, with anyone. He focused his attention not on the success of Gorbachev's reforms, but on their unintended consequences.

Soros would later face the accusation that a number of his grant-ees were dissidents who came from communist families or were themselves communists, rather than longtime anti-communists like Aleksandr Solzhenitsyn. This should come as no surprise. Soros has always maintained a particular affinity to those who stand ready to change their mind, and who have the courage to challenge them-selves—and sometimes to risk their lives for the truth they have learned. He has never been warm to fanatics or cynics. Andrei Sakharov, the legendary Soviet dissident, is an example of a heroic figure for Soros. Sakharov combined the qualities that Soros valued most: firm moral principles, personal courage, intellectual openness, and internationalism.

Most difficult for an outsider to apprehend is that Soros's agenda in Eastern Europe was always changing. There never was a mas-ter plan—how could there be?—but he was instead, in the classic

Popperian sense, improvisatory. This is what has made Soros singular. Writing with the wisdom that comes from both history and the
markets, Soros once noted that "it is characteristic of revolutionary
periods that events outpace the ability of the participants to understand them."[17] "I have tried," he concedes, "to keep abreast of the
revolution, adjusting both my interpretation and my objectives to the
circumstances."[18] For Soros it is not just *what* he sees, but, far more
significantly, his *ways* of seeing.

The concept of a "fertile fallacy" is central to Soros's conceptual
and practical worldview; he deploys psychological explanation to
account for human behavior. "We are capable of acquiring knowledge," Soros writes, "but we can never have enough knowledge to
allow us to base all our decisions on knowledge. It follows that if a
piece of knowledge has proved useful, we are liable to overexploit
it to areas where it no longer applies, so that it becomes a fallacy."[19]
Likely better than anyone else, Soros realizes that we fall victim not to
our failures but to our successes. Unlike those American administra-
tions that universalized the experiences of Eastern Europe, he chose
never to do so. Policies that were efficacious in Poland in 1989 need
not be—indeed most likely could not be—efficacious in Iraq in 2003.
Soros always treated such simple transpositions of ideas and practice
with skepticism.

George Soros did not approach the challenges facing Eastern Europe with the intention to dismantle the Soviet Union or the Federal Republic of Yugoslavia. On the contrary. Unlike most Western
politicians, who saw the end of the Cold War in geopolitical terms,
Soros was afraid that the dissolution of these two multiethnic empires
might give rise not to democracies but to claustrophobic authoritarian regimes, particularly in Central Asia. Yet when Yugoslavia and
the Soviet Union began to implode, he did not press his foundations
to try to re-embroider nations that had lost their historical legitimacy,
but rather to help consolidate the newly emergent democratic states.
The most important condition to influence the direction of the train
is never to get off the train.

In 1990 Soros moved to London to be closer to these places where history was taking shape. While there, he did more than simply operate a handful of national foundations in Eastern Europe: he became Eastern European once again. His Hungary Foundation was established in 1984 and the strategy was to give thousands of small grants to support every initiative that had the potential to subvert the communist system. Unlike the slew of Western advisers and technicians who would soon flood the region, Soros realized that "the people living in the countries where I had foundations understood their countries better than I did . . . and I deferred to the judgments of the local boards. If I seriously disagreed with their judgment, I changed the board."[20] Local knowledge, a hallmark feature of the Soros worldview, was hereby established. "The foundation in Hungary worked like a charm," he wrote later. "It was exempt from all the pitfalls that beset normal foundations because civil society adopted it as its own."[21]

Soros's effectiveness over time may best be explained by his openness to fund scores of diverse (sometimes even contradictory) initiatives concurrently, and to discontinue them when expectations fell short. A striking example was in China. Soros had been enthusiastic about Chinese economic reforms in the 1980s. Yet even before the slaughter at Tiananmen Square in June 1989, he realized that the communist authorities had duped his foundation, and there was grave risk that the foundation could unwittingly legitimize the regime rather than subvert it. Soros then closed its operations. "Be ready to get involved, and be ready to get out" was his credo, and this took form both as an investor and as a philanthropist.

George Soros did not come to Eastern Europe with a plan. He came with a curiosity. He is a strange mixture of a philosophical mind that is in love with abstract ideas and an anthropologist's sensibility and keen interest in small details. Whereas many in the West were convinced that the future of Eastern Europe was to imitate slavishly the West and its institutions, Soros's hope was that the revolutions of the East could also transform the West. In his subconscious, perhaps,

1989 was not exclusively about Eastern Europe: it was about Europe as a whole. Already in 1990 Soros was convinced that "there is only one way. Existing frontiers must be respected, but frontiers must lose their significance. What distinguishes Europe today from the inter-war period is the existence of the European Community."[22] For Soros the defeat of communism would ultimately have been wasted if it did not encourage the enlargement of the European Union, and the transformation of the EU into a model of the open society of the future. This would remain his insistent commitment for the next three decades.

WHAT MAKES GEORGE SOROS'S CODE so difficult to crack is that while he is messianic, in a sense, he is not (nor has he ever been) a missionary. The two concepts need to be understood as related yet distinct.

A messianic sensibility is a common trait of many philanthro-pist-billionaires, be they named Rockefeller, Gates, or Soros. The world, they think, is waiting for them, and improving it is somehow their presumed responsibility. While many on the left tend to believe that what motivates the super-rich is nothing but material self-interest, the reality, for good and for bad, is different. Society's wealthiest have, like any social class, both values and interests. To think otherwise would be a sociological mistake. Many of the richest seek not only to earn profits but also to shape the world. George Soros is no different. "I carried some rather potent messianic fantasies with me from my childhood," he has written, "which I felt I had to control, otherwise I might end up in the loony bin. But when I had made my way in the world I wanted to indulge myself in my fantasies to the extent I could afford."[23] Soros received ultimate "satisfaction to be involved in historic events" and parlayed the prominence he enjoyed from his extreme success in the financial markets to get a hearing in the field of international politics.

Still, Soros never saw himself as a salesperson for an open society ideology. He stands by an open society as an ideal, never as dogma. His insistence that not only others *but he himself* is wrong much of the time in the interpretation of historical events makes him distinctive among those high-net-worth individuals who share his aspiration to change the world. And so at the moment when many Westerners, besotted by the momentous possibilities in the region, insisted that there was no alternative to the political and economic model of the West, Soros demurred. He defined freedom differently. To him, freedom was not a synonym for capitalism; it was the availability of legitimate alternatives and the capacity to choose between them. This necessary but subtle point was lost on many observers. Reflecting later on his own achievements, Soros remained steadfast: his views landed well not because he was wiser but rather because "I recognize my mistakes more quickly."[24]

EASTERN EUROPE WAS also the central stage on which the myth of George Soros, the stateless statesman, emerged. The best illustration of the improvisational approach that Soros adopted in his effort to contribute to the transformation of Eastern Europe is the fact that he did not keep an archive of his grant-giving before 1994. One clear-cut explanation was his concern that this information could be misused by the communist secret police. Another reason has greater resonance for Soros's distinctive approach: a revolutionary time, when the system is navigating disequilibrium, is not the moment to account for past performance. Instead, accelerating the pace of grant distribution was deemed of the highest importance.

Two of Soros's philanthropic initiatives of the early 1990s—his support for Soviet scientists and his efforts to reestablish gas and electricity supplies in besieged Sarajevo—provide the clearest examples of how Soros's interventions worked at scale.

The collapse of the Soviet Union had a devastating effect on its scientific institutions, as there were no funds to pay scientists' salaries. For a time it seemed as if Russia's entire scientific infrastructure would implode, and institutions from Moscow to Novosibirsk to Vladivostok might vanish overnight. These scientists, who played a vital role in the dismantling of the communist system, were facing a simple choice: they could either leave their country or leave their vocation. It was during this moment that George Soros stepped in and committed $100 million to support approximately thirty thousand research scientists across the former Soviet Union who had lost official research funding. Any scientist who had published at least three articles in a leading scientific journal during the previous five years would receive $500, or more than a year's pay. The money that the scientists received so unexpectedly reminded Soros of the cherished bounty of fifty pounds that he had once collected from the Quakers when he was an impoverished student at the London School of Economics in the late 1940s. Securing that check without any fuss or bother led him to conclude at the time that this was an ideal way for charities to function. (A later example of Soros's adoption of this approach would come following the 2008–9 financial crisis, when he gave $200 to school-age children on welfare in New York State for back-to-school supplies.)

"My objective was not only to save the best of Soviet natural science, which I considered one of the crowning achievements of the human intellect," Soros recalled, "but also to demonstrate that foreign aid could be administered effectively."[25] To this day, he calls this intervention perhaps the greatest achievement of his philanthropic life.

It is also worth noting that the idea to provide cash supplements to Soviet scientists was not the brainchild of Soros's Moscow foundation. Just the opposite. The foundation had not been a particular fan of the idea. Soros delegated considerable decision-making autonomy to his national foundations, but he was also always on the hunt for compelling ideas that emerged from outside of it. Priority should be given to local knowledge, yes, but good ideas should be available from as many sources as possible.

Around this same time, the former Yugoslav republic of Bosnia had become one of the most disheartening places on the map. Bosnia had declared its independence, but the country's Serb minority took up arms against the Muslim majority, with military assistance from the rump Yugoslavian government in Belgrade. The Bosnian capital of Sarajevo had been cut off from the rest of the country, and its residents were not only starving: they were subject to constant shelling, sniper fire, and other acts of violence. The West was hesitant to intervene and people were losing hope.

George Soros never believed in traditional charitable giving, but what he learned from his experience in Budapest in 1944 was that fatalism, a sense of ultimate powerlessness, is the worst humiliation a person can endure. At all costs, such powerlessness must be challenged. Thus during the siege of Sarajevo from 1992 to 1996, Soros committed $50 million to support the population of the Bosnian capital by reestablishing gas and electric service during the bitter winter, setting up an alternate water source, and bringing in desperately needed supplies.

"The mere fact that I had to spend $50 million on it is a defeat," Soros said of his Bosnian efforts. "I consider humanitarian spending as a defeat, in the sense that we failed to prevent disaster, that things deteriorated to the point where spending on humanitarian activities became necessary. I'm opposed to humanitarian spending. Generally, I think there is a time when CNN comes with the pictures, and people become aroused, and by then it's too late. The Open Society Foundation has got to be ten years ahead of the curve."[26]

The Sarajevo operation may have been a defeat in Soros's calculus, but it was a hallmark example of his ability to influence international politics. Soros was never one to sink into his armchair. His stock-in-trade has been direct involvement—and once involved, he advances ideas that politicians will customarily claim cannot be achieved, or are too risky for the moment. The effect of such engagement has often been that public pressure on Western political leaders increases in turn.

On his support for the civilian population in Sarajevo, Soros has commented: "It was a political gesture, meant to bring in U.N. troops to protect the nongovernmental organizations."[27] His calculus was that the money would attract NGOs to Sarajevo to carry out programs he would then underwrite. Their presence, in turn, would pressure Western governments to send UN peacekeeping troops to the city to protect the aid workers, thus internationalizing matters on the ground. For Soros and his collaborators, "the whole goal was to make Sarajevo work again . . . to make it a viable city—not a city of helpless victims, but a city of survivors, and to do that you had to involve the locals."[28]

Vital and necessary actions like this placed Soros and his foundation on the political map of Eastern Europe. Empowering civil society, and acting on those often small insights that only participant-observers can acquire, equally helped the foundation distinguish itself from the democratic assistance industry that flourished after the fall of the Berlin Wall. It was after such interventions that the media started using such grandiloquent framings like "George Soros's foreign policy."

Strobe Talbott, then the US deputy secretary of state, told *The New Yorker* magazine that though Soros's role in the region was "not identical to the policy of the U.S. government," it was "compatible" with that policy. "It's like working with a friendly, allied, independent entity, if not government," Talbott said. "We try to synchronize our approach to the former communist countries with Germany, France, Great Britain and with George Soros."[29]

Soros was convinced that the world needs stateless statesmen— leaders who are unconstrained by realpolitik and who see the world through the prism of a persecuted minority. And he saw his role as being such a leader. It was his strategy that by acting in this way, a nonstate actor could force states to redefine their interests.

But while Soros's contribution to the transformation of the region is widely recognized by admirers and critics alike, more often than not his ideas have been misinterpreted. In the expanding "literature" on Soros conspiracy theories, Soros and his foundations are time and again portrayed as the instigators and organizers of the so-called color revolutions in Georgia, Ukraine, and Kyrgyzstan between 2003 and 2005. In reality, Soros was always skeptical about these mass anti-government mobilizations and about their ultimate efficacy. In fact, Soros was at pains to make clear that the impetus for change was always more complex and lacking easy definition—light years different from how those who are conspiracy-minded hoped to portray them.

Soros certainly sympathized with those citizens taking to the streets (although his son Alex noted to me that like many Jews of his generation, his father feels uneasy about crowds), and many of the foundation's grantees were among the active participants in these events, protest movements that were forged in the crucible of democratic aspiration. That said, each of these so-called revolutions has been instructive for Soros, guiding him to the realization that the removal of a corrupt autocrat (and his corrupt henchmen) is hardly the same as becoming a democracy. Soros has learned from experience that corrupt, weak states can be as harmful to the rights of ordinary citizens as the dictatorships they replace.

AT THE BEGINNING of the twenty-first century, the general mood in Eastern Europe and in the world began to shift. Illiberal forces were on the march and George Soros became their prime target. In a bitter twist of fate, Soros became the symbol (and the punching bag) of everything that the new activists sought to extirpate: internationalism (globalism), minority rights, autonomous civil society, and the power of nonstate actors. In the far right media bubble, Soros became the dark symbol of both international capitalism and international socialism.

In Eastern Europe the "war on Soros" has become a rallying cry meant to persuade Eastern European societies that any form of internationalism is antithetical to national cultural traditions. While the illiberals acknowledge that funds from Brussels are useful and should not be rejected, they argue that Eastern Europeans must resist the idea of the European Union as a political community. Many people who knew precious little about George Soros or the work of his foundation, people who lived in places where Open Society Foundations had never even been active, now became convinced that humanity's salvation was predicated upon the defeat of him and his ideas. At a moment when conspiracy theories have replaced ideologies as the instigator of political identity, Soros-related conspiracy writing has become the book club of the far right.

Eastern European populism was already on the rise by the early 2010s, but it was the refugee crisis of 2015 that turned national populists into a major political and intellectual power in the region. Opinion polls indicate that the vast majority of Eastern Europeans are wary of migrants and refugees. A July 2017 study by Ipsos revealed that only 5 percent of Hungarians and 15 percent of Poles believe that immigration had a positive impact on their country, and that 67 percent of Hungarians and 51 percent of Poles think their countries' borders should be closed to refugees entirely.[30]

During the refugee crisis, images of migrants streaming into Europe sparked a demographic panic across Eastern Europe, as people began to fear that their national cultures were under threat of vanishing. The region today is made up of small, aging, ethnically homogeneous societies—for example, only 1.6 percent of those living in Poland were born outside the country, and only 0.1 percent are Muslim.[31] In fact, cultural and ethnic diversity, rather than wealth, is the primary difference between Eastern and Western Europe today. In the Eastern European political imagination, cultural and ethnic diversity are seen as an existential threat, and opposition to this threat forms the core of the new illiberalism.

Some of this fear of diversity may be rooted in historical trauma, such as the disintegration of the multicultural Habsburg empire after World War I and the Soviet occupation of Eastern Europe after World War II. But the political shock of the refugee crisis cannot be explained by the region's history alone. Rather, Eastern Europeans realized during the refugee crisis that they were facing a new global revolution. This was not a revolution of the masses but one of migrants; it was inspired not by ideological visions of the future but by images of real life on the other side of a border. If globalization has made the world a village, it has also subjected nations to the tyranny of global comparisons. These days, people in the poorer parts of the world rarely compare their lives with those of their neighbors; they compare them instead with those of the most prosperous inhabitants of the planet, whose wealth is on full display in movies, on television, and on the Internet. The French liberal philosopher Raymond Aron was right when he observed in 1961 that "with humanity on the way to unification, inequality between peoples takes on the significance that inequality between classes once had."[32] If you are a poor person in Africa who seeks an economically secure life for your children, the best you can do for them is to make sure they are born in a rich country, such as Denmark, Germany, or Sweden—or, failing that, the Czech Republic or Poland. Change increasingly means changing your country, not your government. And Eastern Europeans have felt threatened by this revolution.

The great irony is that although Eastern Europe today is reacting with panic to mass migration, the revolutions of 1989 were the first in which the desire to exit one's country, rather than to gain a greater voice within it, was the primary agent of change. After the fall of the Berlin Wall, many in the former communist bloc expressed their wish for change by emigrating to the West rather than staying home to participate in democratic politics. In 1989, Eastern Europeans were not dreaming of a perfect world; they were dreaming of a normal life in a normal country. If there was a utopia shared by both the left and the right during the region's post-communist transition, it was the utopia of normality.

Revolutions as a rule cause major demographic disruptions. When the French Revolution broke out, many of its opponents ran away. When the Bolsheviks took power in Russia, millions of Russians fled. But in those cases, it was the defeated, the enemies of the revolution, who saw their futures as being outside their own country. After the 1989 revolutions, by contrast, it was those most impatient to see their countries change who were the first to leave. For many liberal-minded Eastern Europeans, a mistrust of nationalist loyalties and the prospect of joining the modern world made emigration a logical and legitimate choice.

As a result, the revolutions of 1989 had the perverse effect of accelerating population decline in the newly liberated countries of Eastern Europe. From 1989 to 2017, Latvia lost 27 percent of its population, Lithuania 23 percent, and Bulgaria almost 21 percent. Hungary lost nearly 3 percent of its population in the 2010s. And in 2016, around one million Poles were living in the United Kingdom. This emigration of the young and talented was occurring in countries that already had aging populations and low birth rates. Together, these trends set the stage for a demographic panic.

It is thus both emigration and the fear of immigration that best explain the rise of populism in Eastern Europe, which feeds off a sense that a country's identity is under threat. Moving to the West was equivalent to rising in social status, and as a result, the Eastern Europeans who stayed in their own countries started feeling like losers who had been left behind. In countries where most young people dream of leaving, success back home is devalued.

In the revolutions of 1989, as in the revolutions of 1848, liberals and nationalists were political allies, a coalition that broke the back of communism in Eastern Europe. The Hungarian prime minister, Viktor Orbán, a nationalist who had been a recipient of a Soros fellowship to the University of Oxford in 1989, is the best illustration of this conjoining of forces. But at the beginning of the twenty-first century, as in the last days of the Habsburg Empire, liberals and nationalists have become the worst of enemies.

George Soros, who advocates for international governance, universal human rights, and a progressive migration policy, is now deemed the major threat to the nation-state. What we might label the "Soros Affair"—the nationalists' obsession to label as a traitor any supporter of the ideas of the open society—plays a lamentably similar role to the Dreyfus Affair in nineteenth-century France. Soros has turned out to be right that the twenty-first century, like the twentieth century, will be defined by the clash between the ideas of open society and those of closed society as an incarnation of the old notion of tribalism.

History is always the world's best ironist. Many Eastern European nationalists have embraced the current right-wing Israeli government in order to challenge on the plane of symbolic politics their oldest and most bitter enemy—Jewish cosmopolitanism, as embodied by George Soros.

This intellectual paradox is plaintively described by Yehuda El-kana, an Auschwitz survivor and the former rector of Central European University. Elkana wrote in 1988: "Two nations, metaphorically speaking, emerged from the ashes of Auschwitz: a minority who assert, 'this must never happen again,' and a frightened and haunted majority who assert, 'this must never happen to us again.' It is self-evident that, if these are the only possible lessons, I have always held to the former and seen the latter as catastrophic."[33] Soros fully shares this conviction.

A Hungarian Jew who became an American financial speculator is now the fiercest defender of the European Union. And he is defending the Union on two fronts: against political elites in Eastern Europe who benefit greatly from the generosity of the Union's subsidies, and against Brussels bureaucrats who resist the need to reinvent the Union. What makes Soros so infuriating to Eastern Europe's illiberal leaders is that he exposes their biggest lie: that open society liberalism is an alien ideological import into the region. And in order to make their fellow citizens believe the lie, the illiberals have had to turn George Soros into a foreigner, a person not from here.

White, the second film of Krzysztof Kieslowski's *Three Colors* trilogy in the early 1990s, masterfully captures Eastern Europeans' ambivalence about the liberal West. Karol, a Polish hairdresser living in Paris, is left divorced, desperate, and humiliated by his younger French wife, Dominique, on the grounds that he cannot perform sexually. His impotence becomes the symbol of the East trapped in the overexpectations of the West in post-1989 Europe. Miserable, penniless, but still obsessed with his former wife, Karol returns to Warsaw hidden in a compatriot's suitcase, and spends the remainder of the film seeking to avenge his humiliation by making his ex-wife feel helpless and lonely in the same way he felt in Paris. His plan succeeds: he gets her imprisoned in Poland, only to realize that he is still in love with her. The East has taken revenge on the arrogance and insensitivity of the West, only to realize that the liberal West remains its only point of reference.

It is clear that if George Soros did not exist, the Eastern European nationalists would have had to invent him.

The Founder's Tale

Michael Ignatieff

GEORGE SOROS BELONGS TO A SMALL and select circle of wealthy men who have founded a university. His story is interesting because it is unlike any other. Other rich men who have founded universities in the past—Leland Stanford, John D. Rockefeller, Johns Hopkins, Andrew Carnegie—did so for reasons that are easy to understand. They wanted to make the final ascent from the ranks of the very wealthy to the exalted realm of the great and the good, and to lift any remaining stain that clung to their money and the way they had made it.

Men like Carnegie and Rockefeller were the robber barons of their era, and their philanthropy was a response to the criticism they sustained: in Carnegie's case for suppressing the Homestead Strike, or in the case of Rockefeller, for the ruthless tactics toward competitors that fueled Standard Oil's expansion. Soros was very different. He was a speculator, not an industrialist. He did not turn from finance to philanthropy; he pursued both simultaneously. He was comfortable with money, free of guilt about it, and fundamentally uninterested in it as an end in itself. There had always been money on both sides of his family, and no shame or embarrassment ever attached to the

All quotations from identified sources, unless otherwise stated, come from interviews with sources conducted by the author in December 2020 and January 2021. See notes on pages 266–267 for a list of those interviewed.

middle-class life he lived in the Budapest of the 1930s. Certainly, he had been miserable and poor when he was studying in London in the 1940s, and doubtless this was a spur to succeed as a speculator when he arrived in New York in the 1950s. But success of the spectacular kind he had achieved by the early 1980s did not produce any sentiment of shame. Speculation was a game that he played superbly well, not a source of guilt he had to expiate.

Founding a university is also a way to celebrate your own greatness. Certainly Soros had the usual human vanities, but on his climb to great wealth, he had avoided self-promotion. For commercial reasons he was not eager to see his name in the newspapers—but some of his deals, especially the shorting of sterling in 1992, earned him global celebrity. Even then, at the apex of his fame, he could have endowed hospitals and clinics, supported orchestras or theater companies—the kind of generosity that celebrates fame rather than inviting controversy. Instead, he took a philanthropic path that was distinctly his own.

Soros seemed to accept that he was destined to remain an outsider, as a European, as a Jew, and as an intellectual, no matter how successful he was. Instead of agonizing about his outsider status, he appears to have reveled in it. He understood that his contrarian streak and outsider status had contributed to his success. So his philanthropy was not driven by a desire to gain social acceptance. He could easily have bestowed a gift on his alma mater, the London School of Economics, as an efficient way to consolidate his reputation in the London elite, but while his foundation did support projects at the school, he never endowed LSE with a benefaction that sought to associate his name with the school.

Instead, beginning in 1990, he bestowed his money, as well as time and energy, on an improbable university start-up in Central Europe. The beneficiaries were not well-heeled and respectable academics in prestigious universities, but a small cluster of dissidents in Budapest, Prague, and Warsaw who, while utterly powerless, had kept their honor as defenders of academic honesty through the communist era.

Certainly, Soros admired their courage, but he saw something more exciting: they might have history on their side.

Under their influence, he allied his philanthropy to a grand historical change—the transition from communism, from closed to open societies. He saw himself as the angel investor at a hinge moment in European history. His goal was not respectability but historical significance.

It takes Olympian self-confidence to believe you can change history. What set Soros apart as an investor was a strategic sixth sense, anchored in a deep understanding of European politics, about how political change could impact, among other things, currency and exchange rates. He specialized in making money from the interaction of markets and politics and made himself a master of volatile and uncertain markets. He was fundamentally at home in uncertain worlds. Risks that made others fly to security were the opportunities from which he sought to profit. This pattern started early. In March 1944, when he was thirteen, the Germans invaded Hungary, and the Jewish middle-class world he had thought was solid disintegrated at the first touch of terror. From this he learned, mostly from his father, that in situations of existential uncertainty, you could never trust what other people told you, only what your own eyes could confirm, and that if you were a Jew, you were on your own. Again, his reaction to this trauma was distinctive. A figure like the entrepreneur Peter Munk, who came from a similar milieu, escaped Hungary in 1944 and never came back, instead building a career and devoting all of his philanthropy to his newly adopted home of Canada. Andrew Grove, another Hungarian Jew who fled to the United States in 1956 and later founded the microchip company Intel, said he would never return to a place that had persecuted his people. Unlike them, Soros not only returned but created an institution. This suggests how deeply he remained attached to Hungary and how deeply he saw himself as a Hungarian.

Even Soros's Hungarian identity was distinctive, for it was deeply influenced by his own father's brand of cosmopolitan internationalism. Tivadar Soros had been one of the leaders in Hungary of

Esperanto, an international language invented in 1887 by L. L. Zamenhof, a Polish Jew from Białystok, as a response to the rise of linguistic nationalism in the Russian and Austro-Hungarian empires. Esperanto promoted itself as a cosmopolitan, transnational alternative to the linguistic nationalism of these empires, and it attracted large numbers of Jewish adherents, including Tivadar Soros. Esperanto was, in a sense, a cosmopolitan competitor to Zionism as a solution to the dangers that increasingly threatened Jewish communities in Central Europe before and after World War I. When Tivadar changed the family name from Schwartz to Soros in 1936, in response to the anti-Semitic legislation of the regime of Admiral Miklós Horthy, he chose an Esperanto word, *soros*, the future tense of the verb "to soar." So the cosmopolitan internationalism and the visceral hostility to nationalism were constitutive features of his outlook from the beginning. In his deepest commitments as a philanthropist and founder of institutions, George Soros has remained, to the last, his father's son.

All of this complex reckoning with the history of Central and Eastern Europe went into the shaping of his historical reflexes. That he made a lot of money betting on these reflexes must have seemed an unchallengeable proof that he should trust them when he moved from investing to giving. In Eastern Europe in the 1980s he saw history being made, and he wanted to be something he had never been before: an architect of history.

The closest parallel to this historical ambition was Andrew Carnegie's attempt before World War I to use philanthropy to avert the headlong rush to war, by creating the international tribunal at The Hague and the Church Peace Union. By investing in international arbitration and an international network of spiritual leaders from different faiths who were supposed to find commonalities of faith and ethics, Carnegie believed philanthropy could stop war by generating international movements in favor of peace. All this turned out to be fanciful, but in its bright-eyed ambition, Soros's project to use money to shape the transition from communism across the former Soviet empire was in the same league as Carnegie's.

There is pathos in how it all turned out: he bet on open societies, but thirty years later, especially in Central and Eastern Europe, open societies are struggling against the rising tide of nationalist dictatorship and single-party rule. The university he founded in the country of his birth has been expelled and has had to start again in Vienna. It is easy to tell his story as a cautionary tale of one man's self-deceptions. Yet he went into his philanthropic adventure in Central Europe with his eyes open. He knew how easily historical progress could be reversed. He retained what he had always displayed as an investor, a cold-eyed realism that sheltered him from euphoria and disillusion alike.

His desire to use philanthropy to make history distinguished him from other founders of universities, but acquiring these ambitions required a radical change in how he thought about his own money and his own success. He had made a fortune through speculation, by taking positions and taking a profit before prices fell. To be a successful speculator, you need to be ruthless and unsentimental: vacating positions at the right time, keeping your options open, and managing risks by staying mobile, agile, light on your feet, and unencumbered by loyalties and past positions. As one of his longtime friends, the Swiss banker Pierre Mirabaud, recalls, Soros liked to joke that investment is a speculation gone wrong.

This attitude toward investment led him to view institutions with instinctive suspicion. He himself had felt throttled inside investment firms in the 1960s, which led him to set off on his own. His own firm deliberately sought to avoid becoming an institution itself. It was essentially a two-man operation for many years. As for academic institutions, his memories of the London School of Economics in the 1940s were not happy. He had been a lonely expatriate in his twenties who made few friends or academic contacts. He idolized one of the faculty's leading figures, the philosopher of science Karl Popper, whose landmark book *The Open Society and Its Enemies* was to have an enduring influence. He fancied himself a philosopher in the style of Popper, but Popper didn't have time for him or his ideas.

Yet this same man invested in an untried academic start-up, in a region with no private universities at all, and put his faith in dissident professors who had never run anything in their lives. Even more remarkable, he has stayed with the investment, through thick and thin, good years and bad, for thirty years. The university remains his largest single institutional commitment. He has invested $2 billion of his own money in it, and a skeptic might ask what return he has to show for his investment. History has not taken the path he hoped. Central and Eastern Europe are still struggling to escape entrenched patterns of political culture—single-party leaders, nationalist dogma, and corruption—that were shaped by communism. Far from securing recognition to equal Rockefeller or Carnegie, Soros has been targeted as the malign spider at the center of a liberal cosmopolitan conspiracy. He says he is proud of the enemies he has made, but there must have been moments of pain at the venomous hostility of the government that rules his native land. Yet he has stood by CEU, and instead of liquidating a struggling position has doubled down. As for returns on the investment, they are all long-term, to be measured in the lives he has changed, particularly the eighteen thousand CEU graduates who owe their education to him. For someone who was hostile to institutions, he can take consolation in the fact that regimes, good and bad, come and go, but universities—among the oldest institutions in Europe—endure. He has good reason to think that his will, too.

BY THE LATE 1970s and early 1980s, Soros began to explore ways to use his money's power. From the beginning his philanthropy was political, and his conception of political philanthropy was distinctive: it was not a matter of funding politicians or political campaigns—though he does some of that—but the more grandiose ambition of nudging historical change itself. After attending seminars convened by the human rights activists Jeri Laber and Aryeh Neier, he began providing financial support to what eventually became Human Rights Watch. After a visit to South Africa in 1979, he started funding scholarships for Black students there. In the early 1980s he financed a key meeting of South African business leaders and the African National Congress to explore ways to end apartheid without destroying the South African economy. Around this same time he turned his attention to Central and Eastern Europe. He was introduced to Western intellectuals who had established contact with dissident thinkers in the Soviet bloc. The Canadian philosopher Charles Taylor persuaded Soros to fund the Jan Hus Educational Foundation, which had been established by several other philosophers, including Taylor's Oxford colleague William Newton-Smith, along with several Czech dissident émigrés. The foundation channeled books and lecturers to Prague. A few months earlier, Newton-Smith had gone to Prague to give a lecture on the philosophy of science in the apartment of the philosopher Julius Tomin, only to be arrested fifteen minutes into his talk, interrogated, bundled out of the city, and expelled at the West German border. Soros also supported the work of the Paris-based activist Annette Laborey, who ran a small institution that enabled Eastern European intellectuals to visit French universities. In the 1980s few thought that this work would produce imminent change. The dissidents and their Western friends were tunneling under the walls of the communist regimes, but they assumed that it would take a long time for the regimes to collapse under the weight of their accumulating failures.

In 1984 Soros established a foundation in Budapest, with the cooperation of the Hungarian Academy of Sciences, to support Hungarian intellectual and cultural life. It was the first free foundation inside the Soviet bloc, and after tough negotiations, Soros got his way: his foundation, not the academy or the government, would have control over how it spent his money. The foundation imported thousands of Western books and donated them to university and state libraries. It shipped in photocopiers to facilitate the circulation of free scholarly and political opinion. It gave grants to enable Hungarian philosophers, historians, and writers to travel to the West. Many of the eventual founders of Central European University were among the initial recipients of these grants.

János Kis, then the editor of an underground journal and a member of the democratic opposition, received a grant from Soros's foundation to translate Immanuel Kant's *Critique of Pure Reason* into Hungarian, and subsequently received a stipend to spend a year at the New School for Social Research in New York. Soros visited Kis at his apartment in Budapest in 1985. For Kis, it was a strange experience. He had never met a very wealthy expatriate capitalist before, and clearly Soros had not met many people who had chosen internal exile. Kis remembers him asking a rhetorical question: "Why do you do what you do? I couldn't."

Soros would look back with nostalgia to this early period of his philanthropy in Hungary. He was to tell his biographer Michael Kaufman that the Hungarian foundation was "the most fun of all" because he was able to help people of the caliber of Kis, while also importing photocopiers, which broke the party's monopoly on information. Critical essays that once were typed and circulated in a few copies could now be distributed so much more widely that they escaped the control of the party and the secret police altogether. "With just $3 million, we were having a bigger influence on the cultural life of Hungary than the Ministry of Culture," Soros remembered.

Hungary also represented a homecoming of sorts. Soros returned with his mother and other members of his family, renewed contact with childhood friends, and even appeared on the Hungarian media. On one celebrated occasion he used his fluent mother tongue to give the communist regime an ultimatum when it sought to ban publication of a list of recipients of Soros's grants. He told the interviewer that unless the ban was lifted, he would take the foundation out of Hungary. The regime blinked and allowed the list to be published.

These early successes encouraged Soros to support another initiative—funding the Inter-University seminars in the idyllic medieval city of Dubrovnik on Yugoslavia's Adriatic coast. These seminars were established by the Croatian nuclear physicist Ivan Supek, the rector of Zagreb University, in 1970. Dubrovnik became a venue where Russian, Balkan, Central European, and Western European intellectuals could meet in an atmosphere of relative freedom. The Dubrovnik seminars were exciting affairs since they sought to re-unify European intellectual life around the ideals of a shared search for truth free of ideological shackles. In some sense, these academics were trying to live in the future, even though Yugoslavia continued to be repressive, even though the wall still divided Berlin, even though the Soviet empire showed no signs of collapse.

By early 1989, however, the tectonic plates in Europe had begun to shift. The Soviet leader Mikhail Gorbachev had unleashed *perestroika* and *glasnost* but was soon losing control of the Soviet state apparatus and of public opinion in his empire. In Hungary, the regime was losing its capacity to create fear and buy off discontent. A steady stream of samizdat publications, concerts, dance performances, and seminars started a ferment the Communist Party proved incapable of controlling. In the summer of 1989, a young Hungarian dissident named Viktor Orbán made a dramatic public speech in one of Budapest's historic squares calling for the withdrawal of Soviet troops. Shortly thereafter, Soros funded a fellowship for Orbán to spend a semester in Oxford. This was the heady context in which the Inter-University seminar met in Dubrovnik in March 1989. Bill Newton-Smith, who had attended these gatherings for more than a decade, persuaded Soros to take part. Talk was beginning to circulate, both in the Hungarian foundation and in the Inter-University seminar about setting up a new university, but when Soros arrived in Dubrovnik, he remained skeptical. Newton-Smith remembers him grumbling as they came in from the airport together, "They all think Uncle George has come to town to give them a university. Well I will listen to them but I'm not convinced. I think it's better to reform existing institutions."

Soros remained cautious, believing, to use a phrase of Popper's, that "piecemeal social engineering" was the most effective way to make change. This was how he had worked with the Academy of Sciences. Young dissidents like the historian István Rév warned him that the academy was cooperating with him only to maintain its privileged position, but Soros stuck with the collaboration, believing that he should work with existing institutions. In Dubrovnik, however, as he listened to intellectuals and graduate students from Budapest, Belgrade, Prague, Warsaw, and Moscow, he began to change his mind.

He was flattered by their attention, of course, but he also felt a deeper affinity to these Eastern European intellectuals than to the arbitrageurs, stock pickers, and fund managers he worked with in New York. He had been writing down his own theories for years and had just published *The Alchemy of Finance*, a labored and laborious attempt to apply his Popper-influenced theories of reflexivity to moneymaking. The book also included this declaration of his intentions as a philanthropist: "I would value it much more highly than any business success if I could contribute to an understanding of the world in which we live or, better yet, if I could help to preserve the economic and political system that has allowed me to flourish as a participant."

Like the university founders of old, he wanted philanthropy to "preserve the economic and political system," but unlike them, he also wanted to understand the historical transition at hand and use his resources to ensure it succeeded. The intellectuals at the conference may not have taken his philosophical pretensions very seriously, but they certainly regarded him, in the words of one of them, as a "providential person." Here, in Dubrovnik, was this extraordinary Hungarian billionaire who listened, took notes, asked questions, kept his counsel, and watched as the intellectuals debated where the university should be located, what it should teach, who should lead it.

The historian László Kontler, then a young instructor who attended the 1989 Dubrovnik meetings, remembers that while the creation of a university was on the agenda, no one realized how quickly events were moving in the region. The talk was not, he remembered, about transition from communism, but how to support a university curriculum that would "undermine the credibility of Soviet ideology."

A few months later, the fall of the Berlin Wall accelerated the plans and discussions. The question ceased to be whether there should be a university, but when it should start and where. The Hungarian intellectuals said there was only one choice: Budapest. The Slovaks said it had to be in Bratislava, the Czechs in Prague, and so on. There were meetings in Bratislava, where Soros secured a promise by the new Czechoslovak prime minister Petr Pithart, himself a former dissident, that the new university could have a lease on a trade union building in Prague. That seemed to settle the question of location, but Soros still hesitated.

Through the whole of 1990, Soros vacillated, sometimes thinking he should invest in existing universities, sometimes believing he needed partners and couldn't finance a new university all by himself. He gave the impression of a man who changed his mind after every conversation. Bill Newton-Smith disengaged from the process, disillusioned by Soros's apparent indecision. Slowly, Soros realized that if he wanted to start a university, he would have to do so with his money alone. In December 1990, at a meeting in Newton-Smith's rooms in Oxford, he finally told a gathering of Czech, Polish, British, and Hungarian academics that he would fund the start of a new university that would open in Prague in September 1991.

Once he made up his mind, his instincts were radical. Once established in Prague, the university should also have campuses in Warsaw and Budapest. For him, it was evident that Central Europe had a common culture and history and should have a university to reflect that identity. Newton-Smith privately thought the idea was "ridiculous," and as time went on, the fragmentation of Central Europe became ever more evident, but in this bright and hopeful moment of transition, it still seemed possible to have a university in three capitals in the region.

In thinking about what kind of university the region needed, Soros reasoned that in a time of transition, the region needed experts in transition: lawyers to write constitutions, more lawyers to privatize state companies, economists to figure out how to unleash the disciplines of a price system on a socialist command economy, political scientists to assist in the creation of free political parties. Founding a university to change the course of history meant training a new elite to take the place of the discredited and bankrupt communist cadres in government offices, factories, research institutes, and social institutions. The focus of the education offered should be practical, vocational, and policy-oriented. Soros was enamored of intellectuals, but he was even more enamored of "doers," the legal scholar András Sajó remembers, people like himself who "get things done." What the region needed, in other words, was a "trade school for transition," a place that would train a new elite to manage the shift away from communism. If this was what Soros wanted, Newton-Smith reasoned, he wouldn't want a philosophy department.

But that's not how things turned out. Two of the founding faculty members of the university—István Rév and Jiří Musil, the directors of the Budapest and Prague campuses, respectively—persuaded Soros that its graduates would need academic training in the social sciences and humanities. A transition would not be enduring unless its new elite acquired a substantial grounding in purely academic learning. After long months of disagreement and discussions, Soros accepted their arguments. Instead of a training school, the institution George Soros got for his money was entirely different. It was a highly academic graduate school in the social sciences and humanities. It taught medieval history, classical philosophy, the history of Eastern Europe, and environmental sciences. Why? Because these were the disciplines the dissidents knew and because he listened to them. Gábor Klaniczay, a young medievalist, for example, convinced him that medievalists were the custodians of a vanished but vital tradition in the region, before the region became locked in the nineteenth-century prison house of nationalisms. In the Middle Ages, it was in the medieval university in Bologna, for example, that young students from across Central Europe had met and conversed in the lingua franca of Latin. Whenever wars broke out, there remained a regional elite, schooled in a common culture, that could rebuild the bridges. To someone raised on the dreams of Esperanto, this must have struck a chord. Why not a twentieth- and twenty-first-century version of the same: a *universitas* where, with the lingua franca of English and a common devotion to scholarship, a new generation could see themselves as the heirs of these university traditions and escape the imprisoning modern discourse of nationalism? Soros took some convincing, but he listened to people like Klaniczay and the historian Péter Hanák, who made similar arguments. Little by little history and the humanities made their way into the curriculum of Central European University. For someone who thought he was making history happen, for someone whose success with money taught him his instincts were nearly always right, the largest surprise about the university's founding is that Soros listened and learned. Because he did, the institution is what it is today.

János Kis credits Soros with listening, but also ascribes this willingness to listen to Soros's deepest motivations: "It is true that George imagined CEU as a trade school for the transition to democracy. But this is not a complete account of what he had in mind. He also wanted CEU to be the lighthouse of the liberal thought in the region. Regardless of whether he was clear about this (he was not), a trade school couldn't have become a lighthouse of the liberal thought. So George's commitment to liberal values, including the value of open society, was a driving force moving CEU away from his other ideal, a trade school for practicians, and in the direction of a graduate school in social sciences and the humanities."

Once Soros gave the go-ahead in December 1990, the founding of a university in the space of nine months was an almost inconceivable undertaking. At any other time, it would have been absurd to try, but in the euphoria and energy released by the collapse of the Soviet empire, anything seemed possible. There wasn't time to select faculty with formal searches. The dissident intellectuals essentially chose among their own contacts to staff the new departments.

As a result, CEU is among the only universities essentially created by its departments. The inevitable result, over the years, has been that each department became a separate feudal micro-kingdom. At the beginning, however, each department shared the same vision of a new university that would rebuild the broken bridges to the European and North American academic world. Péter Hanák established the history department; Gábor Klaniczay and János Bak founded the medieval studies program; János Kis was asked to set up the political science department; Ernest Gellner, one of the illustrious Western academics recruited to the new university, agreed to found a nationalism studies department in Prague, the city of his birth. Richard Southwood, a distinguished Oxford scholar, established an environmental sciences program. Roman Frydman, from New York University, established the economics department. András Sajó set up the legal studies department, with flying visits from American academics like Stephen Holmes. This created a distinctive CEU collaboration between dissident intellectuals from Central and Eastern Europe and senior faculty from prestigious Western universities.

By September 1991, Central European University opened for classes in the trade union building in Prague, with offerings in art history, economics, political science, and sociology. The sociology department then moved and established itself in Warsaw. The Budapest programs started with legal studies, history, environmental sciences, and a year later with political science and international relations. All students—there were seventy-six in the first year—received full scholarships and stipends, courtesy of Soros, many of them recruited from the Open Society Foundations that he was establishing from the Baltics to Armenia and deep into Central Asia and the Russian Federation. The early students, in the words of the political scientist László Bruszt, were all prime-ministers-in-training, intensely political and committed to returning and leading the transition in their countries. Their eagerness was exciting, but the isolation, ideological rigidity, and provincialism of their communist educations required a lot of remedial work. The early students did not know how to read a text critically. They were accustomed to rote repetition of lectures, copying down ideologically correct sentences from the official texts. Bruszt remembers a student from the Urals who came to him and said he wanted to study political theory. When Bruszt asked him what political theory he knew, he dutifully mentioned Marx, Engels, and Lenin, and then added that in his university library back home he had come across a few copied pages in English of a text by someone called Dworkin, and that had inspired him to study at CEU. This was the Anglo-American legal scholar Ronald Dworkin, who later became a recurrent visitor at CEU. Interactions like this convinced the faculty that their task was nothing less than building their academic disciplines from the ground up, training doctoral candidates to return to their countries and establish true disciplines on the Western model. At the beginning, Soros was cautious about this goal, deciding that in order not to aggravate relations with the existing institutions in the region, CEU should not issue degrees. This quickly changed, and by 1992 the university had secured accreditation in New York and was able to issue US-accredited degrees, making it the only institution in Europe at the time offering American-style master's degrees.

In 1993, Alfred Stepan, a distinguished scholar of political transitions in Latin America, was persuaded to leave Columbia University and become CEU's first rector. Before he took the job, he spent two full days at Soros's summer home in the Hamptons, seeking approval for his plans to create a serious, academically respectable graduate school in the social sciences and humanities. On Stepan's watch, the basic scaffolding of CEU's academic structure was erected: history, political science, medieval studies, environmental science, and gender studies—departments that at their founding were unique in Central Europe. The new university drew European and American scholars with international reputations, to share not only in training a new elite, but in using comparative and historical analysis to understand the transition itself. László Bruszt published a groundbreaking study of the politics of transition. In the department of legal studies, András Sajó and Wiktor Osiatyński made the *East European Constitutional*

Review, the leading journal for constitution-making in the Eastern European countries. Stepan, with Soros's help, established the university's board of trustees and recruited as its founding members Ralf Dahrendorf of Oxford University, Wolf Lepenies of the Wissenschaftskolleg in Berlin, and Leon Botstein, the president of Bard College.

In the first decade, Soros was deeply involved in the university's governance, sitting on the executive council, chairing its board of trustees, overseeing budget discussions, and questioning hiring decisions. In one notable instance, Soros reproved Roman Frydman, the founder of the economics department, for not doing enough to get the new market-based economic thinking into public discourse in the region. This led to Soros funding supplements in key newspapers in Eastern Europe, with articles seeking to popularize market insights and the idea of open society. These supplements, in turn, led to the foundation in Prague of the syndication service Project Syndicate, which to this day disseminates progressive economic and social opinion pieces in newspapers around the world.

Soros committed $5 million a year for five years to CEU, and at every budget meeting would reinforce the message that the university would have to secure additional funding from governments or other philanthropists. "No stock, all flow" was the financial motto. And yet every year would pass, and no additional resources were found. The Austrian government made promises, but nothing came through. The new governments in the Czech Republic, Slovakia, Hungary, and Poland were reluctant to subsidize what they dismissed as an American billionaire's vanity project. A similar thing happened when Bill Newton-Smith went cap in hand to wealthy private donors in the UK or Europe. They asked whether he was kidding. Why did Soros need help with his pet project?

It began to dawn on Soros that if the university was to survive, it would have to be with his money alone. Against his own intentions and contrary to his wishes, he was being driven toward permanent support for an institution that he had thought would be a temporary instrument of transition.

Stepan wanted Soros to endow the new university, but Soros turned down this request, and by 1996 Stepan had left to resume his scholarly career, this time at Oxford. It would not be until 2000, under one of Stepan's successors, Yehuda Elkana, who came from the Van Leer Jerusalem Institute, that Soros agreed to endow the university, initially with $250 million. This reluctance about endowments spoke to Soros's growing desire to keep control of the institution he had founded. This dynamic—constantly supporting the institution, renewing his commitment, sometimes year by year, but being reluctant to capitalize and recapitalize the endowment—was to remain a constant feature of his engagement with the university for the next twenty years.

THE UNIVERSITY GREW rapidly in the 1990s. Students were flooding in from all parts of Central Europe and Central Asia. Distinguished academics began regular visits and new faculty from the region began filling out the ranks of the professoriate. At the same time, the political moment of 1989 was replaced by the return of darker and more disturbing forces: nationalism and authoritarianism.

Soros cannot be charged with naivete about these developments or failure to anticipate their return. As early as April 1990, in a speech, he said, "There is a grave danger that the universal closed system called communism will simply disintegrate into national entities which fall short of an open society."

An authoritarian populist, Vladimír Mečiar, began a campaign to break up Czechoslovakia, and in 1992 Slovakia became an independent nation. In the Balkans, Yugoslavia broke apart and disintegrated into civil war, with catastrophic violence, ethnic cleansing, and outward migration. In 1992, Dubrovnik (now within an independent

Croatia) was shelled by Serb forces, and the Inter-University Centre, where intellectuals across the region had once gathered, was reduced to rubble. In Budapest and Prague, CEU welcomed students from all of the warring republics of the former Yugoslavia, especially those from Serbia who were escaping compulsory military service, and the university provided a safe space, throughout the war, in which they could learn and live together in peace.

For a time, Central Europe seemed to be spared the ethno-nationalist carnage in the Balkans and was proceeding in a market-oriented, liberal democratic direction. As long as this held true, CEU's project—to train the new liberal democratic transition elite—seemed in tune with the direction of history. But even in the early 1990s, there were a few straws in the wind that indicated history might take a different turn. A deep current of right-wing anti-Semitism surfaced here and there. A disgruntled right-wing Hungarian dissident, István Csurka, wrote a deeply anti-Semitic attack on Soros and CEU in 1993, describing him and other Western liberals as termites undermining the foundations of the Hungarian nation. At the time it was easy to dismiss Csurka as a radical outlier.

Another sign of the change in the political climate came with the election of Václav Klaus as prime minister of the Czech Republic in 1992. CEU had been welcomed by Václav Havel and Petr Pithart, and now CEU encountered the other side of Czech politics: right-wing, conservative, authoritarian, and inveterately hostile to Soros. Within six months of coming to power, Klaus had rescinded the lease on the trade union building in Prague, and CEU underwent its first forced relocation, to Budapest. Around this time, the sociology department relocated from Warsaw to Budapest as well. Soros's original dream of a networked university in three capital cities in Central Europe had to bow to the reality that the politics of each country was resolutely national, and the regional identifications, even among intellectuals, were relatively weak. The university still called itself Central European, but by the late 1990s it had become a Hungarian institution, with US accreditation. Soros secured a magnificent former palace, in the heart of the historic downtown, that was to become the home of the university.

While he was increasingly excited by the institution taking shape, Soros himself was immune to the euphoric illusion that the liberal democratic transition was irreversible. He was fiercely critical of the failure of the Americans and the Western Europeans to grasp how epoch-making the collapse of the Soviet Union had been and how fragile the prospects for democracy were. He had been calling for a Marshall Plan for the economic reconstruction of the whole Soviet empire, but his appeals had fallen on deaf ears. In the absence of concerted investment by the "winners" in the Cold War, he had stepped in himself, establishing foundations throughout the region, increasing his annual spending to upward of $300 million, and taking on projects himself, like preventing the emigration of Soviet scientists and the destruction of Soviet scientific culture. Not content with his investment in CEU, he also poured money (as much as $40 million a year) into the Higher Education Support Program, which created new social science departments in universities throughout the region and founded three new universities: the American University of Central Asia in Bishkek, the European Humanities University in Minsk, and the European University at St. Petersburg. He set up a Research Support Scheme to fund social science in the public universities in the region. No founder of universities had ever entertained such extraordinary ambition: to make the transformation of higher education the driver of an entire historical transition.

Soros's ambitions, it could be argued, met the historical moment, but he was disillusioned to discover how few governments and foundations followed his lead. As he watched the West missing its chance to link the former Soviet empire to the West and its democratic ideals, as Yugoslavia descended into a downward spiral of violence, his public commentary on the region became ever darker. In testimony before the US House of Representatives in 1994, he said, "When I embarked on my project, I was planning on a short-term campaign to seize the revolutionary moment and to provide an example that would be followed by the more slowly moving, more cumbersome institutions of our open societies. But I was sadly mistaken. Now I must think in biblical terms—forty years in the wilderness." He could not have imagined how true these words would turn out to be.

All this lay in the future. In the heady 1990s, CEU grew year on year, attracting students from the former Soviet Union, Central and Eastern Europe, and the Balkans. From an enrollment of 76 in 1991, CEU was taking in 674 students by 1998. But slowly the demography of the university changed. At first, it was an attractive option for students in the region, especially if Soros was paying full scholarships. Many of these students then went on to complete doctorates at Oxford, Cambridge, Harvard, and Stanford. Instead of training an elite who would stay in the region and lead it forward, CEU became a means of exiting the region altogether. When Soros and the CEU leadership recognized the danger that CEU might be contributing to the brain drain, the Higher Education Support Program set up a new program to pay salaries for graduates willing to return to their home universities after having finished their doctoral studies at CEU or at Western universities.

At the same time, demographic growth in the Central European region was faltering and the number of young people eligible for graduate education began to decline. A university founded to create a transition elite in the region was slowly losing its core student constituency from the region. In its place, CEU began recruiting worldwide. In 1991, it recruited students exclusively from the twenty-seven countries of the former Soviet bloc. By 2000 it was recruiting from the United States, the UK, and Western Europe, and after 2010 from Africa, Asia, and Latin America. It currently recruits students from 120 countries.

The CEU story, therefore, is about unintended consequences, which should not have surprised its founder. Indeed, a deep sense of human fallibility was foundational to his understanding of market behavior, as well as the ironies of history itself. It is no accident that this quotation from Soros is prominently displayed inside the door of the CEU building on Nador utca in Budapest:

> Thinking can never quite catch up with reality; reality is always richer than our comprehension. Reality has the power to surprise thinking and thinking has the power to create reality. But we must remember the unintended consequences—the outcome always differs from expectations.

By THE TIME of CEU's tenth anniversary in 2001, it was firmly established not as an insurgent start-up or a training school for transition, but as an elite social science and humanities graduate school, distinguished by a unique collaboration between senior figures from the North Atlantic academic elite and dissident intellectuals now transformed into university professors.

The university was increasingly global in its recruitment pattern, and under Yehuda Elkana began to build up its research reputation. In the decade between 2000 and 2010, it launched departments in network and data science and experimental cognitive psychology, with distinguished figures like Dan Sperber (from the Institut Jean Nicod in Paris) making regular professorial visits to the new department. CEU quickly established a reputation for its baby lab and its studies of infant cognition before speech. The university also established a business school and a school of public policy.

By the time Hungary, Slovakia, Poland, Croatia, and the Czech Republic joined the European Union in 2004, Soros could have been forgiven for believing that his investment in transition had paid off. All of these countries had been stabilized by the powerful incentives of the European integration process. The expectation was that, once inside the Union, the European Council, the European Parliament, and the European Commission, together with the European Court of Justice, would exert a transnational regulatory role, ensuring that these countries remained on the democratic path. Guided by this expectation, the Open Society Foundations began scaling back its investments in the Balkans and Central Europe. It believed its job was done.

George Soros's attention shifted to other areas—particularly the foundation's work in the United States and in South Africa—but personally he became ever more attached to Hungary. With his wife, Tamiko, he began spending more time in Budapest, delivering a series of lectures at CEU while staying in a hotel suite around the corner from the university.

Soros's involvement in university life was not without controversy. Any university so dependent on a single donor will want to defend its institutional autonomy. When Yehuda Elkana stepped down as rector, Soros asked him what he could do for the university. Elkana told him that he should step down from the board of trustees and increase the university endowment. In response, Soros took up a new role as the honorary chairman of the board and doubled the endowment to $500 million, but he took care to ensure that the management of the endowment remained not in an independent university endowment committee, as is the practice in most US universities, but with the managers at Soros Fund Management. He respected academic freedom and did not intervene in university hiring or governance, but he kept close control of the purse strings. And even in his more limited governance role, he remained involved in board decisions, supporting the creation of a School for Public Policy to further his aim of a university with a more practical policy orientation.

While the university continued to grow, the political climate in Hungary began to darken. After Hungary joined the European Union, thousands of Hungarians had taken out mortgages with Western banks denominated in euros. When the financial crisis hit in 2007 and 2008, they suddenly found themselves under water, and the government struggled to offer any help. Public finances collapsed. In

2010, the socialist government was swept from office and the Fidesz party under Viktor Orbán took power. Orbán had already served as prime minister between 1998 and 2002 and had prepared the country for entry into the European Union. But after he was turned out of office, he was stung by the defeat and vowed in a famous speech that never again would "the Hungarian nation" be in opposition. The faculty at CEU had never heard rhetoric of this kind before, especially the idea that Orbán and his party incarnated the nation, and that the nation could not be in opposition. During his time out of office, Orbán built a civil society movement of the right, based in the Hungarian churches, and developed an ideology with deep appeal in the small towns and rural areas: hostile to Europe, resentful of Western European condescension, assertive of Hungarian pride and language. Once in power, Orbán's new government rewrote the constitution, slapped down the liberal media, and set about consolidating party control over the Supreme Court and other key institutions. From the beginning, CEU professors joined with the liberal media in analyzing and denouncing these trends. The hope at the time was that the university could ride out the radical change in political climate.

Slowly it became apparent that the Fidesz victory represented a deep-seated change in the direction of the transition itself. Creating a new liberal transition elite had been Soros's explicit strategy, but the problem, which the university's political scientists like Béla Greskovits began to analyze, was that the new elite—drawn from the former dissidents—had been too small to lead a successful transition. To succeed, the liberal dissidents had had to make common cause with members of the former communist elite, individuals who inhabited an ambiguous "gray zone"—inside the communist apparatus while maintaining relations with the dissidents. This political alliance, between former communists who now rebranded themselves as socialists and the liberal democratic dissidents, was necessary for a transition to succeed, but it entailed compromises—for example, an agreement not to purge former police informers or members of the security apparatus. These compromises doomed the liberals and socialists alike.

The new transition elite was also tarnished by the radical economic disruption of the transition itself, which created a political opening to the right, throughout Eastern Europe. By the early 2000s, politicians like Viktor Orbán in Hungary, Jarosław Kaczyński in Poland, Vladimír Mečiar in Slovakia, and Václav Klaus in the Czech Republic were lining up together to accuse the liberal transition elite of weakening national culture and protecting the former communist elite. Dissidents who had been in prison or under surveillance prior to 1989 now were attacked for being insufficiently anti-communist. Still, the attacks worked, in part because the conservatives were more successful than the liberals in building up support in "conservative civil society": the church, small-town professionals, and village dwellers who had known stability under the communist regime. These conservative social groups now looked with alarm at the depopulation of villages, the weakening of the health and social security system, the closure of factories, and the sale of public lands and properties to a wave of private and foreign speculators. The liberal transition elite had laid the foundations for a new Eastern Europe: they had written the constitutions, privatized the state companies, created the new commercial law for a capitalist economy, and prepared the post-communist states for entry into the European Union. But in the process, these changes cost them the support of voters, who gravitated toward right-wing political parties better positioned to exploit their anxieties about identity, community, and religious faith.

Viktor Orbán was himself a former beneficiary of George Soros's support. The sudden attack that Orbán mounted against Soros, beginning in late 2016, was not the pursuit of a personal vendetta or a son's revenge against a father figure. It was purely political. Targeting Soros as the epitome of everything Fidesz stood against—Europe, multiculturalism, immigration, secular tolerance, the open society—was a brilliant way to mobilize a rural, small-town base disoriented by change. Making an alien US-based speculator public enemy number one also appealed to "the national bourgeoisie," the urban middle class whose own fortunes depended on allegiance to a single party with control of state assets and state budgets.

Orbán also understood CEU's vulnerability better than CEU did: a foreign-accredited university, paying high salaries and preaching values of multicultural tolerance and openness, turned out to have solid support in Budapest itself but not in the small towns and villages, the political power base of all Hungarian parties.

In late August and early September 2015, the migration crisis broke upon Europe and shattered the uneasy truce between Viktor Orbán and the European Union. A million Syrian refugees flooded across the Aegean Sea, into Greece, and then northward through the Balkans and across Serbia into Hungary, eager to take advantage of Angela Merkel's call to give them a home in Germany. Orbán tried at first to hold the line, and then opened the border. Migrants engulfed trains in Budapest railway stations, heading to Austria and Germany.

Orbán, whose poll numbers had been languishing that summer, quickly grasped the political opportunity that had been handed to him. He became Europe's most prominent and vituperative opponent of Merkel's generous gamble and an ever more strident critic of Muslim immigration and the supposed threat it posed to European civilization.

Soros was among Orbán's most determined critics. As a Holocaust survivor, as an immigrant, as an American citizen, he believed that Europe should respond with generosity to the plight of the Syrian refugees fleeing the civil war in their home country. In editorials he urged Europe to give the refugees a home. At the CEU, students and faculty went to help the refugees who were camped out at the Budapest railway stations. Students brought plugs to charge refugee phones, food, water, and maps to guide them to safety in Germany.

After the traumatic days of the migration crisis, CEU sought to establish businesslike relations with the Fidesz regime, and for a time the university's leaders believed it had succeeded. But that did not mean CEU professors stopped criticizing the government. The

university's constitutional experts analyzed the gerrymandering of
the electoral system, the neutering of the Supreme Court, and the
new media laws, while other scholars denounced the corruption of
what one university affiliate, Bálint Magyar, called Orbán's "mafia
state." The regime appeared to ignore these criticisms, as the CEU
administration sought to secure the government's consent for a key
project, the rebuilding of its Budapest campus and the erection of a
new classroom and library building. After tortuous negotiations, de-
manding all the diplomatic skill of the university's rector, John Shattuck, CEU secured government approval, and by the autumn of 2016
the new building was ready for opening.

When I succeeded Shattuck as rector that fall, George Soros flew
in for my inauguration and for the opening of the new building. At
the ceremony, key figures close to the Orbán government were in the
audience, including the rector of Corvinus University of Budapest
and the chairman of the parliamentary foreign affairs committee.
The ceremony emphasized the university's Hungarian associations
and pointed to a renewal of a good working relationship between
the Hungarian government and CEU. The university, after all, was a
major employer, paid taxes, and was regularly cited in international
rankings as the best institution of its kind in the country. To signify
all this, there was a speech of welcome in the Hungarian language,
and a student read a poem by the great Hungarian poet Attila József.

As we left the platform together after the ceremony, Soros tugged
my academic gown and whispered sharply, though in good humor,
"You read the wrong poem." He then recited from memory, in Hungarian, a much sharper and more bitter poem written by Attila in
the 1920s, when he had been expelled from university for his radical
political views.

The whole incident, the university's founder reciting a Hungarian
poem from memory—and then telling me later how the poet and
his father had known each other in the 1930s—showed how deeply
Soros's Hungarian identity ran and how strongly he associated himself with Attila's resistance to academic oppression. We did not know

then, but that was the last time George Soros would set foot in his native land.

During the fall of 2016, the university's relations with the Orbán regime appeared good. The minister of higher education, László Palkovics, visited the new building and expressed a mixture of amazement and approval at CEU's new classrooms and library. When I asked him whether our relations with the government were in good shape, he assured me they were. When I pressed him about some recent comments in the government-controlled media that were critical of Soros's stance on the refugee issue, he dismissed them. "It's just politics," he said.

In November, Donald Trump won the US presidential election, and almost immediately CEU's relationship with the Orbán government began to deteriorate. The Obama administration had put the US-Hungarian relationship "in the deep freeze" to express its disapproval of Orbán's corruption and violations of the rule of law. Now with the incoming Trump administration signaling to Orbán's lobbyists in Washington that it would change that policy, Orbán seemed to have decided that the way was clear for a direct attack on George Soros.

The assumption at CEU was that the target of the attack, if it were ever to come, would be the Open Society Foundations hub in Budapest, a substantial administrative center that processed more than $100 million of foundation grants every year. In the event, the attack was directed instead at what many called "the jewel in Soros's crown" in Budapest, the CEU.

The first sign of the attack came just before Christmas, when Orbán delivered a speech rallying Fidesz members of parliament and supporters to prepare for the 2018 national elections. Orbán declared that his objective in the coming campaign was to drive George Soros and all his works from Hungary. This campaign strategy had been proposed by a US Republican campaign adviser, who urged Orbán to label Soros as the man threatening Hungary with mass migration. This is how a populist "politics of enemies" works. Orbán needed an enemy of stature, and the Hungarian opposition was too weak and too divided to give him a really worthwhile target. It was far more effective to make a man not even resident in the country responsible for all its woes, and to make his "open society" the symbol of everything Orbán was running against.

Campaign posters soon filled every available space on the subway, the trams, and the outdoor billboards: a picture of George Soros in profile with a smile on his face, and the slogan, "Don't Let George Soros Have the Last Laugh." When critics pointed out that the figure of the "laughing Jew" had been a trope of the *Völkischer Beobachter*, the Nazi Party newspaper of the 1930s, the regime reacted with indignation: *How dare you accuse us of anti-Semitism!* Thus a new kind of anti-Semitism, directed at Soros, made its first appearance in Europe. It made shameless use of Nazi-era tropes, while indignantly denying that it was doing so.

The campaign of personal defamation was followed by a direct attack on his institution. In March, CEU heard from friends inside the Hungarian government that the regime was preparing a revision of the higher education law. When that revision was proclaimed, in the official gazette, it was instantly clear that while it was nominally directed at all foreign higher education institutions working in Hungary—there are about thirty of them—the legislation was in fact targeting only one. Hence, the law quickly became known as "lex CEU." It required every foreign institution working in Hungary to negotiate a bilateral agreement between its country of origin and the Hungarian government, and to maintain a campus on its native soil. CEU is one of many US institutions overseas—the American University in Cairo, for example—that does not maintain a domestic campus in the United States.

With support from Soros and the board of trustees, the CEU administration publicly opposed the legislation as a discriminatory attack on academic freedom and set about mobilizing support in Hungary, the United States, and European capitals. Immediately, students from CEU, joined by students from universities across Budapest, ringed the campus to protect it from an expected police attack. An international digital campaign seeking international support from fellow institutions attracted letters of support from faculty, student associations, and university administrators from around the world. They flooded Viktor Orbán's inbox for weeks at a time. International condemnation, led by the German president in a speech to the European Parliament, followed soon after.

On a warm Sunday afternoon in late May 2017, a crowd of Budapest citizens, estimated at eighty thousand, gathered on the Buda side of the river, crossed the chain bridge, and marched past CEU to Parliament Square, chanting "Free Universities" in a "Free Society." It was the largest demonstration in Budapest since the heady days of 1989, an unforgettable show of support for the idea that an attack on academic freedom is ultimately an attack on democracy.

Thanks to this outpouring of public pressure, Orbán agreed in early June to enter into negotiations with the State of New York, where CEU is chartered, to see whether an agreement between Hungary and New York could secure a way for CEU to stay in Budapest. Over the summer of 2017, the chief legal counsel of the governor of New York met with Orbán's designated representative, and in late August an apparent breakthrough occurred. CEU would establish a campus at Bard College and conduct educational programs there, satisfying the Hungarian requirement for a US campus, and the Hungarian government would allow CEU to stay in Budapest. The university signed the agreement and waited for Orbán to do the same.

The signature never came. Instead Orbán announced that he would give the university another year to comply with the new law. In October, at a meeting in London, Soros turned on me, as rector, and said sharply that I had been "played." The implication was that I should never have conducted negotiations with Orbán. I vehemently disagreed. I was responsible for the faculty, staff, and students who were fighting to stay in Budapest, and I had to keep faith with them. Soros shared that objective but didn't believe a deal with Orbán was ever possible. It turns out that he was right.

For the remainder of the year, right through until the election in April 2018, the anti-Soros barrage was unrelenting. Not only were subways, buses, and streets plastered with anti-Soros posters, but there were also incessant television attacks claiming that an open society meant submerging Hungary in a deluge of refugees. The strategy, directed by Orbán's US campaign strategists, had the desired result. In the election, Fidesz once again secured the two-thirds majority of the seats in the Parliament necessary to make constitutional changes. Within weeks, Soros ordered the closing of the Open Society Foundations offices in Budapest, and by the fall of 2018 CEU was in advanced negotiations with the city of Vienna and the government of Austria to secure a new home there.

Had a US administration been prepared to defend US institutions overseas, the outcome might have been different, but in the summer of 2018, the Trump administration's new ambassador to Hungary, David Cornstein, a wealthy Republican donor from New York, arrived in Budapest. During his confirmation hearings, under questioning from Democratic and Republican senators (some of whom had visited CEU), Cornstein had promised to keep CEU in Budapest. But instead of fighting to keep a US institution in an ally country, he concentrated instead on securing Orbán a visit to the White House in the spring of 2019.

By the fall of 2019, the university began offering its US-accredited degrees, now illegal in Hungary, in Austria, and by the summer of 2020, it had secured accreditation as an Austrian private university, with the right to offer Austrian degrees. In the fall of 2020, the European Court of Justice ruled that "lex CEU" violated World Trade Organization rules relating to freedom of commerce, European Union law in relation to freedom to establish a business, and European human rights law in relation to freedom of expression. CEU's legal victory was comprehensive, but it came too late. The university by this time had decamped its teaching to Vienna, while retaining research establishments and administrative functions in Budapest.

CEU had survived the most serious crisis in its history. It had remained in Central Europe and had maintained the unbroken continuity of its teaching. More students than ever were applying, and it continued to hire new faculty. None of this would have been possible if the university's founder had decided, as he had done with so many bets in the past, to cut his losses. Instead, in the summer of 2019 Soros agreed to a substantial cash injection of 550 million euros, phased in annual payments over the following twelve years to support the university, and he also committed a further 200 million euros to defray the costs of moving to Vienna. Further, Soros agreed to a loan of 185 million euros to pay for CEU's permanent campus in the Otto-Wagner-Areal in Vienna, with occupancy to begin in 2025.

These astonishing numbers—nearly a billion dollars in total—indicate the full extent of Soros's determination to stay true to his commitment to the university he founded. On top of that, in February 2020 he committed a further billion dollars to support the creation of an Open Society University Network, to enable universities across the world to develop curricula, exchange students, and facilitate social change in their societies. Other wealthy founders might have chosen to bail out in the face of the unremitting hostility of the Hungarian government, the general darkening of the prospects for open society in Eastern Europe, and the democratic recession worldwide. The speculator that George once was might have done so, but the CEU experience had changed him. He had originally thought of his adventure in Eastern Europe as a temporary venture, a risky speculation that might pay off. Over time, he had discovered just how difficult it was to change the political culture of a whole region. His foundations had been expelled from Russia. His philanthropy had been unable to stop the consolidation of single-party authoritarian rule in Belarus and Hungary. He had sought to mobilize Western European governments to bring down the divide with Eastern Europe and genuinely integrate the two halves of the continent. He had been rebuffed, and instead of his philanthropy drawing support and encouragement from governments or private donors, he ended up having to go it alone.

Nothing had turned out quite as he had hoped, but he was not surprised. Unintended consequences are the stuff of history, he knew, and history is never over. The future of Hungary will have many chapters after the one written by Viktor Orbán. Poland is more than Jarosław Kaczyński, just as Turkey is more than Recep Tayyip Erdoğan. These rulers seek to foreclose the future, to define it in their image, but their hold on power is not eternal. As Soros turned ninety-one, his commitments to CEU indicated that he had come to an important insight that might not have occurred to him in the 1980s, when he began his efforts to change the history of his native region. He had grasped that regimes come and go, single-party rulers come and go, but institutions, universities especially, endure. Some of what Soros had tried to build had been swept away, but there were institutions, CEU among them, that would survive, prosper, and endure as his lasting legacy.

A Network of Networks

Orville Schell

WHEN ONE JANUARY MORNING IN 2021 headlines around the world announced that the Chinese corporation Hainan Airlines Holding Co., Ltd. had gone bankrupt,[1] I found myself reliving a visit to this very company with George Soros in 2005. Soros was interested in this upstart private airline as an investor rather than as a philanthropist, and so we found ourselves bound for the island province of Hainan in China's far south.

Soros had become interested in China during the mid-1980s after being involved in bringing a group of reform-minded Hungarian economists—who as he put it "were greatly admired in the Communist world"[2]—to the People's Republic of China. His China Fund was set up in 1986 under the patronage of Chen Yizi, director of the Research Institute for the Reform of the Economic Structure, a government-sponsored Chinese think tank established during the tenure of liberal Party General Secretary Zhao Ziyang.[3] Although Soros shut it down in early 1989, after false allegations of connections to the CIA were lofted, some projects were nonetheless allowed to continue, and from time to time he was still able to travel to China. However, he came under ever-closer scrutiny after General Secretary Hu Jintao attended the 2005 Shanghai Cooperation Organization meeting in Astana, Kazakhstan, and was reportedly warned (falsely) by President Vladimir Putin of Russia that Soros and his foundations had

almost single-handedly fomented the so-called color revolutions—
the Rose Revolution in Georgia, the Orange Revolution in Ukraine,
and the Tulip Revolution in Kyrgyzstan—that had recently shaken
these former Soviet republics. Putin was said to have warned Hu that
China, too, should be very wary of Soros's activities.

Putin's warning notwithstanding, these were years when China's
leaders were interested in almost any foreign investment, even from
the likes of "the crocodile," as Soros had been dubbed in China
because of his presumed ruthlessness as an investor. He was thus
allowed to continue to make occasional trips, as long as his activities were ostensibly focused on business and finance. During these
years he met with state-run think tank economists and officials from
the China Investment Corporation, China's sovereign wealth fund
(which was just organizing itself), as well entrepreneurs such as Jack
Ma (Alibaba), Edward Tian (AsianInfo Technologies), and Chauncey
Shey (SB China Venture Capital), ostensibly to explore investment
opportunities. But at the same time, Soros also availed himself of
every opportunity to meet with representatives of civil society organizations and to sound out officials about their appetite for engaging
with his foundations on relatively unsensitive topics, such as the rule
of law, the environment, and academic exchange.

I accompanied Soros on some of these trips, and so I was able to
observe his involvement in China's development boom and how he
managed to fit together his own bifurcated life as both a businessman
and a philanthropist. But I also became aware of another distinguishing feature of the larger universe that George Soros inhabited: the
immense galaxy of people swirling around him who helped irrigate
his own life with an ongoing sense of intellectual purpose as a global
actor. While some of these people came from the world of business
and profit, most of them came from the second side of his life, where
Soros gave away the money he'd earned to promote open societies.

The truth was that in his philanthropic life Soros had by the first
decade of this century become a catalytic force that would give any
one-party state cause to worry. For he had woven a web of interlocking

foundations and people that stretched around the world like a string of personal embassies, funding programs dedicated to free speech, legal reform, environmental justice, freedom of assembly, and universal human rights with hundreds of millions of dollars annually. Collectively these programs had made him as famous as a foe of autocracy as he was for being a successful investor. Needless to say, his reputation as the Johnny Appleseed of the notion of "open society" did not endear him with hardliners in the Chinese Communist Party, or any other authoritarian regime for that matter. Ultimately he would be considered so "unfriendly" in Beijing that party leaders would refuse to issue him any kind of visa at all.

But in 2005 these restrictions still lay in the future. As our plane—a corporate jet from China's first private charter company, Deer Jet—drifted down through the fluffy tropical clouds over the palm-fringed coastline of Hainan, I marveled at the anomaly of a US hedge fund mogul being feted by a billionaire entrepreneur in this country that had once pilloried their ilk as "capitalist roaders" and "counter-revolutionaries." We were heading to Haikou, the provincial capital, to visit Chen Feng, the founder and chairman of Hainan Airlines, China's largest private air carrier. Soros had already invested in the company, making him its largest outside investor, and Chen was now courting him to put in a second round. But it was not just investment capital that Chen wanted. He also wanted the cachet of someone like Soros to lure other investors to the firm.

As our plane set down at Haikou Meilan International Airport, everyone in Soros's party felt they were on an adventure. After all, we were about to be admitted into a world that normally was sealed off from the prying eyes of outsiders. What is more, this southern island province was far from Beijing and well known for its unrestrained economic development. Chen Feng would tell us of having been involved in his own share of dubious activities, some of which sounded almost mafia-like. But, as the age-old Chinese expression put it, "The mountains are high and the emperor far away" (山高皇帝远). With Beijing's controlling hand far away and Hainanese entrepreneurs and officials often in league with each other on ambitious development projects (usually involving land and bank loans, two key aspects of China's madcap economic boom), some unprecedented, not to say unholy, dealmaking had been going on and Hainan's cowboy communist capitalists had ended up creating some surprising new companies. Chen Feng's Hainan Airlines was just one of the best known examples of the kind of boomtown economic development that was making the island province an epicenter of go-go entrepreneurial energy, if also of questionable business practices.

But how could it have been otherwise? In a country where there were still no private property rights, where all land was controlled by low-paid local government officials, and where loan making was largely in the hands of only slightly better-paid state bankers, dealmaking was an endless series of invitations for embezzlement and kickbacks.

As we stepped off our private jet (Deer Jet was also owned by Chen Feng) into the steam-room-like tropical air of Hainan, we were met by a bevy of smiling young women with ruby-red lips, each bearing a bouquet of obscenely exotic flowers. Then, like the entourage of a visiting potentate, we were squired to a cortege of awaiting black limousines, delivered to Chen's seaside estate, and installed in his opulent neighboring guest house.

At the appointed time came an audience with Chen himself. After greeting us effusively at the door of his home, instead of regaling us with the success and virtues of his airline or numerous other business ventures, he instead began telling us about his interest in Tibetan Buddhism. Then, with evident pride, he led us on a tour of the upstairs meditation room he'd built especially for his spiritual practice. It was here before a lovely Buddha image that he meditated, studied with his in-house Tibetan lama, and thought through the corpus of the crypto-Buddhist corporate *kultur* that Hainan Airways employees were encouraged "to study (学习)." Indeed, he'd made it easy for them by printing a special tasseled bookmark-like card emblazoned with condensed prescriptions for how his version of Buddhist teachings could lead to a more successful corporate culture. What is more, he was in the process of writing a tract on the seminal role of Buddhist self-cultivation in Chinese civilization. After this two volume opus, *Lifetime Cultivation of Body and Soul*, was finally finished, he calligraphed it with a traditional writing brush and inkstone (his calligraphy was not bad), self-published it in a traditional thread-bound (线装本) Chinese edition, and distributed it to friends and colleagues. When he presented me with a signed copy several years later, he seemed as proud of this work as of his airline.

As I watched Soros gaze around Chen's meditation chamber, it occurred to me that, despite the fact that he was not religious, there was an interesting parallel between him and this fellow Chinese mogul. Both were successful capitalists and very rich men, but each seemed to find his life as a businessman and his growing wealth insufficient recompense and was reaching for some deeper meaning and nourishment, whether spiritual or intellectual, to complement his obvious material success. Soros had long sought to express himself as a philosopher and as a theoretical economist. Chen was evidently seeking deeper meaning through his study of Tibetan Buddhist thought and practice.

In truth, Soros had never found that trading stocks and bonds or running a hedge fund completely fulfilled his life's expectations, and he'd always aspired to a more complete intellectual, if not spiritual, life. In his early years after leaving Hungary for London, he'd spent endless hours writing philosophical treatises, most of which were never published. Ever since, he has been a wistful philosopher manqué, someone who has craved the idea of being in a larger discussion with some pantheon of philosopher kings.

"I would have liked to be a philosopher," he once honestly declared in an interview.[4] This sense of being incomplete as just a businessman has been a leitmotif in the arc of Soros's life.

"The big difference between my business life and my foundation life is that in the latter I was genuinely engaged," he admitted to his biographer Michael Kaufman. He went on to declare that if he had a heart attack doing business, he'd consider himself "really a loser." However, "if I got shot doing something in Russia or China, I wouldn't have that feeling."[5] Having been largely shut out from being able to work toward a more open society in China, he'd now turned, and not unenthusiastically, to business. After all, both fields of endeavor gave him a privileged view into what was happening in this dynamic, unpredictable, but very consequential country.

Most people have come to know Soros on one side or the other of the trader/investor – philosopher/philanthropist divide that has represented the distinguishing poles of his epic life. By being able to follow his experiences dealing with the People's Republic of China, I've been able not only to see how his views on that important country have evolved, but also to understand better how these multiple parts of his divided personality actually fit together, and how he has used his wealth to create a unifying global commons.

On our first night in Hainan, Chen Feng had assembled members of the elite Golden Ding Club (金鼎俱乐部) in Soros's honor. (A *ding* [鼎] is a form of an ancient bronze wine vessel used for ceremonial and ritual purposes.) Chen's club consisted of some of China's most successful private entrepreneurs who rallied together from time to time to banquet, bond, and share their collective experiences as capitalists living and working within the context of a "socialist society" and a Leninist one-party state. At the dinner Soros was called on to make some remarks, not so much because he had anything relevant to tell this gathering of self-made Chinese titans, but because Chen knew that his guest was a "get," and whatever Soros said would serve as a benediction on his own rapidly expanding airline group.

As guest of honor, Soros was seated beside his beaming host at an enormous round table. He seemed to be enjoying the idea of having been granted entrance to this sanctum sanctorum of Chinese entrepreneurial energy. Many international businessmen might have seen the occasion as an irresistible opportunity to expand their "*guanxi* network" (关系网), those webs of personal relationships upon which Chinese dealmaking so often depends: collecting new name cards and making new deals. But Soros viewed the dinner more as an opportunity to understand the subterranean forces at play inside China, which were rapidly changing the country in ways that outsiders often had great difficulty seeing and understanding.

I was seated next to one of China's largest private manufacturers of motorbikes, whose company was situated in Sichuan Province. In spite of the fact that he had been pilloried and persecuted during the Cultural Revolution, and that his distinctly capitalist enterprise had been forced to grow inside a socialist state cage, this man evinced optimism about the future of his business. For to help drive China's economy forward and maintain high growth rates, the Chinese Communist Party still needed privateers like him. And despite the fact that many of them had generated distinctly un-communist amounts of personal wealth (and economic power), the party still admiringly referred to them as "national champions" (全国冠军) and they continued to be able to operate relatively freely within the otherwise often rigid confines of the Chinese state. Hainan Airways was in many ways a poster child for all the other private enterprises represented around the Golden Ding Club banquet table. Collectively they were not only supercharging China's economy with new energy, but also lending luster to China as a global trade powerhouse.

It was a heady time just then in China. Many of these dinner guests had concluded that the Chinese Communist Party was likely to allow private companies like theirs to continue to expand and prosper, and even compete with the state-owned enterprises that had comprised the heart of the Chinese economy since 1949. The private firms were outperforming most state-owned enterprises, and it was not farfetched to think that the companies represented by the Golden Ding Club might even replace them one day. This scenario beguiled those Americans who still hoped that greater "engagement" would lead China to continue reforming and opening up. Soros himself had always been intrigued by this vision, which had, after all, been at the heart of the logic of his philanthropy as the communist world broke up after 1989. And because he felt that the businessmen gathered together in Hainan were living evidence that such reform-minded change had happened and was still possible, sitting around this banquet allowed all of us in Soros's small traveling party to feel that we were very much in the right place, with the right people, at the right moment.

And indeed, before our private jet whisked us away from Chen Feng and Hainan, Soros had ponied up another round of investment for his airline.

"It's a fine company, and I don't have enough exposure in China," a smiling Soros told the press.[6]

In retrospect we were perhaps somewhat naive in believing that the promise of reform justified looking toward the future with such hopefulness. Although Soros's Open Society Institute still had a few lingering philanthropic projects continuing in China, the party was increasingly ambivalent about civil society, particularly foreign funding for its domestic NGOs. With Soros's foundation banished, and he as its progenitor viewed by the party with growing ambivalence, there was no longer much promise for his "open society" evangelism in China. So, with his civil society wings clipped, why not do a little business? After all, China was in an exciting period of economic development, and Soros wanted to keep his front-row seat as the drama unfolded. And Hainan Airlines was one of the most dynamic players in this always surprising drama.

After having started in 1993 with a single plane, by the time we arrived in 2005 Hainan Airlines was China's largest private passenger carrier and was destined to become the fourth-largest airline in the country. For Chen Feng, a private businessman struggling in a system where almost all enterprises in the transport, media, telecommunications, and banking sectors were still state-owned, this was no small accomplishment. As his ambitions grew, the Hainan Airlines Group became one of a rapidly expanding number of multinational Chinese conglomerates gaining a global name for itself. But often the growth of these companies was so rapid, chaotic, and sometimes lawless and distorted by government interference and patronage that it was difficult, especially for foreigners, to evaluate them and then to know just how their investments might end up being used.

With their high-rise headquarters and slick promotional materials, companies like Hainan Airlines certainly radiated an air of dynamism and success. But their reality was often far different. These companies were almost always encumbered by hidden "Chinese characteristics" (中国特色) that made them very different animals from their counterparts elsewhere in the world. Many of these new Chinese enterprises lacked transparency, had dodgy governance structures, were plagued by murky ownership, were overdependent on their founders, and were subject to the whims of the party and its leaders. Even more important, their success or failure was invariably dependent on their relationships with government leaders and the state-owned bank chieftains who provided most of the available investment capital in China, where financial markets were still weak. And then there was the reality that whenever a private company wanted to expand, the CEO needed to have good contacts with local officials, because all property, permitting procedures, and lending institutions were state-controlled. Such market-distorting dependencies made corruption almost inevitable. Foreign investors undertaking due diligence were left peering through a glass darkly.

As Soros would only belatedly understand, his investments in Hainan Airlines were ascribed to a less profitable part of the larger HNA Group, so that even as the airline prospered, he ended up getting poor returns. This Chinese legerdemain and lack of transparency often left foreign investors at the mercy of a system that was opaque and unfathomable. Each case was too often just a variation on a theme: An overseas investor would initially be shown enormous deference by being feted with a degree of pomp and ceremony that would lead him to conclude that he had somehow managed to bridge the difficult divide separating the two worlds that the Chinese demarcate as "inside the country" (国内) and "outside the country" (国外). Transactions considered "inside" between Chinese players are those where everyone more or less understands how things work because they've been living "inside the country" their whole lives. But matters pertaining to emissaries from "outside the country"—such as joint-venture business deals with foreigners—are subject to a different set of protocols and rituals that hark back to the dynastic days of "barbarian management," when outsiders were plied with ritual and ceremony designed to keep them at bay with flattery. Such indirect strategies of stealth and deception were far less costly and more effective management tools than brute force.

In an investment or joint venture involving foreigners, the preliminary wooing is often as elaborate as any ardent personal courtship. It may involve private jets, exotic bouquets, extravagant gifts, luxurious guest houses, tours of meditation rooms, seats of honor at elaborate banquets, and other blandishments that leave a guest of honor feeling nonpareil. But once the deal is done, the money has been transferred, and there is no longer any possibility of retreat, the "foreigner friend" often finds himself quietly shunted onto a siding and to confront opacity, where it's easier for the Chinese partner to quietly relieve said "friend" of his company's intellectual property, make his investment vanish down the Chinese rabbit hole, or otherwise fleece him.

Soros was not, of course, unaware of the refractory nature of totalitarian states, whose signature is secrecy and paranoia. After all, as a youth he'd lived through both the Nazis and then the advent of communist rule in his native Hungary. And yet, despite the skepticism born from this experience about one-party governments (much less the likelihood of them ever voluntarily relinquishing unilateral state control), Soros nonetheless tried to maintain a fundamentally optimistic attitude about China. This had enabled him to continue hoping that his activities as a philanthropist might help bend the metal of Chinese authoritarianism. Part of his optimism derived from his abiding belief in the tonic effect of liberal democracies: that if they made an effort to engage with regimes like the People's Republic of China through business, trade, civil society interactions, academic exchanges, and philanthropic activities, they might have a salutary effect. This was the dream of "engagement" that had been set in motion by Richard Nixon and Henry Kissinger's game-changing trip to Beijing in 1972, when they'd met with Mao Zedong and Zhou Enlai, agreed on an anti-USSR strategy, and transformed the Cold War global order. And even after Soros's repeated failures in other formerly communist countries—most monumentally in Russia and then in China—he seemed unfazed. Indeed, the idea that he might still somehow help facilitate a peaceful transition from autocracy to a more democratic form of government remained his dream. Surprisingly his expulsion from numerous communist countries has led to no regrets and has precipitated no apologies. As he bluntly put it in an article entitled "A Selfish Man with a Selfless Foundation," his life had taught him to "believe that in philanthropy one should do the right thing whether or not it succeeds."[7]

"It's a very cultured way of influencing people," observed fellow Hungarian investor György Jaksity. "You can say, 'I am Napoleon Bonaparte—I will kill thousands of people unless you give me Moscow.' Or there's the other way, the Soros way."[8]

Traveling with Soros in China over the years, I was always amazed by how, even after repeated rebukes and setbacks, he kept his equanimity, kept going, and kept spending hundreds of millions of dollars a year in the hope of encouraging the "better angels" of various refractory countries to evolve in a more open, just, and humane direction. The dream that China, even if the Communist Party stayed in power, might also evolve away from its Maoist roots endured during the first decade of the 2000s. The hope—for Soros and others—was that if the United States and other liberal democracies were patient and provided encouragement and financial support, the gap between authoritarian China and the democratic world would slowly narrow. China might not immediately emerge as a full-blown democracy, but it might develop in a progressively more open direction. Such faith was characterized by the former World Bank president Robert Zoellick when he hopefully suggested in 2005 (the same year we went to Hainan) that China might yet end up a "responsible stakeholder" in the world order.[9]

Just such a convergence seemed to promise itself during the ensuing decade, when the Chinese Communist Party launched its
so-called "going out" (走出去) policy and began encouraging both
private and state-owned enterprises to leverage themselves with capital from state-owned banks and acquire companies and investments
abroad. Chen Feng was one of those entrepreneurs who took this bit
in his teeth and went on a madcap, global buying spree. Like so many
other ambitious private Chinese entrepreneurs who were fueled by
seemingly inexhaustible supplies of state capital, he began hoovering
up assets around the world. Hainan soon had stakes in Hilton Hotels
and Resorts, Deutsche Bank, Swissport, Ingram Micro, and hundreds
of other global assets. By 2017, HNA Group ranked no. 170 in the
Fortune Global 500 list.[10] And by endowing Hainan Airways with his
valuable global investment cachet early on, George Soros contributed
to getting this enormous Chinese snowball rolling. "Soros' investment
clearly shows that Hainan Airlines' performance is outstanding, on
a par with international airlines," Chen had proudly proclaimed
shortly after our visit.[11]

By January 2021, Hainan Airlines had grown to have some 220
aircraft and 290,000 employees, and its parent, the Haihang Group,
owned more than 2,300 other businesses around the world, including
stakes in fourteen other global airlines with some 900 planes!

But then, after its spree of debt-fueled acquisitions both home
and abroad, it was suddenly revealed that the company was not only
going bankrupt, but its executives stood accused of embezzling $10
billion in assets. Hainan Airlines was, it turned out, still something
of a poster child for Chinese private enterprise. However, instead of
being a model of responsible Buddhist business practices and corporate shareholder value, by then it had become a symbol of overreach,
hubris, corruption, and failure.

The full eclipse of the promise of engagement came after the
investiture of Xi Jinping as general secretary and president, as he
made it increasingly evident that China was no longer on a reformist, liberalizing trajectory. What is more, Xi was coming to view the

ballooning independent economic power of private moguls like Chen Feng, Jack Ma, and Wang Jianlin as potential political threats. And once in office he began reining in some of them while at the same time initiating a host of quasi neo-Maoist campaigns and controls: he promulgated a new "civil society law" in 2016, the Overseas Non-Governmental Organization (NGO) Law, that circumscribed foreign NGO collaboration with Chinese counterparts; detained many of the country's human rights lawyers in 2017; canceled term limits for presidency in 2018; began expelling members of the foreign press corps; also unleashed an era of belligerent "wolf warrior diplomacy" (战狼外交) in 2020, and promulgated the sweeping Anti-Foreign Sanctions Law that spelled out how China can retaliate against those who sanction, or even advocate for sanctions, against China.[12] In serial fashion such belligerence antagonized one country after another that had once been favorably disposed to it. Norway, Korea, Sweden, the Philippines, Canada, Australia, India, and then even the European Union have all been vindictively punished by Beijing for refusing to yield to Chinese threats of retaliation for perceived slights and criticisms.

As Xi's tenure evinced ever more autocratic tendencies, Soros's attitude began shifting as well. He seemed to conclude that his efforts had not, in fact, bent any Chinese metal, and with increasing frequency he began speaking of China as a growing threat, a "mortal danger" to the liberal democratic world.[13]

During the earlier halcyon period when "engagement" still possessed an almost alchemical promise among policy makers of being able to promote "convergence," there was a logic for Soros, and others, to continue supporting collaborative activities in China, whether through business or civil society interactions. But with the advent of Xi's hardline policies, this logic vanished, and in Soros's own evolution, the earlier version of him as the implacable opponent of "closed societies" began to reemerge and take ascendancy over Soros the hopeful reformer. In his 2019 and 2020 speeches at the World Economic Forum in Davos, he described this very different China, one that under Xi had evolved from being a "strategic competitor" to one that was becoming a genuine threat, particularly in the world of technology. China had, Soros unambiguously declared, become "the most dangerous opponent of open societies" in the world today.[14]

As far as the Chinese Communist Party was concerned, Soros had returned irrevocably to his roots. He was now unambiguously opposed to authoritarianism and resolutely in support of open society. He has not visited China since 2014.

I FIRST MET George Soros long ago, when he became involved in setting up Helsinki Watch and Human Rights Watch with my father, Orville Schell Jr., and Robert Bernstein, then the CEO of Random House. Soros had also been associated with my mother when both became critical of American policy during the Vietnam War and worked on some common projects together. But it was not until the 1990s—when my Chinese-born wife, Baifang Schell, began accompanying Aryeh Neier, the president of Soros's Open Society Institute, to China and then also began helping Soros on his own trips there— that I got to know him better.

As I have watched Soros over the past few decades, I have come to see that besides his urge to make money and his quest to have an impact as a philanthropist, there was another aspect of him as public citizen that had previously eluded me. His foundations were not just a way for him to advance those causes he cared about, but also a way to nourish his intellect and soul from the world of ideas. What became evident was that whether he was doing business or engaging civil society, he was also weaving together another important part of his life, a unique fabric of people that help sustain him as a thinking activist person.

By helping set up the Golden Ding Club as a fraternity of private entrepreneurs, Chen Feng had created an alternative capitalist chamber of commerce within China's socialist state as a support mechanism for his own business fraternity. But Soros had done something even more creative and rewarding: he had used his considerable wealth to help others while also helping himself by establishing a global community that afforded him the ability to interact with a broad network of scholars, diplomats, university presidents, government officials, filmmakers, writers, artists, journalists, activists, and sundry others whose work interested him. He has referred to this growing community of people and institutions as his "network of networks."[15] But as he also began consorting with this growing nebula of people in a more direct and regular way, he found it so congenial that he began intellectually, and sometimes physically, to live in it.

While the web of networks was global, it came to life in miniature cell-like form through the meetings that Soros and his wife, Tamiko, tirelessly convened over lunches and dinners in their New York City apartment, long weekends at their houses in Southampton and Bedford, work trips to their townhouse in London, Thanksgiving celebrations at Central European University in Budapest, winter retreats in the Bahamas, and numerous more public get-togethers and conferences. Each gathering was irrigated by the many tributaries feeding Soros's networks, whose headwaters all rose in the activities that composed his enormously diverse life. And as these tributaries fed into these intimate salon-like gatherings, they slowly formed a greater body of interconnected, interesting, and politically active people whose portfolios ranged from finance, banking, and investment to world affairs, revolution, election reform, technology, democracy, human rights, and even drug use, education, and palliative care. Many had, of course, been directly or indirectly nourished by one of Soros's philanthropic programs. But then, often without quite realizing what was happening, these recipients found themselves becoming enmeshed in this larger Soros network and being able to offer their benefactor some recompense. While he nourished supplicants with financial support they, in turn, nourished him and his insatiable appetite to learn by sharing their knowledge and work. As convener in chief, Soros has constructed a feedback loop that has given him the incomparable benefit of being able to learn from and interact with his own grantees. And as part of this unspoken reciprocal compact, participants and guests not only get to interact with him and other guests, but are also offered the opportunity to forge new partnerships with these others in ways that only expanded their progenitor's vaunted "network of networks."

"I regard altruism and philanthropy not as a duty, but as a pleasure and a source of satisfaction," Soros wrote in his book *In Defense of Open Society*. "It gives me a great sense of satisfaction to be engaged in an activity for which it would be worth dying."[16]

Being invited to one of Soros's meals, weekends, vacations, or conferences—even a phone discussion or Zoom meeting—is for many like getting a summons from a head of state. Indeed, if (as some who know him have joked) he is something like a head of state, he is perhaps better described as the head of a "stateless state" that nonetheless has its own foreign policy and embassies around the world. And an invitation to one of his weekend retreats is like being handed a ticket for a cruise on a small but very well-run ship open only to the most interesting and accomplished list of passengers. But unlike a cruise ship, the Good Ship Soros has no slot machines, floor shows, stand-up comics, or lounge acts. Instead its entertainment features discussions about genocide, American politics, the global order, human rights abuses, climate change, pandemics, and the occasional film (usually a documentary). It is not everyone's version of recreational fun, but for Soros and his acolytes it fits the bill.

Once on board one of these land-locked cruises, except for a possible jog, bike ride, or stroll on the beach, most guests never leave the confines of Soros's all-encompassing estate compounds, especially El Mirador, in Southampton. And why should they, when everything—tennis, swimming, films, patio lounging, chess and backgammon, meals cooked by his team of gourmet chefs, more films, and nonstop intellectual content—is provided within?

Even as urgent global affairs are discussed, the outside world can feel a little more tractable and time within even seems to slow down. Once in the embrace of a Soros sojourn, one has the childlike sensation of having passed through a portal into a secret garden, a sheltered, privileged preserve that offers a reassuring sense that here, at least, things still work, people still make sense, and the world still coheres. The quiet, well-manicured gardens, verdant lawns, arching trees, delicious food, and conversations with well-informed people create a welcome sense of respite from the craven world outside. And yes, perhaps it is all just an expensive illusion, an elaborate form of conjury that only wealth can create, like looking into a Fabergé egg. But however one construes it, there is no denying that such weekends offer entrants a welcome interlude of surcease from the travails of life outside.

Usually there are ten or so guests in residence at a time, and it's always a surprise to learn who will show up on a particular invitation list. Making sure that the guests all fit together and enjoy one another's company is a board game at which Tamiko has become the tireless grand master, even as George remains the unifying presence.

At El Mirador, each day starts with a casual breakfast set outside on a well-provisioned patio table where copies of *The New York Times* and *Financial Times* are at the ready. Thereafter guests are left to go about their own affairs, as does Soros, and there is no further collective activity until luncheon time. Then an elegant buffet is set up at the pool house, and guests sit at tables arrayed along a patio under the spreading boughs of enormous shade trees. Like Soros himself, house guests usually come barefoot and dressed in the most casual manner. (Outside guests are invariably dressed with a little more smartness.) But Soros's own informality gives everyone else permission to relax, let their hair down, and linger in casual discussion over coffee long after the luncheon dishes have been cleared. Then guests repair to their rooms to nap, work, talk on the phone, or read.

Not until 7 P.M. do guests reconvene, this time for cocktails, usually with a few outsiders who have also been invited for dinner. It is at these evening meals where guests get a chance to exchange experiences and ideas with Soros and one another. However, as Soros's hearing has declined and he found himself less able to participate fully in the conversation, a single large dinner table became unworkable and so guests now sit in smaller groups situated at smaller tables. At Soros's own table, each place is equipped with a microphone that allows him to hear clearly, through an earpiece, what his tablemates are saying and thereby to join fully in the discussion. Guests must get used to pressing a button on their microphone stands before speaking, but Soros evinces no apology for this system's awkwardness. What matters is that it works and that he is able to continue participating fully in all interactions with his guests, almost as if there were no impediment at all.

During the COVID pandemic, when everyone was confined to their homes, there was an interruption to this regimen. But Soros was paradoxically less inconvenienced by the challenges of engaging in conversations over Zoom or Signal. In fact, he was at no greater disadvantage because of his hearing loss than anyone else. So, instead of spending weekends with guests at one of his estates, his collegium simply moved online, where he was easily able to electronically stay in touch.

Uninitiates at Soros weekends often consider the table at which he sits as the "important table," or at least as primus inter pares, and they have sometimes been left smarting when they find themselves parked at a table populated by the spouses and children of the worthies who are engaged in animated debate with his eminence. But they soon learn that seating charts shift night by night and there is reprieve at ensuing dinners.

It is undeniably true that such house parties are dependent on Soros's seemingly infinite wealth and considerable global standing. But their uniqueness also depends on his own very special sensibility. Many other billionaires put their fortunes to far baser purposes, too often calculated to simply impress others. But never in all the years I've enjoyed Soros's gatherings have I ever felt that his affluence was being deployed in a way that was designed to announce itself or calculated to impress or intimidate. Instead he arrays his wealth in an understated way, with the aspiration of generating a full and free exchange of ideas centering on issues that interest and concern him. Because he takes deep pleasure in interacting with his guests, he does this not simply to please them, but to please himself. That his guests happen to include some of the most brilliant, accomplished, and engaged people on the planet only makes the experience more rewarding for him and for them.

Soros's aspiration is the same as that of great universities—namely, to create an open academic fraternity where wide-ranging discourse can take place. This is perhaps one of the reasons why he also created and endowed a whole new university, Central European University, that specializes in addressing real-world problems in a practical way. Soros calls CEU "a university that takes its principles and its social responsibilities seriously."[17]

Soros likes thinkers who are also doers, and so academic jargon, repetition of turgid theories, and the incantation of behavioral science mumbo-jumbo are not the currency of his realm. Instead, his focus is on understanding how a global problem arose and how it can best be ameliorated.

Yes, Soros reigns over his dominion of networks like a latter-day sovereign, with Tamiko as his consort and his system of foundation offices arrayed around the world like his own legations. And yet despite his dominion, he is disinclined to dominate discussions. He has strong views and can sometimes be arbitrary in his decision-making, even make mistakes, but he is a good listener who seems to have concluded that the best pathway to continued learning is to be open to what others have to say.

One of my sons has described a stay at Chateau Soros as a little like being summoned to the court of Louis XIV. However, he adds, "whereas what counted in Bourbon France was aristocratic rank, how one dressed, and what jewelry one could boast, at the Soros court what matters is how interesting and au courant one can be." He added that there is sometimes such pressure to produce scintillating contributions that at dinner some conversations "become like a competitive sport." There is a bit of *Downton Abbey* or *Brideshead Revisited* here, except that Soros's guests don't dress that well for dinner, with the host usually presiding in an open floral shirt.

It would be easy to write off such a lifestyle as upper-class self-indulgence, except for the fact that Soros has given away more than $30 billion of his own money, and both the financial beneficiaries and most of those on his guest lists come from much more modest circumstances than he. While wealthy business associates do sometimes stray into his fold, the lion's share of Soros's guests work for environmental organizations, governments, multinational organizations, universities, civic groups, think tanks, the media, or cultural organizations. And while he himself wants for nothing, he is one of the few billionaires who has not indulged himself in a private plane, a luxury yacht, a chic vineyard, or similar pretentious affectations favored by others among the super-rich.

But what should one make of the grander events, such as his epic-scale wedding to Tamiko Bolton in 2013 or his equally grand occasional tented birthday parties? Seen from one perspective, these extravaganzas are over the top. Does anyone need to assemble many hundreds of people in enormous tents and spend a million dollars just to celebrate a birthday?

Here, too, though, there is method in the seeming excess. While these large events are costly, they do serve the important role of collectively rallying the bigger dramatis personae from Soros's diverse, larger-than-life web of networks. These big-tent events are a chance for orbiting members from his many worlds to get connected to Soros Central and become a more organic part of his larger enterprise, even though they may have only joined a lunch, dinner, or weekend at one of his houses.

As a whole, Soros's various gatherings play an important role in integrating his network of networks and helping his acolytes, friends, and associates feel like members of a larger society of fellows. And such a sense of solidarity helps fortify these global civil society members almost as much as his financial support itself. For what propels

Soros's collective civil society enterprise forward is not just his funding, but his ability to make his recipients feel they are part of a unique, collective global effort. One might even call it a movement. And as the solutions to an increasing number of contemporary problems turn out to be global in scope, such an integrative force is precisely what such diverse and often isolated open society institutions and leaders need to feel connected.

Soros has devised a way of making the process of spreading his money generously around the world also nourish and inspire him with new thinking. In this process he is doubtless answering a need that has smoldered within him since his youth: to be more than just a businessman, to be someone actively engaged in the broad world of ideas, philosophy, and politics. As I have watched the great whirlpool of global actors that he's managed to set spinning around him, I have often had the sense that it is precisely the intellectual and political excitement they generate that has helped him keep not just up-to-date, but inspired and active, even as he enters his tenth decade.

Proud of his own economic theory of "reflexivity," Soros has unconsciously managed to put it into practice in his own life. His economic theory presupposes that "if investors believe that markets are efficient, then that belief will change the way they invest, which will in turn change the behavior of the markets in which they are participating."[18] By building this network of networks, he hopes to change the world's behavior, and in the process enhance his own ongoing learning and evolution.

"In the course of my life, I have developed a conceptual framework which has helped me both to make money as a hedge fund manager and to spend money as a policy-oriented philanthropist," he cheerfully wrote in the *Financial Times* in 2009. "But the framework itself is not about money, it is about the relationship between thinking and reality, a subject that has been extensively studied by philosophers from early on." In a word, he adds, reflexivity postulates that "participants' views influence the course of events, and the course of events influences the participants' views."[19]

As one of the many planets that have long orbited in the Soros solar system, I have worked with many institutions over the decades that have benefited from his largesse. While I was a dean at the University of California, Berkeley, Soros funded several programs to bring young Chinese and Burmese journalists to the graduate school I oversaw. When I moved to the Asia Society in New York, his foundation began funding programs in media, climate change, and US-China relations. At the same time he generously supported Chinese writers and intellectuals who had run afoul of China's one-party state. Despite the fact that Soros's critics and detractors are many, I cannot say that in my long association with him I have ever seen any such grounds for criticism. Soros is not a demonstrative or sentimental man, but his commitment to trying to make the world a better place by building a constructive community of well-informed doers seems irrefutable.

Indeed, as I write these paragraphs I sit in Pasadena, California, with my dying wife. Even here Soros's multifaceted generosity and interlocking networks have touched our lives. When his own Hungarian-born mother lay on her deathbed in his New York City home, as Soros attended her, he decided to set up a program in palliative care to teach hospitals and caregivers how to better help families confronting the tragedy of losing loved ones. As he explained in launching his Project on Death in America, "First and foremost, doctors, nurses, and other health professionals need better training in the care of the dying, especially in the relief of pain. Physical pain is what people fear most about dying. A dying person in pain cannot think about anything else, leaving no room for coming to terms with death, for reviewing one's life, putting one's affairs in order, for saying good-bye."[20]

When I called him and Tamiko to tell them that my wife would be joining a drug trial at the City of Hope cancer research center and hospital, they immediately connected me with Katherine Foley, a neurologist at Memorial Sloan Kettering in New York City. Having headed the pioneering pain management service at the hospital's cancer center, she became the medical director of the Supportive

Care Program that Soros funded. There, a new generation of medical personnel have been trained to help hospitals, patients, and families manage end-of-life issues in a more informed and humane way. And in her intelligent, business-like manner, Foley introduced us to one of her Soros program–trained colleagues, Matthew Loscalzo, who had become the executive director of the Department of Supportive Care Medicine at the City of Hope where his wife, Dr. Joanne Mortimer, directed the Women's Cancer Programs. Without their help and good counsel, the death of my wife would have been even more painful and trying than it was.

For me, here in the most concrete way was one more illustration of how George Soros's seemingly endless network of interlocking networks was succeeding in helping people in need, in the most basic and human of ways. His efforts may not have always been successful in bringing about radical changes and in opening societies in countries like Russia and China, but he has, at least, helped many individuals in those countries while supporting the better instincts of others in myriad walks of life around the world.

The Challenge and Legacy of Being a Jew from Hungary

Leon Botstein

THE MOST ENDURING AND INFLUENTIAL FACT in the life of George Soros is that he was born a Jew. His encounter with the escalating consequences of that fundamental and permanent fact during the first fifteen years of his life in Budapest began with segregation and exclusion, and ended in deprivation, terror, and the fear of death. Yet unlike some of his Jewish contemporaries, including members of his immediate family, George resolved to accept the basic and indelible fact that he was a Jew and would always be regarded as a Jew. When confronted with his identity as a Jew, he did not deny it. He remembers just one occasion when he was tempted. In 1949, on a trip to Switzerland, he shared lodgings in Davos with a man he had been skiing with, a young Israeli, probably an agent of the newly established Mossad who sought to recruit him to the cause of the still very young State of Israel. After nearly a week, the Israeli confronted him; he asked George directly, "Why won't you admit to being a Jew?" George was taken aback. After all, during the most dangerous months of 1944 it was repeatedly observed that George really did not look Jewish (with his blond hair) and therefore could pass easily. But the Israeli was not fooled. George was embarrassed. He replied that he would not deny that he was Jewish. But, he was equally disinclined to highlight the fact.

It would be unfair, if not unjust, to fault this reluctance on the part of a young Jewish man for whom anything approximating a "normal" life, such as using his real name, had begun only four years earlier, when he was fifteen. For slightly less than three-quarters of George Soros's life, being a Jew had been an unrelenting cause of uncertainty and anxiety. Admitting to being Jewish in 1944 would have easily put his life in danger. George survived only by successfully taking on a new name, different from any of the non-Jewish names assumed by his parents and brother, each officially documented with false Christian identity papers. There was no "right" or dignified way for any Jew of any age on the European continent to emerge as a survivor from the genocide of the Jews of Europe that ended in 1945, just a few years before George's encounter in Switzerland. The genocide was calculated and efficient as well as random and haphazard, and succeeded in murdering six million Jews.

After 1945 George Soros held on to his identity as a Jew but submerged it within an overarching commitment to universalism in which the multiplicity of subjective identities would all be devalued. For the young George Soros, the decisive formulation of this credo came from Henri Bergson's idea of "open society" driven by a "dynamic religion" defined by empathy as well as reason. In his influential book *The Two Sources of Morality and Religion*, published in 1932,[1] Bergson juxtaposed such an "open" society against a "closed" society buttressed by a "static" religion reliant on "totemism" and mythological fantasies. Like Bergson, who himself became increasingly distant from his own identity as a Jew, in the end Soros acknowledged it, and like Bergson, even credited his having been born a Jew with supplying him with the capacity to reformulate and defend Bergson's cosmopolitan vision of an "open" society. For Bergson and Soros—both Jews—fighting for an "open society" was a "moral obligation."

In Soros's later years being Jewish would become a visible and central aspect of his fame and notoriety. But his youthful allegiance and dedication to the struggle to transcend the provincial and regressively sectarian and to cultivate the universal were shaped not merely by ideas, but also by the encounter with the mendacity and brutality of anti-Semitism in Budapest, before and during World War II—and the courage and wisdom his father demonstrated by confronting it and eluding its worst consequences. These experiences decisively shaped his own character, ambitions, and outlook, all for the better. The war years taught him about the unintended consequences of passivity and the pitfalls of unexamined adherence to seemingly civilized standards of behavior, including the routine respect for authority in the face of unprecedented and extreme conditions. Following rules and conventional thinking exacerbated the fatal risks created by abnormal conditions. Survival required intuition and courage; Soros was inspired to emulate the fierce independence of mind and appetite for risk his father displayed.

Being Jewish shaped George Soros's approach to life by encouraging him to take advantage of being an outsider, and being an exception. His self-awareness, his capacity to observe how he was seen by others and to think for himself, became inseparable from the memory that he had been born into a minority, born Jewish into a family of Jews. This singular fact lent an exceptional intensity and determination to his beliefs and ideals, particularly to his commitment to the idea of an "open society." It sustained his desire to assist the neglected and helpless, particularly minorities who were victims of the abuse of political, legal, and economic power by majorities and authoritarian governments. It inspired him to resist the imposition of political ideologies and systems that assumed the mantle of absolute truth. The experience of living through the war years framed his fascination with epistemology and the limits of reason; it led him to develop theories of reflexivity, certainty, fallibility, the limits of science, and unintended consequences.

In her 1956 Walgreen Lectures, published as *The Human Condition* in 1958, Hannah Arendt argued that coming to terms with "natality," the unique and indelible circumstances of a person's entrance into the world (given that, as she put it, "we are all the same, that is, human, in such a way that nobody is ever the same as anyone else who ever lived, lives or will live") determines the possibilities of how an individual will act in the world, particularly in the realm of politics.[2] The case of George Soros validates Arendt's idea; by acknowledging and ultimately embracing his natality as a Jew, he made it possible to become an independent thinker, and unique as a man of action in politics. History will remember George Soros as having been the most influential private citizen and philanthropist in the late twentieth and early twenty-first centuries.

GEORGE SOROS WAS born in 1930 in Budapest to upper-middle-class parents. They were second cousins and both from Jewish families, one of which—his mother's—was quite well off. George's father, Tivadar Soros, was respected as a skilled lawyer, but he was not inclined to hard work. The decisive experience in Tivadar's life had been his time as a prisoner of war in Siberia during World War I, and his dramatic and improbable escape. Having barely survived, Tivadar preferred to concentrate on the comparatively easy task of managing his wife's real estate holdings; this allowed him to live well and pursue, leisurely, his many hobbies and interests. Although George's parents' home was predominantly secular, George's Jewish identity was marked, in a concrete sense, and sealed by circumcision; Jewish males seeking to conceal their identities as Jews from would-be captors and killers were at a distinct disadvantage. George had, in addition, a bar mitzvah, as did his older brother, Paul. George voluntarily took advantage of the religious instruction provided in school and even relished challenging the teacher.

George grew up in a nonobservant home that nonetheless recognized the High Holidays with festive meals and celebrated Passover. As the youngest child, George asked the "Four Questions" in the Haggadah, in Hebrew, at the annual family Seder. His extended family included pious Orthodox Jews, whom George knew and liked.

But he would never forget seeing, as a child, an aunt remove her wig to take a nap. It frightened him; the image came to represent the sacrifice required to maintain a rigorous Jewish life and the gulf between the aspiration to the universal visible in his parental home and an allegiance to the sectarian.

The community into which George was born, the Hungarian Jews of Budapest, was truly distinct. Arendt's phrase, that "nobody is ever the same as anyone else," applies with uncanny precision to the Jews of Hungary during the seventy-seven years between the Compromise (*Ausgleich*) of 1867 that transformed the Habsburg dynasty into the Austro-Hungarian Empire and instituted legal emancipation for Jews, and one catastrophic date during the final years of World War II, March 19, 1944. Consider the array of "geniuses" who were born Hungarian Jews—most, but not all, in Budapest—between the mid-1880s and the 1930s.[3] The list is astonishing and has become the stuff of legend. It includes László Bíró, the inventor of the first commercially successful ballpoint pen; athletes who won Olympic medals (most famously the champion fencer Attila Petschauer); pioneers in photography, film, and music; entrepreneurs; and above all scientists and mathematicians. In the pantheon of great Hungarian Jews from that period are, among others, world-renowned scientists and mathematicians (John von Neumann and Leo Szilard), historians and philosophers (Arnold Hauser, Karl Mannheim, György Lukács, Michael and Karl Polanyi), filmmakers (Michael Curtiz), composers and performers (Emmerich Kálmán, Leó Weiner, Fritz Reiner, Joseph Szigeti, George Szell, Georg Solti), and artists (László Moholy-Nagy—Solti's cousin, born Weisz—and André Kertész). Most of these future celebrities were closer in age to Tivadar Soros, who was born in 1894. But many, such as the writer and Nobel laureate Imre Kertész, the composers György Ligeti and György Kurtág, and Andrew Grove, the entrepreneur who created the microchip company Intel, belong to George's generation; like George they were born in the interwar era, in the 1920s and 1930s.

According to the census of 1910, the Hungarian half of Austria-Hungary, the "Dual Monarchy," contained 911,000 Jews,

203,000 of whom lived in Budapest.[4] After World War I, half of those Hungarian Jews, 473,000 of them, found themselves within the borders of the new, truncated Hungarian state created by the controversial Treaty of Trianon of 1920, which became and remains a persistent source of resentment, anger, and fierce nationalism among Hungarians. Slightly over half of the Jews within the new borders, 240,000, lived outside of Budapest, dispersed throughout the country. This fact distinguished the Hungarian Jewish community from that of Poland (where more than 90 percent of Jews lived in cities) and Germany (where 70 percent of Jews were urban). Jews accounted for 5 percent of the population of post-Trianon Hungary. The half cut off from the radically smaller new Hungarian nation ultimately came under German rule and influence during World War II; between 1938 and 1941 Hungary took back territory in Slovakia, Transylvania, and Serbia and proceeded to deport the Jews in those regions.

Of the over 860,000 Hungarian Jews alive in 1941 (counting those living outside the Trianon borders), two-thirds perished in the Holocaust. In Trianon Hungary alone, between March 1944 and the Soviet victory in Budapest in January 1945, the Nazis and Hungarian fascists, led by the Arrow Cross Party under the leadership of Ferenc Szálasi, murdered more than 430,000 Hungarian Jews. At the end of the war, 119,000 Jews in Budapest survived, a remarkable percentage when compared with other Eastern and Central European cities with significant Jewish populations. Consider Lodz in Poland, where the Jewish population in 1931 also numbered more than 200,000, making up a third of the city's inhabitants. Fewer than 900 of them were still alive in the city when the Russians liberated it in 1945; only another 10,000 Jews from Lodz are estimated to have survived elsewhere. Yet 24,000 Budapest Jews eluded extermination by hiding in the city and its environs with false identities. That number included George Soros, his parents, his older brother, and his grandmother.

In the Budapest of George's childhood, the more than 200,000 Jews in a city of 1 million represented 46 percent of all Hungarian Jews within the Trianon borders. Owing to the high percentage of

Jewish inhabitants in the city since the 1880s, Budapest earned a dubious nickname. It was dubbed, humorously among Jews and derisively by anti-Semites, as "Judapest," which means, in German, "the Jewish plague." In the district of the city where George lived during his childhood, on Kossuth Square, 37 percent of the inhabitants were Jews.

This demographic presence and distribution were evidence of the exceptional history of Jews in Hungary. The Hungarian Revolution of 1848, led by Lajos Kossuth, sought independence and liberal political reform. The Jewish community aligned itself with the national revolution; in the years leading up to 1848 many Jews elected to take Hungarian names. That process was halted in the 1850s during the period of reaction following the brutal suppression of Kossuth's movement in 1849 (with the aid of Russia). Nonetheless, from 1850 on, and particularly after 1867, a stable alliance was forged between the Magyar nobility and Hungarian Jewry.[5] Leading Hungarian aristocrats recognized how crucial Jews were to economic growth and modernization. By 1910, 60 percent of Hungarian merchants, 58 percent of printers, 42 percent of innkeepers, 25 percent of butchers and bakers, and 21 percent of all tailors were Jews. Economic productivity was generously rewarded. There were only eight Jewish noble families before 1867, but between that date and 1918, 330 Jewish families were ennobled by the Habsburg monarchy. More than half of these, 220, received their status of nobility after 1900. Jews in commerce and industry and in the free professions were embraced by the elites of the nation between 1848 and 1920. Jews had become partners in the struggle for liberty and autonomy for the Hungarian people beginning in the 1840s. They were welcomed by the Hungarian aristocratic and bourgeois elite on account of their willingness to embrace Magyarization, particularly the adoption of the Hungarian language.[6]

The contrast with Poland is instructive. Both Poland and Hungary share idiosyncratic centuries-old mythic aristocratic self-images. The fervent nationalism that flourished during the nineteenth century was not only spearheaded by the nobility but also defined by it. The ideal of a modern "nation of nobles" lingered well into the 1920s and 1930s during the regency of Admiral Miklós Horthy, long after the aristocracy abandoned its historic commitment to liberalism. In Poland, the *szlachta*, or noble class, was more broadly defined and represented—depending on how one counted, as much as 12 percent of the total population and as little as 6 percent—and nearly all its families were Catholic, making Polish nationalism, as expressed in the uprisings of 1830 and 1863, a movement that excluded Jews. In contrast, the Hungarian nobility in 1840 represented only 5 percent of the population, but its ranks expanded over the course of the nineteenth century to include Catholics, Protestants, and Jews. Thus, even though nineteenth-century Hungarian nationalism was a movement framed by the aristocracy, it was a cause to which Hungarian Jews attached themselves.

By forging a political alliance with the Jewish population of Hungary during the era of liberalism and rapid economic and demographic growth after 1867, the Magyar nobility triggered Jewish migration from neighboring Galicia, a densely populated Polish province at the northern end of the Austro-Hungarian Empire. This influx was most visible in Budapest. The city, after growing by more than a third between 1880 and 1890, expanded by another 46 percent in the decade between 1890 and 1900. The Jewish population of Budapest increased from 70,000 in 1880 to 215,000 in 1920. But significant Jewish communities also thrived throughout rural Hungary, albeit not as aggressively as in the capital. Tivadar Soros, George's father, was born in Nyíregyháza, a town in northeast Hungary that in the 1890s had 33,000 inhabitants, 5,000 of whom (15 percent) were Jews. He was subsequently sent to a famous Calvinist secondary school in Sárospatak, in the Tokaj wine region, a picturesque town with a population of approximately 9,000 inhabitants. One thousand Jews lived in Sárospatak, including a Hasidic community, only a minority of whom could trace their roots back to the seventeenth century.

The alliance between the Hungarian elite and the Jewish community influenced the choice of language among Jews. After 1867, autonomy within the framework of loyalty to the Habsburg dynasty largely supplanted the 1848 dream of independence, and Hungarian national sentiment shifted from participatory politics to the cultural renewal of the distinctly Hungarian. Jews enthusiastically adopted the Hungarian language. In 1880, 42 percent of the Jews of Hungary identified some other language, including Yiddish, as their primary language. A third were German speakers. By 1910, a dramatic shift had taken place, as 77 percent of the Hungarian Jewish population now claimed Hungarian as their primary and preferred language, with nearly all of them (70 percent) identifying German as their second language. More than 90 percent of Jews living in Budapest reported that Hungarian was their mother tongue; another 5 percent preferred German but spoke Hungarian as well.

By the end of World War I, 50,000 Hungarian Jews, most of them residents of Budapest, had adopted Magyar family names. Shortly thereafter, in the wake of the collapse of the monarchy and under far less auspicious circumstances, the pace of the Magyarization of names among Jews accelerated. The defeat of the short-lived communist Hungarian Soviet Republic of 1919, which held power for a mere 133 days, cleared the path for the ascendancy of an exclusionary, conservative, and increasingly anti-Semitic Hungarian nationalism. In a single year, 1919, a year of political reaction marked by widespread anti-Semitism on account of the linkage in the popular mind between Béla Kun's identity as a Budapest Jew and his allegiance to communism, Magyarization took a leap forward, inspiring 10,000 Hungarian Jewish religious conversions, a number that had taken twenty years to reach before the fall of the Dual Monarchy.

The leading myths and framing premises of post–Béla Kun Hungarian nationalism offered no place for Jews comparable to the pre-1918 acceptance of Jews into the national family. On September 26, 1920, the newly installed reactionary regime promulgated a *numerus clausus* law that limited the number of Jews who could enroll in institutions of higher education. Faced with a radical version of Hungarian nationalism based on an explicitly reductive ethnic definition of who could be regarded as authentically Hungarian, even more Jews in Budapest chose to Magyarize their names. In the wake of the 1920 law, the father of the future legendary orchestra conductor Georg Solti changed his children's name, but not his own, in order to protect them and enhance their prospects. Stern became Solti.

This trend continued during the 1930s, in tandem with the increasing popularity of anti-Semitic sentiment in the general population, much to the dismay (largely expressed privately) of a few members of the Hungarian aristocracy. George started school in 1936, two years before the first of the three explicitly anti-Semitic "Jewish laws" was passed in May 1938 (the next two anti-Jewish laws date from 1939 and 1941). That year Tivadar Soros changed the family name from Schwartz to Soros, without religious conversion, for the same reasons George Solti's parents and thousands of other Budapest Jews did so: to mask, superficially, their identities as Jews.

But some thought this step was not enough. During the first eight years of George's life, 31,000 Hungarian Jews, almost all of them from Budapest, converted to Christianity. Between 1938 and 1941, more Jews sought safety in this way; 8,000 converted in 1938 alone. Under the monarchy, Hungarian Jews wanting to convert usually chose Protestant denominations. Unlike Poland, Hungary had a significant and historic Calvinist minority. Protestantism seemed more closely aligned to Judaism and lacked Catholicism's emphasis on Trinitarian theology, the panoply of saints, and the deity of Christ. Even in Vienna and the postwar Austrian Republic, where Catholicism was dominant, Jewish converts preferred Protestantism. Indeed, most of Vienna's Protestant inhabitants had once been Jews.

Despite the virulent anti-Semitism ever more present after World War I, conversion remained an exceptional response among Hungary's Jews. The reason for this reluctance to convert was the experience of history. Conversion to any form of Christianity in Central and Eastern Europe—once regarded, particularly in the seventeenth and early eighteenth centuries, as the only plausible solution to the "Jewish Question"—never proved entirely persuasive either to the adherents of a race-based anti-Semitism or to the region's Jewish population as an antidote to or escape from anti-Semitism, even if that prejudice appeared to be a matter of religion. The anti-Semitism that blossomed in the late nineteenth century and took hold in the politics of post-Trianon Hungary was overtly based on notions of racial purity.

The Jews of the generation of George's parents discovered what Felix Mendelssohn, Rahel Varnhagen, Heinrich Heine, and the ancestors of the Arnhold & S. Bleichroeder banking firm (which would employ George Soros in America) had learned earlier in the nineteenth century: no amount of holy water could wash away one's identity as a Jew in the eyes of the rest of the world. By the turn of the twentieth century, being Jewish had ceased to be something one could erase. It had become defined, by Jews and anti-Semites alike, as a matter of inheritance and pseudo-biology. Somehow, no one ever forgot that a converted family had once been Jewish.

Furthermore, the example of late nineteenth-century Vienna seemed reassuring to Budapest's Jews. Despite the rise of anti-Semitic politics in the empire after 1867, culminating in the election of the explicitly anti-Semitic politician Karl Lueger as mayor of Vienna in 1895, most Habsburg empire Jews, particularly the Hungarian contingent, felt safe under the Dual Monarchy. Emperor Franz Joseph refused at first to recognize the results of Lueger's initial election, a clear sign of his distaste for the political exploitation of anti-Semitism. Jews and liberals were encouraged; the emperor was even-handed in his treatment of the multiethnic, multireligious, and multilingual population of his realm, so long as the members of these communities demonstrated dynastic loyalty and patriotism. In 1897, the emperor finally gave in, after Lueger's fifth election as mayor. But he never abandoned his view that all inhabitants of the monarchy—all ethnicities, religions, and nationalities—were equal as subjects of the crown. After all, the multinational empire was thriving economically and functioning efficiently; the well-rehearsed historical orthodoxy that the Austro-Hungarian Empire was a disintegrating, dying, and decrepit entity is, if the relevant social and economic data are taken into consideration, false.[7]

As the new racialist anti-Semitism flourished before World War I, Jews throughout the empire, especially in Hungary, became (as the writer Joseph Roth observed) the monarchy's most loyal subjects. They resisted, for the most part, the sense of fin de siècle doom found in literature that mirrored a cultural self-image that feared the inevitable collapse of the Habsburg ideology of a stable multiethnic and multilinguistic state.[8] Hungarian Jews in particular clung to the hope that national autonomy within a larger political entity could survive the fall of the monarchy, in a Switzerland writ large. The dream of a post-Habsburg multinational state would shape the post–World War I vision developed by the Hungarian historian and political theorist Oscar Jászi (who was born a Jew with the name Jakubovits in 1875), who called for the formation of a "Danubian Confederation."[9] By the time George Soros's parents married and began their family, this idea was fanciful at best and clearly unrealistic.

To the Jews who found themselves, after 1918, residents of the several new nation-states to emerge out of the defunct Austro-Hungarian Empire and who were confronted with the rapid rise in modern and radical nationalist sentiment, particularly in Hungary, there were three contrasting political options. The first option was to emulate the new nationalism by embracing a parallel modern Jewish nationalism. Indeed, Jewish national sentiment found its potent expression in secular Zionism, whose principal architect was a Budapest Jew who had made his career as a journalist in Vienna, Theodor Herzl. Herzl's modern political Zionism flourished in Galicia and in Russia, both before World War I and after, but it failed to captivate his fellow Hungarian Jews. Only after 1920, particularly during the era of anti-Jewish legislation in the late 1930s, did Zionism take hold in Hungary. Alexander Grossman, who later became a resistance fighter in World War II and then a journalist in Switzerland, turned to Zionism in the 1920s as a teenager in Miskolc (an industrial city with 76,000 inhabitants, 10,000 of whom were Jewish) after repeated encounters with anti-Semitism on the streets. Even so, Zionism remained a minority choice among Hungarian Jews, as it never found a way to compete effectively with more promising alternatives.

The second option was to resist nationalism altogether. The leading movements within this option, socialism and communism, gained a solid following among Jews. Marxism, in all its various forms, promised to break with history in the name of the objective destiny of the human race. Nationalist politics, religion, privilege, and class would be abolished and a postnationalist and postcapitalist society would emerge. Among the Hungarian Jews who joined this cause was Béla Kun, who led the ill-fated communist regime that held power briefly in 1919. A preponderance of those in Kun's government were also Jewish, even though the majority of Hungarian Jews, including those in Budapest, clung to nineteenth-century liberalism as a viable political credo.

Kun would not be the last prominent communist with roots in the Hungarian Jewish community, as the history of Hungary after World War II would make painfully clear. Mátyás Rákosi, who ruled communist Hungary from 1948 to 1956 in direct imitation and emulation of Stalin (replete with terror, show trials, and a personality cult) was born Mátyás Rosenfeld in 1892 to a poor Jewish family from a town now in Serbia, and went to secondary school in Szeged before coming to Budapest. Rákosi was a veteran of Béla Kun's 1919 Soviet Republic, which became, for most Hungarians, a nightmare that cast a shadow over the 1920s and 1930s and inspired more local anti-Semitism. Jews were already widely regarded by the Hungarian middle classes and peasants as archetypical capitalists (consider that in 1921, 88 percent of the members of the Budapest Stock Exchange were Jews, as were 91 percent of all currency traders); they now emerged simultaneously as shrewd radicals with a left-wing ideology at odds with traditional Hungarian values.

Another avenue through which the Jews of Hungary sought to cultivate a viable internationalist political credo and sensibility, without embracing socialism, was the Esperanto movement. Esperanto was invented by a Polish Jewish ophthalmologist and linguist, L. L. Zamenhof. He published his new language in 1887 and subsequently promoted it as a potential universally shared second language that would advance world peace by bridging linguistic barriers and rendering linguistic differences benign. Tivadar Soros, in the early 1920s, chose to lead the Hungarian Esperanto movement. He wrote articles in Esperanto (as well as his memoirs), represented Hungary at international Esperanto conferences, and funded Esperanto's main publication. Tivadar believed that "international life will never be healthy until we change current notions of national sovereignty."[10] In the post-Habsburg world, he pinned his hopes not on nationalism but on cultural movements that might succeed in supplanting it with internationalism.

It was, however, the third option that ultimately distinguished Hungarian Jewry from other Jewish communities that flourished under Habsburg rule: the stubborn but collective and unified choice to remain loyal to Hungarian nationalism as Jewish patriots, despite the growth of anti-Semitism. They chose to rely on the memory of a shared history dating back to 1848 whose rapid descent into irrelevance went largely unnoticed.

In no other Jewish community in Eastern Europe was there such a long history of a political alignment between Jews and non-Jews. In prerevolutionary Russia such a notion had always been inconceivable. Czarist monarchical autocracy was based on the three-part credo articulated by Sergei Uvarov in 1833 that began with religion: "orthodoxy, autocracy, and nationality." The Russian revolution in 1917 initially inspired optimism that Jews might achieve equal status, but its radicalism failed to appeal to most Hungarian Jews, who remained attached both to their religion and to old liberal ideals. In Poland, too, nationalist fervor was closely tied to religious homogeneity; Polish nationalism required exclusive loyalty to the Catholic Church. As a result, anti-Semitism among both the elite and the peasantry was far too ingrained for Polish Jews to aspire to membership in the newly formed Polish nation after 1918, whose construct of national identity had been decisively shaped, after the failure of the 1863 uprising against Russia, by a reactionary and romantic self-image that excluded Jews.

In contrast to this, a unique, stable, and collective consensus among Hungarian Jews that had begun in the mid-nineteenth century persisted even beyond World War II, aligning the Jewish community with Hungarian national aspirations. It had been made possible by two factors.

First, during the first half of the nineteenth century, dynamic religious leadership among Hungarian Jews remained decentralized as the region adapted slowly to the economic and social consequences of industrialization. The modernization of Jewish religious practices that had originated in the late eighteenth century, inspired initially by Moses Mendelssohn, did not gain significant traction beyond the borders of northern German-speaking Europe, except, later in the nineteenth century, in America. Nonetheless, disparate attempts to modernize Jewish practice appeared in Hungarian Jewish communities, inspired partly by the German reform example and influenced by the distinct character of the Viennese liturgy. By the early 1840s, the pressure to reform Jewish customs and life intensified, fueled by impatience among leading Jews to keep pace with the rise of Hungarian liberal sentiment. Religious reform and national liberal politics went hand in hand. When the 1848 revolution reached Pest, a Jewish reform community was formed in which the Sabbath was moved to Sunday and the practice of circumcision entirely abandoned.

Second, the Hungarian revolution of 1848 was liberal and explicitly national in a manner that made it possible for its leadership, including Kossuth himself, to link the issue of full legal and civic emancipation for Jews to the requirement that the Jews of Hungary modernize their religion and thereby make themselves capable of becoming integrated into the idealized coherent linguistic and cultural Magyar nation. In the two decades that followed, Jews pursued the path to become culturally and politically patriots of Hungary—"Magyars of the faith of Israel." The result of that ideal was the evolution of an idiosyncratic, specifically Hungarian religious reform movement that struck a compromise between tradition and the need to abolish practices and lift restrictions sufficiently to permit social and cultural integration with the Gentile community.

Not all Hungarian Jews were persuaded. A sizeable contingent of Hungarian Jewry, the Orthodox, resisted any reform of religious observance; but they did not abandon the political goal of becoming Hungarian. In 1868, right after the *Ausgleich*, a schism occurred in the Hungarian Jewish community between traditionalists and the reformers, whose movement came to be known as Neolog Judaism, with a liturgical practice and theology similar to Conservative and Reconstructionist Judaism in America today. In 1930, the year George Soros was born, 62 percent of Hungarian Jews were affiliated with the Neologs; 36 percent chose to remain Orthodox. The Neologs dominated in Budapest, whereas the Orthodox maintained a slight majority in the rest of the country, except in larger provincial cities. A small remainder chose to stand apart, most of them members of various Orthodox sects, such as the Satmar Hasidim. Divided as the community was on matters of religion, the schism did not damage the consensus with the Jewish community regarding a shared political vision: integration by Jews, as Jews, into the Hungarian nation.[11]

This explains their enthusiastic, overwhelming, and singular adoption of Hungarian as the language of choice. On account of respect for German culture and loyalty to the Habsburg crown, German remained the preferred second language. Yiddish survived, but much less significantly than in, for example, Galicia. Hungarian patriotism suppressed enthusiasm for Zionism and consequently blunted the revival of Hebrew as a modern national language. By 1900, Hungarian Jews, particularly in Budapest, prided themselves as exemplars of all things Hungarian in culture, manners, and mores—a spiritual if not sentimental nationalism that offered a sense of security. One could be a proud Jewish Hungarian, not a Jew in Hungary or a Hungarian Jew; no wonder Louis Spitz, a well-to-do Neolog and an engineer, changed the family name in 1900 from Spitz to Szilard (which in Hungarian means "firm" or "solid") when his son Leo, the future nuclear physicist, was two years old.

In order to understand why the community held on to this self-image, despite 1919 and the radical historical discontinuity it represented, one has to grasp how deep and widespread were the roots of the ideology of compatibility between being Jewish and being Hungarian. In 1892, the notorious Austrian writer Leopold von Sacher-Masoch, to whose name we owe the word "masochism," published a new edition of his exceptionally popular pseudo-anthropological-ethnographic tales about Jews. A Christian himself, Sacher-Masoch specialized in studying so-called exotic cultures, mostly in or adjacent to Europe; he wrote on the daily life and local wisdom of Poles, Russians, the peoples of the Ottoman Empire, and, with some regularity throughout his career, Jews. His lavishly illustrated coffee-table book, *Jüdisches Leben in Wort und Bild* (Jewish Life in Words and Pictures), featured characteristic tales about Jews from all over the world. Two came from Hungary. For his Jewish and non-Jewish readers alike, Sacher-Masoch ventured to capture the unique self-image of the Jews as proud Hungarians.

In the first vignette, we encounter a bookbinder in Hort, a small town in northern Hungary. He is a master bookbinder, enamored of Shakespeare and Schiller, who is reluctant to part from the books he is hired to bind. Learning by observing the people who come to him with their books and by reading those books (since he could not afford them himself) becomes his life's work. The bookbinder recounts that as a young man he was so enthusiastic about 1848 and Kossuth that he took on a Magyar surname. His epiphany was that "the Hungarian Jew has found a fatherland, and simultaneously, this fearful, derided human type has found the courage to defend that very fatherland."

Having embraced this newfound patriotic self-image, the bookbinder observes, in the Hungary of 1867, the Jews achieved for themselves religious freedom, tolerance, reconciliation, and the end of prejudice. His wife, however, has little patience with the bookbinder's unquenchable thirst for reading, but she humors him, particularly his enthusiasm for Neolog religious reform. The husband never ceases to teach his wife moral principles drawn from modernized Judaism, promoting the rational and critical inquiry into the nature of the external world. The bookbinder derides superstition and chooses freely which Jewish laws to follow. He is constantly rationalizing the Bible, claiming Moses as the discoverer of trichinosis, thereby justifying with science the dietary ban on pork.

But for all his patriotism and reformist convictions, especially his regard for the progress of science, the bookbinder is a cultural conservative. When a wealthy woman of society (herself a Jew with a Magyarized name) gives him Émile Zola's novel *Nana* to bind, he not only refuses but burns the book, exclaiming, "This is no book for a Jewish woman." As compensation he gives her instead a framed illustration of a scene from a Schiller play. Sacher-Masoch's tale ends with the bookbinder realizing his frustrated literary gifts and his acute understanding of the complexities and contradictions of the human psyche by acting as a love-letter writer for the wealthy woman's illiterate cook, a trusting adherent of Orthodoxy. In the process he encounters a rival Jewish ghostwriter from a neighboring town. The happy end: the bookbinder and the wealthy woman conspire to wed the cook to a prosperous merchant. The bookbinder is the honored guest at their Neolog wedding and toasts the happy couple with a verse from Schiller.

Sacher-Masoch's second Hungarian Jewish tale is set in a single year between two Kol Nidre nights, the start of Yom Kippur. The setting is in the Hungarian countryside, in a midsized town. The heroine is the unhappy daughter of a strict conservative Orthodox man. The daughter has a close friend, the town doctor, who is a modern, enlightened Neolog who derides her father as a "zealot," a man of unbending Orthodox ways. The doctor brings a guest to the holiday meal before the fast: a young aspiring medical student. He is a man of a new generation and even more radically Neolog.

The heroine and the medical student fall in love. Her parents forbid the relationship, even though their trusted doctor friend assures them of the young man's future professional and material success. But the young student is too much of a freethinker and "despises the laws" of Judaism. Consequently, the father schemes to marry his unhappy daughter to a rich and presumably reliably Orthodox grain merchant. As the year progresses, the daughter falls ill. The only cure, the elder doctor informs the father, is the "prescription of love," and the only person who can write that prescription is the apostate medical student. On the eve of the subsequent Yom Kippur, the father finally relents. All ends well. The medical student passes his exams; the two lovebirds marry and move to Budapest, where, fully supplied with the newest medical equipment, the young doctor makes a success of himself and the couple lives happily ever after in the nation's capital.[12]

Sacher-Masoch captured the conceits and the unique character of Hungarian Jews. The reader encounters the gap between Orthodoxy and Neolog beliefs and the growing preference for the latter. Jews represent the vanguard of learning, craftsmanship, taste, and science. The apex of culture remains German, represented by Weimar classicism, particularly Schiller and his commitment to an inherent linkage of beauty (aesthetics), the good (ethics), and rational enlightenment. Jews are hard-working and noted for their industriousness and sense of quality. Although they are pioneers of economic and scientific progress—apostles of rationality—Jews are portrayed as conservative defenders of cultural and moral traditions shared by Jewish and non-Jewish Hungarians. These include a fierce patriotism and a rejection of the ascendant philosophical challenges to traditional sexual mores and historic aesthetic values. The Neolog credo enabled Jews to become part of Hungarian society and lead the transformation of Budapest into a modern city by banishing superstition, illiteracy, and ignorance. At the same time, Jews strengthened a conservative construct of traditions and mores shared by Gentile and Jew alike.

∾

THIS IDEALIZED PERCEPTION of a symbiotic relationship between Hungarian identity and an affirmative Jewish identity based on Neolog Judaism, making Jews as equal as Hungarians as their Catholic and Calvinist countrymen, turned out, not slowly but quickly, to be outdated.

Exactly one year after the passage of the 1938 law restricting access by Jews to most white-collar professions, the Hungarian government clamped down further on Jews, limiting not only their right to work but also their right to own property, "in order to prevent the expansion of Jews in public life and the economy."[13] Count Pál Teleki, the prime minister in Horthy's regency, in his statement in support for the 1939 anti-Jewish law, officially severed the historic bond between Hungarian Jews and the Hungarian nobility and elite: "Had I submitted a bill drafted entirely by me, certain portions would have been much stricter . . . this Act introduces the alien ideology of race and blood into Hungarian legislation and mentality . . . I have been convinced of the appropriateness of this attitude in its scientific and social aspects for more than twenty years."[14] In August 1941, under Teleki's successor, László Bárdossy, the Hungarian government enacted a still harsher anti-Jewish law, in order to "defend the race"; it forbade marriage and sexual relations between Jews and non-Jews.[15]

The Jews of Poland and Russia suffered few such illusions about the world they inhabited. Even German Jewry, despite its cooperation with liberalism, had no history comparable to that of Hungarian Jews of an alliance, through nationalism, with the German aristocracy. The irony is that the long history of Jewish Magyarization made it possible for George Soros and his family to survive World War II, along with 24,000 other Jews who successfully hid in Budapest. Despite the fragility in the acceptance of Jews as Hungarians, and the weakness in the loyalty of the Hungarian aristocracy, Hungary managed to delay the start of the Final Solution, the extermination of Jews, until March 1944, albeit as an unintended consequence of an alliance with Nazi Germany that kept German troops out of the country.

The nineteenth-century link between Hungarian nationalism and liberalism and the Gentile support for Jewish emancipation and integration into the Hungarian nation, particularly within the Hungarian high aristocracy, turned out to be tenuous. Consider the contrast between two prominent members of the same noble clan: the hero of liberalism and nationalist reformer, a man routinely called "the greatest Hungarian," Count István Széchenyi (1791–1860), and his great-nephew, Count László Széchenyi (1879–1938), the husband of Gladys Vanderbilt. István Széchenyi opposed the more radical nationalism of Kossuth but made common cause with him in 1848. He was a proponent of liberal ideals and declared, "I happily sacrifice my aristocratic ideals as a lesser good, and trade for a greater good, for *true freedom*."[16] He argued openly for the acceptance of Jews into the national movement. In contrast, László Széchenyi, Hungary's minister to the United Kingdom and the United States in the 1920s and 1930s, promoted the idea of Hungary as an exclusively Christian nation led by an authoritarian government.[17]

The Hungarian Jewish community and the reactionary governments under Admiral Horthy both tacitly accepted that the era of Sacher-Masoch's tales was over—one side with a mix of denial and resignation, the other with polite indifference. Each went along with tightening discrimination, limiting the freedom of Jews and resisting pressures from Germany for harsher measures, through to the end of 1943. The brutality of the Arrow Cross notwithstanding, there were still enough Hungarians to help create the conditions that allowed more than half the city's Jews to survive.

The extent of the Magyarization of Hungarian Jewry, particularly in Budapest, did not entirely obscure an awareness of the marked rise, beginning at the turn of the twentieth century, in anti-Semitic sentiment from below, among the peasantry, the lower middle classes, and the working classes. These groups saw economic modernization as a threat to their way of life, not only in terms of material well-being but also in terms of cultural traditions whose content and symbolism were reframed in revisionist and reactionary terms. Their Jewish neighbors now appeared in a new light, not as fellow Hungarians who prayed to a different God on a different day, but as the pioneers of new practices that ranged from novel means of production, the making of ready-to-wear clothes in large workshops, the development of heavy industry, the introduction of technology into agriculture, and the establishment of an unfamiliar world of banking, credit, and finance, including speculation in real estate. The Hungarian Jew became an avatar of class inequality, a purveyor of capitalist exploitation through competition based on the rationalization of economic life.

Anti-Semitism became an integral component of a new ethnic nationalism that, in cities and towns after 1919, defined Jews not only as exponents of a heartless individualism, but also as a coherent body of foreigners and interlopers who undermined a sense of community based on sentiments of national solidarity. Among peasants, Jews were further suspect as allies of the landed aristocracy and feudal privilege. The new anti-Semitism was therefore not only an urban phenomenon; uniquely in Eastern and Central Europe, Jews accounted for nearly 20 percent of all large landowners in Hungary before 1930. The more "authentic" ethnic Hungarian peasantry with deep historic ties to the land, as opposed to those with German or Slavic origins who arrived after 1867, may have been less virulently anti-Semitic than their counterparts elsewhere in Eastern Europe. But even if true, this was a distinction that made at best a marginal difference, given the end result.[18]

Tivadar Soros was keenly aware, even as a child, of the changing reality around him. He recalled children taunting him, shouting "Hep-Hep" at him in the street during his childhood in Nyíregyháza in the late 1890s. The anti-Semitic slogan "Hep-Hep" ("Hep" being an acronym for "Hierosolyma est Perdita," or in English, "Jerusalem is lost") was a legacy of the widespread anti-Semitic riots of 1819 that occurred throughout the German states during a period when the emancipation of Jews had reemerged as a fiercely contested political

issue. After the fall of Napoleon, the debate over whether to extend
Jews equal rights, or reverse the first steps toward emancipation taken
before the French Revolution and under Napoleon, triggered violent
public unrest. Emancipation from the ghetto had already occurred in
the leading cities of Germany, and a generation of prosperous and
educated Jews had acculturated themselves. They assumed German
manners and habits, pioneered the development of a modernized
reformed practice of Judaism, and spawned a distinctly Jewish era of
enlightenment (*Haskalah*).

The "Hep-Hep" rioters attacked these Jews who resided outside
the confines of ghettos—Jews who looked just like everyone else, even
Jews who had converted to Christianity. The "Hep-Hep" riots therefore came as a shock. A half century before the triumph of race-
based anti-Semitism and the radical new definition of nationalism in
European politics, the "Hep-Hep" riots were a harbinger of the virulent anti-Semitism that would come to haunt the political landscape
of modern Europe.

Attempts to understand the roots of late nineteenth-century and
early twentieth-century anti-Semitism are fraught with danger. Cau-
tion is required so that an irrational prejudice is not inadvertently
transformed into a demonstrable, seemingly rational, and causally
legitimate belief. Numbers and lists represent static moments; they do
not in and of themselves tell a story. Just because something may be
the case does not justify transforming it into an explanation. Consider
the Budapest in which George's parents married and started a family.
In 1930, when George was born, just over 88 percent of Jews in Budapest had finished at least twelve years of elementary and secondary
education; 8 percent had earned a university diploma. In the general
population, apart from the Jews, fewer than 17 percent had completed
twelve years of school, and only 2 percent held a university degree.
No wonder the first Hungarian anti-Jewish law, from 1920, limited
Jewish enrollment in Hungarian universities; before it was enacted
Jews made up nearly 40 percent of the enrollment in the two leading
universities of Budapest.

That same year, in 1930, Jews, who were 20 percent of the city's population, accounted for 56 percent of all lawyers (Tivadar Soros's profession), 40 percent of all doctors, 25 percent of all pharmacists, 33 percent of veterinarians, 36 percent of journalists, 36 percent of engineers, 30 percent of all actors, 55 percent of bank employees, 40 percent of nonfactory workers in manufacturing industries, 57 percent of independent self-employed persons in commerce, and 29 percent of self-employed industrialists. Economic prominence had already been countered by ostracism in politics. Jews amounted to only 2 percent of judges (a decline from 6 percent in 1910) and fewer than 5 percent within the municipal, regional, and state civil service (also representing a sharp drop from 1910 levels).

The material rewards of modern urban life were distributed, it seemed, disproportionally to Jews. In the Austro-Hungarian Empire between 1893 and 1914, peasants with failing farms and urban artisans who were organized into guilds found themselves increasingly unable to compete. Small landowners and homeowners were often outbid by dynamic real estate developers. Furthermore, both Catholic and Calvinist Hungarians were less motivated than Jews to adapt to novel economic circumstances. They were slow to seize the opportunities offered by new knowledge-based professions, particularly in medicine and engineering.

If one adds to that the uncertainties and losses investors encountered in the volatile, relatively new world of the stock market and investment banking, it is hardly surprising that a wide swath of the Hungarian population seethed with resentment about their fate. The shared myth of a Magyar nation of nobles and gentry spread throughout the country made citing economic factors such as class conflict and the evils of capitalism insufficiently persuasive as explanations for a new and increasingly inhospitable world. It was simpler to assign the blame to a discrete, strangely powerful enemy in one's midst whom everyone could see. Jews were different, comparatively small in number, and their success and influence were visible. They were plausibly a nefarious presence. Yet in Hungary, the success of Neolog Judaism deepened the Jewish community's sense of security, particularly its deep faith in the liberal legacy of mid-nineteenth-century Hungarian nationalism. Neolog Jews did not feel compelled to hide their Jewishness, an attitude that had the unintended effect of strengthening the Orthodox community's sense of belonging in Hungary.

In this context there is little doubt that the young George Soros, between his infancy and the year of his bar mitzvah in 1943, was entirely aware that he was Jewish and, given the comparatively well-to-do economic status of his family, sensed more of its advantages than its dangers. After 1940, he went to school with Jews. His family circle consisted of Jews of varying convictions, a source of conflict within the family concerning what being Jewish meant and how best to deal with the prejudice that surrounded them. George had a strong attachment to his uncle Zoltan, a devout member of the Orthodox community, but he was also close to his mother, Erzebet, who was far more skeptical and reserved about her Jewish identity—even though her ancestors included prominent rabbinic scholars connected to a center of Jewish learning in Pozsony, then known as Pressburg and now called Bratislava, the capital of Slovakia, once a multiethnic city where the composer Béla Bartók spent much of his later childhood.

During World War II, while hiding in the Lake Balaton region, Erzebet Soros came under the influence of a Central European mystical Christian movement, Rosicrucianism, that dated from the early seventeenth century. It posited an all-encompassing universal order, concealed from ordinary mortals, a spiritual space accessible exclusively through the means of a rosy cross and rare sacred texts that revealed hidden truths beyond the natural world. Rosicrucianism's methods were reminiscent of Freemasonry and Masonic rites. Toward the end of her life, after her husband's death, George's mother underwent baptism by immersion while visiting her aged mother and her sister's family in Florida. She had, understandably, enough of being Jewish without faith.

Tivadar, on the other hand, was more like the young doctor in Sacher-Masoch's Jewish tale. He saw to it that the family maintained a nominal membership in a Neolog synagogue; his enthusiasm for Esperanto was entirely compatible with radical Neolog convictions. As he makes plain in his eloquent and moving memoir, *Masquerade*, which chronicles how he and his family survived the Gestapo and the Arrow Cross, he, like Sacher-Masoch's bookbinder, credited Judaism for leading him to the basic ethical principles that guided his life. He drew from traditional Judaism those beliefs that could be defended by human reason, beliefs that were universally applicable and therefore free from reliance on divine authority, miracles, and superstitions.

These included charity (Tivadar admired his Orthodox grand-father, who gave 10 percent of his income away to charitable causes); a respect for learning (he was proud of having attended university in Heidelberg), particularly the close scrutiny and analysis of hu-man nature; and he embraced a belief in the sanctity of all human life. He rejected ritual but pondered the question of the existence of God, a common preoccupation among Jews, even among the most observant. "Understanding, a love of people," and "tolerance," he wrote—and therefore a set of universal, transnational, and cross-cul-tural ethics—were what Tivadar took from his own rigorous Jewish upbringing. These modernized derivatives of Neolog Judaism he as-signed to his adult self-image as a Jew. After surviving the Holocaust, Tivadar not only adhered to these fundamental beliefs but sought to deepen them. He felt increasingly "ashamed" by all forms of perse-cution. He took them as "offenses" against himself and became ever more determined to feel responsible "for the whole world."[19]

The residue of the successful Magyarization of Jews in Hungary that remained in Tivadar Soros was that he never doubted the legiti-macy of his status as a Hungarian, despite the brutality of the Arrow Cross, the collaboration of many Hungarians in the persecution of Jews, and the presence of political anti-Semitism. That psychologi-cal security in his Hungarian identity enabled him to graduate to a lifelong allegiance to internationalism. Tivadar betrayed little enthu-siasm for any form of patriotism, or solidarity with some presumably coherent social group. He therefore did not emerge from the war with the sense that the experiences of the war years in Budapest required of him a rejection of his Hungarian identity or its replacement by a newfound patriotism for the America to which he emigrated in 1956. Neither did he wish to privilege his Jewish identity through Zionism. Instead he renewed his hope for a new internationalism based on the rights of the individual and focused on the injustices to minorities and the poor that he witnessed in America, and in the apartheid regime in South Africa. Although two of his brothers were murdered by the Nazis, he rejected any notion of collective guilt: a wholesale identification of Nazism with the German people was anathema.

Even a cursory glance at George Soros's beliefs and actions suggests that Tivadar succeeded in his goal to raise his sons in the "same spirit" that had animated his own life. Given that Tivadar credited his own Jewish upbringing with helping him shape a personal ethical credo and an analytical approach to understanding the world as it really was, particularly human behavior, the question becomes: What did Tivadar communicate to his son about the Jewish character and origins of his own beliefs, and how did he do so?

Given his lifelong engagement with philosophical speculation, particularly theories of knowledge and the philosophy of science, it comes as no surprise that George was inclined to confront and contest the religious instruction he received in school; no doubt the teachers were mediocre and the curriculum rigid. However, one aspect of his Jewish upbringing did leave its mark—an aspect consistent with George's subsequent engagement with formulations of "open society." It came from his father's habit of reading to him, systematically, from a book entitled *Die Sagen der Juden* (The Myths of the Jews), published first in German in 1913. This compendium of stories became extremely popular and by 1927 had expanded, posthumously, with the help of the author's son, into a five-volume edition. Tivadar owned the most widely disseminated original one-volume version from 1913 (which was reprinted many times) of over eight hundred pages.[20]

The author of this remarkable book was Micha Josef Berdyczewski, later known by the surname Bin-Gorion. He was born in 1865 in

Polodia in south-central Ukraine and died in 1921 in Berlin. Berdyczewski wrote in Hebrew, German, and Yiddish and was among the most brilliant and controversial Jewish writers of the fin de siècle. He rebelled against traditional rabbinic Judaism and vigorously opposed the cultural Zionism pioneered by Ahad Ha'am (Asher Zvi Ginsberg) and the political Zionism of Herzl. Berdyczewski argued for the free expression of individuality and remained fiercely skeptical of static ideologies and practices that claimed the prestige of absolute truth, particularly those derived from traditional religious doctrine.[21]

He pursued the upending of standard canons of ethics and conventional morality. Instead of limiting himself to writing critical essays and engaging in philosophical debate, Berdyczewski also wrote fiction about the daily lives of Jews, particularly those living in the Russian "Pale of Settlement" whose primary language was Yiddish. His writings on Hasidic life overlapped with the early works of Martin Buber (which Tivadar also admired) that recounted and reimagined the wisdom of the Hasidic masters. Berdyczewski's purpose was not, however, philosophical or theological. He sought to convey penetrating and critical psychological insight into the existential predicament of a community he believed was under siege and in decline.

The purpose of *Die Sagen der Juden* was to "display and interpret the fate of humankind and the world" using the structure and sequence of the Old Testament narrative. The fate of man chronicled in the Jewish Bible, according to Berdyczewski, was humanity's destiny: the eternal struggle to "break free" of an inevitable sense of guilt that all mortal creatures are born with. Although the book follows the structure of the Bible, the author integrated myths, parables, and stories from a wide range of traditions and eras—what Berdyczewski termed the "chaos of myths"—in order to fashion a contemporary "myth-midrash," a modern, universally applicable syncretic exegesis and interpretation of the foundational Jewish religious texts, augmented by references to related cultures and all the wisdom that can be gleaned from the history of the Jewish experience. For all its expansive and eclectic range, *Die Sagen der Juden* was intended to provide the reader with a reimagined picture of traditional Jewish religious beliefs. Berdyczewski divided the book into twelve chapters, beginning with the story of Creation, followed by Adam, the Flood, Babel and Canaan, Abraham, Esau and Jacob, the Children of Jacob, Exodus, the Wandering in the Desert, Joshua and David, the Two Kingdoms, the Babylonian Exile, and the Return.

Each chapter consisted of as many as twenty-five short stories. In addition to the books of the Old Testament, Berdyczewski inserted material from a massive number of tractates and scholarly sources spanning several centuries, up to the late 1890s. His primary subjects were heroes; women in the Bible; the sages of the Talmud; non-Jewish figures such as Alexander the Great, Cyrus, Hippocrates, and Zoroaster; angels; and divinities outside of Judaism like Astarte, Moloch, and Baal. But he also told stories about geographic locations and mythic places, including heaven, the stars, fire, water, the sun and wind, plants and trees, animals, days in the calendar, and, of course, books. He had a particular affection for similes and parables.

Die Sagen der Juden mirrored Tivadar's conviction that the essence and value of Judaism rested in the universal truths revealed through its traditions, particularly its insights into the human condition and its emphasis on human action and the ethics of individual responsibility framed by a determination to understand the world and the human character. Berdyczewski's wide-ranging and eclectic amalgam of insights and range of interpretations fit with the basic premise of Neolog Judaism. He rendered traditions and myths into instruments of rational understanding. But Berdyczewski went further. He fashioned a radical challenge to the Orthodox use of sacred texts, and contested the monopoly of prayer and ritual—and therefore the tradition of locating the source of Jewish life in the synagogue. Berdyczewski was, at best, ambivalent about the effort to preserve, among Jews, a sense of separation and distance, although in *Die Sagen der Juden* he rigorously excluded integrating texts and stories from Christianity.

The primary reason why Tivadar chose this book as a means of communicating his own understanding of Judaism was because

Berdyczewski, an opponent of Zionism and socialism and skeptical of the exclusionary and tyrannical use of secular political power, used the standard texts of Judaism to support his own belief that "we must place limits on the absolute power of the individual state" and that there is a "moral responsibility" to intervene anywhere in order to defend "fundamental principles of justice," including "human rights."[22] Tivadar recognized that the lessons of *Die Sagen der Juden* lent authority to his belief that "we all of us have an obligation to help the helpless when their human rights are violated and when atrocities are perpetrated against them." The truth of modern ethics based on Jewish principles found—in Berdyczewski, as it did for Sacher-Masoch's bookbinder—direct confirmation in the poetry of Friedrich Schiller, who was, not surprisingly, Tivadar's favorite German writer.

Tivadar's readings from *Die Sagen der Juden* continued during the war years, which encompassed, by far, the most significant and formative period in George Soros's life. In terms of shaping his outlook on life—including his estimate of his father's attitude to Judaism, his own identity as a Jew, and his relationship to the Jewish community, particularly its organizations and representatives—the months between March 1944 and January 1945 (when the Red Army captured and took control of Budapest) were decisive. The Nazi occupation of Budapest, followed by the assumption of power by the Arrow Cross Party, brought terror and death to the Jews. Until the Germans arrived, the Jews of Budapest, all the other indignities notwithstanding, had been spared mass deportation and extermination.

The Germans made up for lost time; under Adolf Eichmann a relentless and rapid program of extermination was realized. But it must be said that the long history of acculturation within Hungarian Jewry made hiding and survival possible and plausible, as the Soros family discovered. It might have been anticipated that the local population, particularly in Budapest, would be less aggressive in denouncing Jews and unmasking their false identities than their counterparts in Berlin, Amsterdam, or Warsaw. As the denunciation of George's mother made plain, that turned out not to be true. But the period during which extermination was undertaken in Hungary was significantly shorter and far closer to the military defeat of Nazi Germany. The locals had less opportunity to pursue collaboration by rounding up Jews and ferreting them out of hiding places.

Most survivors will attest to the role fate, chance, and luck played; careful planning alone was never enough. In Budapest, false identities and finding hiding places for one's family were necessary but not sufficient; the expected and the unexpected demanded exceptional qualities of mind, intuition, and courage. Three outstanding features of Tivadar's command of a desperate situation left the most permanent impression on his younger son. First was the focus and discipline his father displayed in confronting the stark facts of reality without reacting to them in standard, predictable, or conventional ways. He was resolutely alert and reflective, thereby retaining the power of surprise by taking the unanticipated and uncommon action. He relished the adventure, and the challenge of outwitting the enemy. Second was his father's recurring willingness to assume risks to himself in order to help others, not only relatives and friends but strangers as well. And third was his father's deep mistrust of, contempt for, and fury at the behavior of the official Jewish organizations of Budapest, particularly their leadership and highly placed functionaries. They used their prominence and prestige within the Jewish community to convey, knowingly and unknowingly, a false sense of security and a misplaced confidence in their understanding and influence, despite a reality that demanded the recognition of its radical incomprehensibility, unpredictability, and unprecedented danger.

Tivadar's capacity, under duress and in hard times, to face things as they are and not as one might wish them to be played a role in guiding George's approach to finance and investing. His father's sense of the essential equality of human beings and his mix of loyalty to family and kindness to strangers set the underlying tone for George's pursuit of political philanthropy. Tivadar's third outstanding wartime virtue—his mistrust of authority—influenced George's skeptical attitude to politicians and political and institutional power, not only of the state but also in voluntary nongovernmental organizations and bureaucracies, particularly those defined by the rhetoric of altruism and charity.

Like his father, George developed a lifelong allergy to the arrogance and ambitions of leaders who claimed to be representative of and dedicated to fraternal, group, and communal solidarity. George, as a witness, absorbed his father's criticism of the leaders of the Budapest Jewish community. They ended up cooperating with the Nazis either naively (because they sincerely believed if they did what they were told, fewer people would suffer and die) or on account of self-interest (because they thought they could cut a better deal for themselves, which some succeeded in doing). The people they were chosen to represent and had agreed to protect—their fellow Jews, trusting, disoriented, and powerless—were only made more vulnerable by the egotism and lack of self-criticism and humility exhibited by the community's leaders.

During the nearly ten months of murder, uncertainty, and the mayhem of war after March 1944, George came to understand why his father's distaste for the official Jewish community was justified. Tivadar, an avid listener to the BBC, was aware of the advance of the Allies, particularly the Soviets on the eastern front, and thought that noncompliance would work because it would buy time, which was on the side of survival of Hungarian Jews. Had the Jewish community not cooperated, had it resisted by destroying lists, refusing to comply with decrees, declining to negotiate, and ignoring threats, and had it counseled the community not to respond to demands and instead to disperse, the Germans and their Hungarian accomplices might never have succeeded in rounding up hundreds of thousands of Jews in an orderly manner and efficiently deporting them to their death. Chaos and disorder would have been better than compliance. George and Tivadar's experiences vindicate the harsh critique of the behavior of the Jewish Councils, Hungary included, in Hannah Arendt's controversial 1963 book *Eichmann in Jerusalem*.

Writing about those who survived the persecution and genocide of the Jews between 1933 and 1945 requires the suspension of the criteria of judgment of behavior that would be valid in ordinary circumstances. Among the keenly sadistic practices adopted by the Nazis and their collaborators was to force their victims to shed whatever remnants of dignity and self-respect they still had before killing them. For example, in 1939 Wehrmacht tanks deliberately drove through the streets of the Jewish quarter in Kraków, running over civilians, targeting families of many generations that were fleeing together, to see whether or not the young would abandon the old, whether children would let their parents be killed as they struggled to save themselves. Likewise, the SS delighted in provoking quarrels among starving concentration camp inmates over scraps of food.

No one who did not live through these years as victims can properly judge those who survived, either for their behavior then or afterward. It is hard to imagine the impression humanity made on a fourteen-year-old Jewish teenager in hiding, fearing for his life, at the hands not only of the Nazis but also of the Hungarian fascists and collaborators, who shot thousands, many tied together, on the banks of the Danube and shoved them into the water.[23] Apart from physical brutality, George and his father were forced to encounter deceit, hypocrisy, and betrayal. The suffering and hopelessness among the victims were not hidden.

The face of human nature showed little improvement during the subsequent occupation and presumed liberation of Budapest by Soviet troops, when Paul Soros fought off abuse and Erzebet Soros was raped. George's fierce opposition to Soviet communism was not based on theory alone, but on observation as well. At the same time George also saw the reverse—courage, heroism, generosity, humility, kindness, innocence, and warmth—that was expressed, often from unexpected quarters, in extreme and abnormal conditions.

In 1947 GEORGE SOROS found himself in London, where he lived for almost a decade. He came as a refugee, armed with his father's skepticism about Jewish communal organizations and the psychology and motivation of their leaders and subordinates. George appealed to the Jewish Board of Guardians for support, only to encounter condescension and refusal. He needed financial help to study at the London School of Economics, but the Jewish relief authorities dismissed this ambition and indicated that they would support him only if he chose to train for a trade. He eventually found ways to maneuver around the obstacles placed before him and in the end was given assistance as a Jew, but only after he appealed to the head of a Jewish charity, who had the grace and good sense to answer and reverse the refusal of George's request. The initial rejection by a Jewish organization of a young person's ambition to learn for learning's sake struck a dissonant chord in George's mind; it served to confirm his resistance to identifying himself as a member of any group or movement. His mistrust of the representative organizations of the Jewish community only deepened.

He went on to study with Karl Popper, whose two-volume work, *The Open Society and Its Enemies*, had appeared just a few years earlier. The book captivated George. It presented a developed historical and philosophical framework that explored the attitudes and perceptions of his father and extended the framework outlined by Bergson to which George was committed. Popper's arguments also bore considerable family resemblances to Berdyczewski's radical reframing of Jewish thought and tradition.

At the time George met him, Popper was in his mid-forties. He was born in Vienna to well-to-do parents whose own families were entirely Jewish. But his parents, like the composer Arnold Schoenberg and Arnold Rosé, the longtime concertmaster of the Vienna Philharmonic, had converted to Protestantism and joined the list of approximately 12,000 Viennese Jews who converted between 1891 and 1914. Although Vienna boasted the highest conversion rate in

Europe, the annual rate still represented less than 0.5 percent of Vienna's Jewish population.[24]

Popper may have been baptized, but he never harbored any illusion that his status, both in Vienna and later in England, would not remain that of a Jew. Popper's father, like George's, was a lawyer, albeit a more prominent one, and Popper's mother was part Hungarian. His uncle, Josef Popper-Lynkeus, was famous as a writer and engineer who wrote on social issues, military music, electric power, and the need for Jews to have their own political state. Popper grew up in a more academic home than George, replete with a massive library and more self-consciously "cultured" in its habits and manners; he also cultivated a lifelong passion for music. But the similarities were unmistakable; both Karl Popper and George Soros were scions of Jewish households that had used the instruments of economic well-being, culture, and learning to integrate into the surrounding non-Jewish world of the two leading cities of the former Habsburg empire. They had also witnessed the shattering political realities created by modern anti-Semitism that had engulfed Jews, particularly the acculturated ones, in both Vienna and Budapest.[25]

Among Popper's teachers was Moritz Schlick, the leading voice of the Vienna Circle, the center of logical positivism. Schlick was assassinated in June 1936 on his way to teach at the university, not because he was Jewish (which he was not) but, according to the testimony of the perpetrator, on account of the injury to public morality inherent in Schlick's mistrust of the truth value of metaphysical claims, including the existence of God. In his defense, Schlick's killer justified his act by referring to Schlick's close association with Jews; this alone was a clear warning about the impending victory of radical political anti-Semitism. After the *Anschluss* two years later, the Nazis released him.

Before emigrating in the mid-1930s to England, Popper had completed his doctorate on the psychology and methods of how we acquire and judge knowledge. George was drawn to Popper's analysis of habits of thinking, acquiring, and validating knowledge, especially the necessity of subjecting the claims of science to rigorous scrutiny. The intuitive psychological dimension of epistemology was one on which George's father had proven himself a shrewd observer who was able to act on his insights. George would ultimately integrate Popper's systematic analysis and his father's instincts into his own work as a thinker and practitioner in both finance and philanthropy.

Popper's background, upbringing, manner, and, above all, interests made him an ideal mentor for George. Under Popper's tutelage, the basic prejudices and insights he had gleaned from his father found plausible philosophical, social psychological, and historical elaborations that enabled George to link systematic skepticism with ethics and freedom. *The Open Society and Its Enemies*, Popper's celebrated extension of his views on epistemology into political theory—his vision of a modern political ideal, the "open society"—offered a reasoned and devastating contemporary critique of both fascism and communism. These political ideologies legitimated the tyranny of state power over the individual by appropriating, falsely, the prestige of truth. They abused the language of science and insulated themselves from criticism by assuming the justification of objective absolute truth. Popper provided to George a reasoned philosophical argument in sympathy with the ideas and beliefs he had nurtured during the war years in Budapest.

George's brother, Paul, emigrated to America in 1948 and with his wife Daisy started a new life that did not include assuming their original identities as Jews. They joined a Unitarian church and a restricted country club in Connecticut (Paul was an avid and excellent sportsman) and took the opportunity of a new country and home to reinvent themselves. George came to America in 1956 to begin a career in finance in New York City. His parents, after the failed Hungarian revolution of 1956, joined their two sons in the United States.

The postwar America to which Paul had arrived was still the one made popular by the controversial Academy Award–winning 1947 film *Gentleman's Agreement*. The film exposed the prevalence of anti-Semitism in America. This was particularly true for Paul's field, engineering. By the time George arrived, however, being a Jew (with or without any connection to a synagogue or Jewish community organization)—despite the existence of parallel "white shoe" Gentile and "Jewish" law firms and investment banks—was becoming increasingly irrelevant, especially in New York. The significant barriers created by anti-Semitism in the United States to careers in law and finance had remained formidable before World War II and throughout the 1940s. But by the mid-1950s, they were rapidly vanishing, along with other prejudices and rivalries among and between white ethnic groups.

The civil rights movement had gotten its dramatic jump start with the Supreme Court's 1954 decision in *Brown v. Board of Education*. White America, now faced with the prospect of the end to de jure segregation for Black Americans, swiftly placed its historic internal differences aside. The dominant corrosive prejudice in the United States had always been race and the color line. After 1954, the Italians, Poles, and Irish conveniently forgot their rivalries; Protestants and Catholics fostered a spirit of ecumenicalism and in 1960 the country elected its first Catholic president. The Christian white population tacitly realized that if it had to choose between a Jew and a Black person as the object of discrimination, the Jew seemed the lesser of the evils. Jews, who had recently been vilified by the Nazis as polluters of "whiteness," were, in the America of the 1950s, granted the dubious right to consider themselves equal, if not exemplary, members of a "white" majority.

The Jews of America whom George encountered—apart from fellow refugees, exiles, survivors, and veterans—had been insulated from the horrors of the war and in particular the extermination of Jews. Some harbored discomfort and guilt about whether they had shown as much solidarity and help as they could have to protect and rescue the Jews of Europe. Yet on the matter of segregation, they viewed the white majority with suspicion. Since the early years of the twentieth century, Jews had made common cause with Black people in fighting prejudice and discrimination. The Jews of New York were largely liberal, and staunch admirers of the New Deal. They were active on the political left in fighting McCarthyism. But the 1950s were a breakthrough era for American Jews in terms of employment and access to education. The Jewishness of George Soros, even on Wall Street, was entirely unexceptional. In practical terms, one's status as a Jew was, at worst, a social embarrassment in the unenviable enclaves of restricted society. Unlike Hungary, there was, as Tocqueville understood, no stable landed aristocracy or noble class.

George's first wife, Annaliese, the mother of his three eldest children, was not Jewish, and religion never presented itself as an issue during their marriage. But after his divorce, when he decided to marry his second wife, Susan Weber, George found himself joining a family that had absorbed the spirit of Jewish New York, shaped profoundly by the massive Yiddish-speaking emigration between 1880 and 1920 from Eastern Europe. Yiddish national culture—something rare in Hungary—rather than religion marked New York's secular Jewish character. Though Susan (who subsequently became a distinguished historian of material culture and the decorative arts) had been raised in a resolutely secular home, with only a nominal acknowledgment of religious traditions, she was outwardly proud of her Jewish identity.

George and Susan initially contemplated having a rabbi officiate at their 1983 wedding, but in view of George's extended family's ambivalence about being Jewish, they settled on a civil ceremony. The couple had two sons, and George gladly saw to it that they received some religious instruction; each had a bar mitzvah. At their elder son Alexander's bar mitzvah, in the late 1990s, a shift in attitude within the Soros family was evident. George, Paul, and Susan's father Murray all had *aliyot* at the reading of the Torah, and they recited the Hebrew prayers required.

George's attitude toward his own Jewishness changed not only because of Susan and their children but also because by the mid-1980s his status and visibility had risen dramatically. He was on his way to becoming a public citizen. He had developed a reputation as a financial wizard and innovator and had become wealthy. In 1987 he published a highly respected and technical treatise on the market-place entitled *The Alchemy of Finance*. Most significant, however, was that George recognized the gift of American citizenship. As a Jew in America, there was nothing to stop him from becoming a political activist. He started his own philanthropic enterprise. Among his first actions was to exploit the weaknesses of state communism in Eastern Europe, starting with his homeland, Hungary. In 1984 he established a foundation there, cutting a deal with the communist government of János Kádár to provide hard currency in exchange for the right to directly support seemingly innocent humanitarian and cultural initia-tives. George ended up supporting health care, the Roma, childhood education, musical projects, and artists and writers; his ambition was to break the monopoly of the state in the public sphere.

George soon became a celebrity in Hungary. He gave radio and television interviews, and met with dissidents and leading intellectu-als. It is hard not to empathize with the sense of psychological closure and victory in the return of a fifty-four-year-old Hungarian Jew—after having survived 1944 and fled communism—as a public bene-factor intent on restoring freedom and defeating the tyranny of the state. His explicit intention was to accelerate the collapse of commu-nism and the Soviet domination of Eastern Europe by helping people in need and supporting independent initiatives in culture, above all the arts and humanities.

His success and achievement were stunning. The tenth anniver-sary of Soros's Hungarian foundation, now named the Open Society Foundation (in honor of Popper), took place in 1994 at the National Gallery in the Castle District in Budapest. Dignitaries and officials lauded George before a packed audience and television cameras. The Budapest Festival Orchestra, funded by George and conducted by Iván Fischer, performed. László Somfai, the eminent Hungarian mu-sicologist and Bartók and Haydn scholar, who had neither sought nor needed funding from George, commented to me on the day of the event, "Every single Hungarian owes a debt of gratitude to Soros for his aid to people in need of essential services and for providing the momentum to defeat communism in the service of freedom."

In 2000, at the end of his ten years as president of Hungary, Árpád Göncz, himself a writer and translator, observed, "George Soros is one of the vital personalities who has shaped our age . . . I can also surely say that in Hungary . . . tens of thousands of people directly—and hundreds of thousands indirectly—have experienced the power of his support."[26]

For some of George Soros's fellow Hungarian Jewish émigrés, the spectacle of his triumphant return was hard to contemplate. Andrew Grove, a somewhat younger Budapest Jew who arrived in America after the 1956 Hungarian uprising and attended City College in New York, expressed amazement. Grove commented that although he had the highest respect for George, not only would he not give the Hungarians or Hungary a nickel, but he had no intention of ever setting foot in the place where he grew up and lived for the first twenty years of his life.

In this contrast, one can recognize the idiosyncratic yet characteristic living residue of George's lifelong self-image as a Jew from Hungary. Grove's response was equally understandable; he wished to turn his back, retaining his vivid memory of the war years, and put an end to the illusion of any compatibility between the Hungarians and the Jews. Resentment and anger prevailed. In George's case, the transmission of values, through his father and extended family, remained connected not only to Neolog Judaism, but to the historic link between Jewish life and Hungarian nationalism first forged in the nineteenth century. Soros's philanthropy—its idealism, grandeur, and range—mirror what Tivadar termed his "little Jewish philosophy," his own version of a Hungarian Jewish outlook.[27]

Soros's fame after 2000 was such that any remaining effort by his extended family to disavow being Jewish was doomed to failure. In the decade following the fall of the Berlin Wall and the collapse of the Soviet Union, Soros had become a household name, and everyone understood him to be a Jew.

One of George's dreams was to foster internationalism at the expense of nationalism in Eastern Europe. In 1991 he founded the Central European University in three capitals—Warsaw, Prague, and Budapest—though he eventually consolidated the university in downtown Budapest, within walking distance of where he grew up. Its mission was to bring students from all the nations once within the Soviet Union and its sphere of influence, and to counter the rise of divisive nationalisms. English would be a common language of instruction, and the university was imbued with a commitment to academic freedom and a vision of shared ideals and cross-cultural co-operation through higher education in the social sciences. Ironically, such regional collaboration had already been fostered, with different objectives, under communism in the Comintern.

If a contemporary writer wished to imitate Sacher-Masoch and chronicle Jewish life through real-life stories representing the habits and values of Jews living in varying parts of the world, George Soros's life story would be an ideal morality tale to reveal the unique residue of the historical experience of Hungarian Jews. Soros, the Jew, in keeping with the liberal ideals of the nineteenth century, became modern Hungary's most generous patron of its culture and Hungary's most courageous advocate of freedom, dignity, and democracy for all its people.

THERE IS CLEARLY a dark side to George Soros's identity as a Jew, now that he has become world-famous. His global prominence as a political philanthropist and legendary man of finance has helped nourish the long-standing calumny of an international Jewish conspiracy that seeks to control the world with money and power using deceit. There are many versions of this notion. Soros's big financial wins, such as betting against the British pound, have routinely been viewed as evidence of such a Jewish conspiracy. His personal diplomacy in the years before the fall of communism and immediately thereafter in the former Soviet space has been consistently distorted by the lens of anti-Semitism, notably in Russia itself.

Nowhere, tragically, has this been more the case than in contemporary Hungary. In the mid-1990s, from the windows of the Budapest apartment of one of George's relatives, I watched with him a Sunday afternoon demonstration by opponents of the then liberal social democratic government. This was an anti-government demonstration featuring banners with Soros's name accusing the government of being puppets of an international Jewish conspiracy intent on undermining the true native Hungarian character of the nation. This was a harbinger of the politics that would come to power with the current Hungarian prime minister, Viktor Orbán. He (ironically a past beneficiary of Soros scholarship to Oxford) has defined himself, to popular acclaim, as the defender of the authentic Hungarian against the corrupting influence of Soros, the Jew. His electoral campaigns featured photographs of George Soros manipulated to make Soros look as close as possible to the standard anti-Semitic visual caricature of a Jew, accusing him of being a "puppet master" and warning, "Don't let this man have the last laugh in the end."[28]

Since the 1990s, Soros's brilliance as a capitalist has eclipsed his hard-earned reputation as a political actor on the world stage in the fight to end communist rule. As the politics in Eastern Europe have shifted to the anti-democratic right, he has become the symbol of a foreign cosmopolitan liberalism that seeks to defend the ideals of a pluralist, free, and open nation. The tropes of the anti-Semitism of the 1920s and 1930s have been revived not only in Hungary, but throughout Eastern Europe, including Russia. The echoes of the notorious 1903 Russian forgery *The Protocols of the Elders of Zion* are unmistakable: the "rootless" cosmopolitan Jews who supposedly control the commerce and finances of the world actually seek to destroy the traditional ethnic and national groups in the name of a degenerate and demeaning universalism. The plausibility of this conspiracy theory rests squarely on the prominence of Soros as a rich Jewish international financier and activist, a wolf in sheep's clothing.

The irony is that in the United States, Soros's civic home, where he is a citizen, a parallel conspiracy theory persists. His foundation philanthropy in America has focused on humanizing criminal justice, eradicating racial inequities, guaranteeing the right to vote for all, safeguarding the freedom of the press, assisting the poor, ending the war on drugs, encouraging transparency in government, and protecting immigrants. His personal political philanthropy has been directed at helping to defeat candidates such as George W. Bush and Donald Trump and elect candidates such as Barack Obama, Hillary Clinton, and Joe Biden. The far right has waged a campaign that also conveniently forgets Soros's role in bringing down communism and his support for a properly regulated capitalist economy. The American version of the Jewish conspiracy presents Soros as a puppet master of the liberal wing of the Democratic Party. The threat he represents to America bears a family resemblance to the manner in which his danger to Hungary is framed. In both cases, the explicit alternate ideal is nativist and anti-immigrant: the vision of an ethnically homogeneous Christian state, not an open pluralist democracy.

One factor that fuels the plausibility of the American version of a hidden Jewish left-wing conspiracy led by George Soros is misinformation and confusion about his attitude to Israel. Like many of his Hungarian Jewish contemporaries and predecessors, Zionism never appealed to him; it seemed too imitative of other exclusionary nationalist ideologies dating from the nineteenth century. To Americans, including many American Jews, Soros, owing to his distance from active public support of Israel, seems not quite Jewish enough, and perhaps even an exemplar of a "self-hating" Jew, itself a dubious historical construct.

A failure of historical memory and an anti-historical reductive conception of the diversity of self-images among European and American Jewry are at work here. There never was a shortage of Jewish critics of modern Zionism, even in Israel. These have included members of the "Bund," for whom the Jewish nation was defined by the Yiddish language and as a distinct unit within non-Jewish nation-states. There are ultra-Orthodox religious Jews for whom Israel remains illegitimate because the Messiah has not yet made his appearance in history. In America, a strong current of anti-Zionism flourished before World War II among highly acculturated and largely secular Jewish citizens, who feared being accused of dual loyalty were they to support the Zionist dream.

Not only has Soros never opposed Israel, he has invested in Israeli companies. More significantly, he has encouraged his son Alexander to help Israel strengthen its democracy by ending second-class citizenship status for Israeli Arabs and by promoting a just solution for peace that delivers to the Palestinian community a viable independent political entity. Soros has taken pride in Alexander's wholehearted enthusiasm for crafting his own separate identity as a Jew, and his scholarly work on European Jewish history.

What has been entirely forgotten in all this implied and explicit criticism is that George Soros's self-image as a Jew was decisively Hungarian in character, rooted in the nineteenth-century liberal tradition. Furthermore, George's experience as a survivor made him mistrust not only organized religion but nationalism of any kind. He has taken up his father's cause on behalf of international and universal goals designed to protect the rights and freedom of individuals, particularly those who dissent and those minorities at risk from intolerant majorities.

Successful conspiracy theories, including the notion of a covert manipulation on behalf of pluralism, freedom, the virtues of cosmopolitanism, and reasoned skepticism with respect to political ideologies and religious systems—animated by a mistrust of authority and power—consistently draw sustenance from some obvious fact whose meaning is grossly distorted.

In the case of George Soros, the key fact is the resemblance of his career to the impressive and visible cultural, scientific, and economic achievements by individual Hungarian Jews during the first half of the twentieth century. Furthermore, his ideas and actions echo not only his father's ideas but those of many great thinkers who are all too often categorized at the outset as Jews. Among them, Baruch (Benedict) Spinoza, Moses Mendelssohn, Karl Marx, Karl Mannheim, and Karl Popper might well be counted.

Soros has indeed remained committed to a belief in the shared destiny, potential, and character of all human beings, which overrides the exclusionary categories that disfigure the pursuit of politics away from its proper objective: the provision of freedom, security, happiness, and well-being to all individuals in the service of the sacred dignity of every living soul. Soros's experience as a Jew has only strengthened his allegiance to a politics throughout the world that, as Hannah Arendt put it, can ensure that "plurality" thrives.[29] He wishes to demonstrate that "because we are the same, that is, human," "nobody is ever the same as anyone else who ever lived, lives, or will live." From the angle of vision he nurtured first in Hungary and later cultivated as a citizen of the United States, George Soros has acted, in the finest tradition of Jewish ethics, as a Jew in the modern world.

Notes

EVA HOFFMAN / ORIGINS

1. George Soros, foreword to Tivadar Soros, *Masquerade: The Incredible True Story of How George Soros' Father Outsmarted the Gestapo*, trans. Humphrey Tonkin (1965; repr., New York: Arcade, 2011), x.

2. Paul Soros, *American (Con)quest* (Oxford: Joshua Horgan Print Partnership, 2006), 4.

3. Michael T. Kaufman, *Soros: The Life and Times of a Messianic Billionaire* (New York: Alfred A. Knopf, 2002), 13.

4. George Soros, foreword to Tivadar Soros, *Masquerade*.

5. George Soros, foreword to Tivadar Soros, *Masquerade*.

6. "George Soros in Luppa [*sic*] Island," blog entry, posted August 6, 2017, http://riowang.blogspot.com/2017/08.

7. Kaufman, *Soros*, 21.

8. Erzebet Soros, oral history, private archive, 1985.

9. George Soros, afterword to Paul Soros, *American (Con)quest*, 187.

10. George Soros, afterword to Paul Soros, *American (Con)quest*, 187.

11. Erzebet Soros, oral history.

12. Kaufman, *Soros*, 20.

13. Erzebet Soros, oral history.

14. Tivadar Soros, *Masquerade*, 3.

15. Tivadar Soros, *Masquerade*, 9.

16. Tivadar Soros, *Masquerade*, 16.

17. Tivadar Soros, *Masquerade*, 21.

18. Tivadar Soros, *Masquerade*, 141.

19. Tivadar Soros, *Masquerade*, 141.

20. Tivadar Soros, *Masquerade*, 150.

21. Tivadar Soros, *Masquerade*, 204.

22. Tivadar Soros, *Masquerade*, 205.

23. Tivadar Soros, *Masquerade*, 203.

24. Kaufman, *Soros*, 46.

25. Kaufman, *Soros*, 52.

SEBASTIAN MALLABY / THE FINANCIER

1. George Soros, interviews with the author, September 23, 2020, and January 12, 2021. The author also conducted multiple interviews with Soros and his financial associates in the late 2000s.

2. The "chicken crap" line belonged to Alan "Ace" Greenberg of Bear Stearns. See Michael T. Kaufman, *Soros: The Life and Times of a Messianic Billionaire* (New York: Alfred A. Knopf, 2002), 87.

3. Soros, author interviews.

4. Kaufman, *Soros*, 108.

5. George Soros, Monthly Report, November 1, 1967. Report provided to the author by Antonio Foglia.

6. George Soros, "The Case for Two Trucking Stocks," Arnhold and S. Bleichroeder Statistical Department Memorandum, November 1966.

7. Soros, author interviews.

8. George Soros, *The Alchemy of Finance* (New York: John Wiley & Sons, 1987), 40.

9. Kaufman, *Soros*, 122.

10. Soros, *Alchemy of Finance*, 60.

11. George Soros, "The Case for Mortgage Trusts," February 1970. This note is reprinted verbatim in *The Alchemy of Finance*, 64–67.

12. Kaufman, *Soros*, 121.

13. Kaufman, *Soros*, 134.

14. Anise Wallace, "The World's Greatest Money Manager," *Institutional Investor*, June 1981.

15. Kaufman, *Soros*, 139.

16. George Soros, *Soros on Soros: Staying Ahead of the Curve* (New York: John Wiley & Sons, 1995), 49. Soros adds, "If a story is interesting enough, one can probably make money buying it even if further investigation would reveal flaws. Then later, if you discern the flaw, you feel good, because you are ahead of the game. So I used to say, 'Jump in with both feet; take one out later.'" Soros, interview with the author, June 10, 2008.

17. Kaufman, *Soros*, 137.

18. Soros, *Soros on Soros*, 56–57.

19. Soros, *Alchemy of Finance*, 149.

20. Soros, *Alchemy of Finance*, 149.

21. Soros confesses that he hung on to his dollar shorts by the skin of his teeth. Soros, *Alchemy of Finance*, 163.

22. These yen and German mark accumulations are over the baseline established on September 6, 1985, the date of the previous diary entry. However, the buying seems to have occurred in the five days after Plaza. See Soros, *Alchemy of Finance*, 164.

23. Soros airs the question of policy makers' commitment in his diary entry of September 28, 1985. See Soros, *Alchemy of Finance*, 165.

24. The additional buying took place between September 27 and December 6. Soros, *Alchemy of Finance*, 164, 177.

25. Soros, *Alchemy of Finance*, 176. Gary Gladstein, who joined Soros's firm in October 1985 to serve as chief operating officer, was astonished by the leverage in his new firm's portfolio. Gladstein interview, March 18, 2008.

26. Soros, *Alchemy of Finance*, 309.

27. Soros, *Soros on Soros*, 59. Soros pointed out that Quantum's return over the full fifteen months of the experiment, which included a "control period" in 1986, came to 114 percent.

28. The most influential academic paper to argue for exchange-rate overshooting was Rudiger Dornbusch, "Expectations and Exchange Rate Dynamics," *Journal of Political Economy*, December 1976. Dornbusch's argument did not hinge on the trend-following by speculators that Soros emphasized; instead, he explained that currencies overshoot in response to monetary shocks because of the interplay between sticky prices for goods and fast-adjusting capital markets. However, Dornbusch's sticky-price contention was a minority view within academic macroeconomics through the 1980s. See Kenneth Rogoff, "Dornbusch's Overshooting Model After Twenty-Five Years," Mundell Fleming Lecture, IMF Staff Papers, vol. 49, Special Issue, revised January 22, 2002.

29. Soros, *Alchemy of Finance*, 176.

30. This exchange and the wider drama of the sterling trade is presented at greater length in Sebastian Mallaby, *More Money Than God: Hedge Funds and the Making of a New Elite* (New York: Penguin Press, 2010), 152–71. The principal original source for this dialogue is Robert Johnson, although others also commented.

31. Speaking of Soros's advice to go for the jugular, Druckenmiller says, "I can have the concepts, I can do the economics, and I can even have the timing, but one simple statement like that in terms of size . . . We probably

got twice the profit I would have had without that snide comment he made about 'Well, if you love it so much . . . '" Druckenmiller, interview with the author, March 13, 2008.

32. Louis Bacon, interview with the author, July 21, 2009.

33. Anatole Kaletsky, "How Mr. Soros Made a Billion by Betting Against the Pound," *The Times* (London), October 26, 1992.

34. William Keegan, "Unnecessary, Unproductive, and Immoral," *The Observer* (London), September 28, 1997.

35. Soros, *Alchemy of Finance*, 372.

36. Soros, *Soros on Soros*, 143.

37. Author calculations based on hedge fund data in Mallaby, *More Money Than God*, 402–7, and Berkshire Hathaway Inc., *2019 Annual Report*, 2, www .berkshirehathaway.com/2019ar/2019ar.pdf. Note that Berkshire's more recent returns have been disappointing, bringing down the average.

DARREN WALKER / PHILANTHROPY WITH A VISION

1. The question of which philanthropist gave away more is probably unanswerable. Carnegie is said to have given $350 million during his philanthropic career, which lasted from 1901 until his death in 1919; Rockefeller, $540 million from 1897 to his death in 1937; Soros, $32 billion from 1979 to the present. After adjusting for inflation on a consumer price index basis, Soros can be said to have given more than Rockefeller or Carnegie. Comparing on a percentage-of-GDP basis, Rockefeller and Carnegie can be said to have given more.

2. Michael T. Kaufman, *Soros: The Life and Times of a Messianic Billionaire* (New York: Alfred A. Knopf, 2002), 95.

3. George Soros, *Soros on Soros: Staying Ahead of the Curve* (New York: John Wiley & Sons, 1995), 105.

4. Soros, *Soros on Soros*, 107.

5. Soros, *Soros on Soros*, 105.

6. Kaufman, *Soros*, 170.

7. Chuck Sudetic, *The Philanthropy of George Soros: Building Open Societies* (New York: PublicAffairs, 2011), 12.

8. Kaufman, *Soros*, 171.

9. Soros, *Soros on Soros*, 107.

10. Kaufman, *Soros*, 172.

11. Kaufman, *Soros*, 191.

12. Soros, *Soros on Soros*, 110.

13. Kaufman, *Soros*, 194.

14. Kaufman, *Soros*, 195.

15. Kaufman, *Soros*, 196; see also Endre Dányi, "Xerox Project: Photocopy Machines as a Metaphor for an 'Open Society,'" *The Information Society* 22:2 (2006), 111–15.

16. Soros, *Soros on Soros*, 113.

17. Soros, *Soros on Soros*, 112.

18. Soros, *Soros on Soros*, 116.

19. Kaufman, *Soros*, 258.

20. Soros, *Soros on Soros*, 114–15.

21. Kaufman, *Soros*, 259.

22. Soros, *Soros on Soros*, 114–15.

23. Soros, *Soros on Soros*, 115–16.

24. Soros, *Soros on Soros*, 115.

25. Interview with Aryeh Neier, January 15, 2021.

26. As Soros once remarked, "I have an enormous network and I must hustle to keep it going." Soros, *Soros on Soros*, 176.

27. Kaufman, *Soros*, 254.

28. Soros, *Soros on Soros*, 120; Lee Hockstader, "U.S. Financier Gives Russia $100 Million for Internet Link," *Washington Post*, March 16, 1996.

29. Open Society's anti-corruption mission was further informed by its support of IDASA, an independent South African think tank that, after apartheid, became a watchdog monitoring the performance and accountability of the new government.

30. "Angola," Open Society Initiative for Southern Africa, n.d., osisa.org /angola/.

31. George Soros, "Capitalism versus Democracy," Project Syndicate, June 27, 2000, www.project-syndicate.org/commentary/capitalism-versus -democracy.

32. The public-health approach to drug abuse built on the work of the Lindesmith Center, an advocacy group funded in 1994 by Soros.

33. "A 'Forgotten History' of How the U.S. Government Segregated America," *Fresh Air*, NPR, May 3, 2017, available at www.npr.org/2017/05 /03/526655831/a-forgotten-history-of-how-the-u-s-government-segregated -america.

34. Sudetic, *Philanthropy of George Soros*, 276; see also "Our Programs and Impact," Open Society Institute–Baltimore, n.d., www.osibaltimore.org /programs-and-impact/our-programs-and-impact/.

35. Sudetic, *Philanthropy of George Soros*, 281. The drug is buprenorphine.

36. Gara LaMarche, "In Defense of Unstrategic Philanthropy," Hist Phil.org, posted December 17, 2019.

37. "The National Memorial for Peace and Justice," info block on landing page, Equal Justice Initiative, n.d., https://museumandmemorial.eji .org/.

38. "History: We are the Country's First and Foremost Civil and Human Rights Law Firm," Legal Defense and Educational Fund, n.d., www .naacpldf.org/about-us/history/full/.

39. Center for Effective Philanthropy, "New Attitudes, Old Practices: The Provision of Multiyear General Operating Support," 2020, http://cep .org/wp-content/uploads/2020/11/Ford_MYGOS_FNL.pdf.

40. "Transforming the Culture of Dying: The Project on Death in America 1994–2003," Open Society Foundations, October 1, 2004, www.open societyfoundations.org/publications/transforming-culture-dying-project -death-america-1994-2003.

41. George Soros, "Keeping America Open: Chairman's Message," OSI US 10 (Tenth Anniversary US Programs 2006), Open Society Foundations, 7, www.opensocietyfoundations.org/uploads/37660798-2e5e-4aac-8d01-1cc feabe93d4/tenth_20061116.pdf.

GARA LAMARCHE / POLITICS WITH A PURPOSE

Unless otherwise indicated in the notes below, all quotations are from interviews conducted by the author.

1. Quoted in Sally Jacobsen, "George Soros: Philanthropist or Opportunist?," *South Florida Sun-Sentinel*, October 26, 1997.

2. George W. Bush, "President Bush, President Kwasniewski Hold Joint Press Conference," press release, White House Archives, July 17, 2002, https://georgewbush-whitehouse.archives.gov/news/releases/2002/07 /text/20020717-3.html.

3. George Soros, *The Age of Fallibility: Consequences of the War on Terror* (New York: PublicAffairs, 2006), 80.

4. Thomas B. Edsall, "Soros-Backed Activist Group Disbands as Interest Fades," *Washington Post*, August 3, 2005.

5. Sally Covington, *Moving a Public Policy Agenda: The Strategic Philanthropy of Conservative Foundations*, National Committee for Responsive Philanthropy, 1997.

6. Chuck Sudetic, *The Philanthropy of George Soros: Building Open Societies* (New York: PublicAffairs, 2011), 49.

7. George Soros and Rob Johnson, "A Better Bailout Was Possible," Project Syndicate, September 18, 2018.

8. Sudetic, *Philanthropy of George Soros*, 54.

9. George Soros, *Soros on Soros: Staying Ahead of the Curve* (New York: John Wiley & Sons, 1995), 250.

10. John Cassidy, "The Ringleader," *The New Yorker*, July 25, 2005.

11. Soros, *Age of Fallibility*, 96.

IVAN KRASTEV / AN EASTERN EUROPEAN MIND

1. Michael T. Kaufman, *Soros: The Life and Times of a Messianic Billionaire* (New York: Alfred A. Knopf, 2002), 25.

2. Milan Kundera, "Zachód porwany albo tragedia Europy Środkowej," *Zeszyty Literackie*, no. 5 (Paris, 1984), 14–31.

3. István Bibó, "The Miseries of East European Small States," in István Bibó and Iván Z. Dénes, *The Art of Peacemaking: Political Essays by István Bibó* (New Haven, CT: Yale University Press, 2015), available at www.university pressscholarship.com/view/10.12987/yale/9780300203783.001.0001/upso -9780300203783.

4. George Soros, *In Defense of Open Society* (New York: PublicAffairs, 2019), 1.

5. Samuel Moyn, *The Last Utopia: Human Rights in History*, reprint edition (Cambridge, MA: Harvard University Press / Belknap Press, 2012).

6. George Soros, *Underwriting Democracy* (New York: Free Press, 1991), 20, available at www.georgesoros.com/wp-content/uploads/2017/10/under writing_democracy-chap-11-2017_10_05.pdf.

7. George Soros, *The Soros Lectures: At the Central European University* (New York: PublicAffairs, 2010), 46.

8. George Soros, *Opening the Soviet System* (London: Weidenfeld & Nicolson, 1990), ch. 1.

9. George Soros, *The Age of Fallibility: Consequences of the War on Terror* (New York: PublicAffairs, 2006), 31–32.

10. Soros, *Underwriting Democracy*, 25.

11. Connie Bruck, "The World According to George Soros," *The New Yorker*, January 23, 1995, available at www.newyorker.com/magazine/1995 /01/23/the-world-according-to-soros.

12. Ernest Gellner, *Language and Solitude: Wittgenstein, Malinowski and the Habsburg Dilemma* (Cambridge: Cambridge University Press, 1998), 37.

13. Francis Fukuyama, "The End of History?," *The National Interest*, Summer 1989, available at www.wesjones.com/eoh.htm#source.

14. Soros, *Underwriting Democracy*, 14.

15. Hans Magnus Enzensberger, "The State of Europe: Christmas Eve 1989," *Granta*, February 2, 1990, available at https://granta.com/the-state-of-europe-christmas-eve-1989/.

16. Soros, *Opening the Soviet System*, ch. 5.

17. Soros, *Opening the Soviet System*, ch. 1.

18. Soros, *Opening the Soviet System*, ch. 1.

19. Soros, *Soros Lectures*, 57.

20. Chuck Sudetic, *The Philanthropy of George Soros: Building Open Societies* (New York: PublicAffairs, 2011), 19.

21. Sudetic, *Philanthropy of George Soros*, 15.

22. Soros, *Opening the Soviet System*, ch. 5.

23. Soros, *Underwriting Democracy*, 3.

24. Bruck, "World According to George Soros."

25. Soros, *In Defense of Open Society*, 64.

26. Kaufman, *Soros*, 274–75.

27. Kaufman, *Soros*, 278–79.

28. Kaufman, *Soros*, 279.

29. Bruck, "World According to George Soros."

30. "Global Views on Immigration and the Refugee Crisis," IPSOS, July 2017, available at www.ipsos.com/sites/default/files/ct/news/documents/2017-09/Global_Advisor_Immigration.pdf.

31. "People in the EU—Statistics on Origin of Residents," EUROSTAT, 2017, available at https://ec.europa.eu/eurostat/statistics-explained/index.php?title=People_in_the_EU_%E2%80%93_statistics_on_origin_of_residents&oldid=374953.

32. Raymond Aron, *The Dawn of Universal History: Selected Essays from a Witness to the Twentieth Century* (New York: Basic Books, 2002), 482.

33. Yehuda Elkana, "The Need to Forget," *Ha'aretz*, March 2, 1988, 3, available at http://web.ceu.hu/yehuda_the_need_to_forget.pdf.

MICHAEL IGNATIEFF / THE FOUNDER'S TALE

I wish to gratefully acknowledge assistance from the following colleagues and friends who were "present at the creation" and whom I interviewed at length, starting with István Rév and the staff of the Open Society Archives in Budapest, where the founding documents and records of Central European University are stored. I also want to acknowledge Agi Benedek of CEU's Institutional Research Office for her help in providing figures on CEU enrollment growth in the 1990s.

I interviewed the following colleagues, who were among the founders of CEU: the political philosopher János Kis; the medieval historian Gábor Klaniczay, whom I thank for the use of his memoir on the founding of medieval studies at CEU; the historian of ideas László Kontler; the political scientist Béla Greskovits; András Sajó, professor of legal studies and former judge of the European Court of Human Rights; the provost of CEU, Liviu Matei; Bill Newton-Smith, Oxford philosopher of science, to whom I am especially grateful for making available unpublished chapters of his memoir on his role in the founding of CEU in 1990–92; and Pierre Mirabaud, Swiss banker and former CEU trustee. I made use of the memoir by Alfred Stepan, the first rector of CEU, in *Social Research*, 2009. I consulted Jacques Rupnik, professor of political science at Sciences Po, Paris, on his role in the early meetings on the founding of CEU. I spoke with the political scientist László Bruszt. Leon Botstein, the chairman of the board at CEU and a fellow contributor to this volume, offered insights into Soros's motivations in founding CEU. Michael Vachon, Soros's longstanding political counselor, provided helpful insights into the Soros-Orbán relationship. I want to thank these colleagues and friends for their recollections. They bear no responsibility for my interpretation of events or for the mistakes that remain in my account.

ORVILLE SCHELL / A NETWORK OF NETWORKS

1. Iris Ouyang, "HNA Group Enters Bankruptcy Restructuring As China's Largest Asset Buyer Succumbs to Debt After Decade-Long Shopping Spree," *South China Morning Post*, January 29, 2021, https://www.scmp.com/business/companies/article/3119812/hna-group-goes-bankrupt-chinas-largest-global-asset-buyer.

2. See his annual speech at the 2019 World Economic Forum: https://www.georgesoros.com/2019/01/24/remarks-delivered-at-the-world-economic-forum-2/.

3. "Chen Yizi, Chinese Communist Party Reformer," Human Rights Watch, n.d., www.hrw.org/legacy/campaigns/china-99/chenyizi.htm.

4. Michael T. Kaufman, *Soros: The Life and Times of a Messianic Billionaire* (New York: Alfred A. Knopf, 2002), 107.

5. Kaufman, *Soros*, 265.

6. "Soros Keen to Go Deeper into China," *Sydney Morning Herald*, January 27, 2004, www.smh.com.au/national/soros-keen-to-go-deeper-into-china -20040127-gdi8i1.html.

7. George Soros, *In Defense of Open Society* (New York: PublicAffairs, 2019), 73.

8. Connie Bruck, "The World According to George Soros," *The New Yorker*, January 23, 1995.

9. "Robert Zoellick's Responsible Stakeholder Speech," National Committee on United States-China Relations, n.d., www.ncuscr.org/content /robert-zoellicks-responsible-stakeholder-speech.

10. Wikipedia, s.v. "*Fortune* Global 500," last modified July 12, 2021, at 16:59, https://en.wikipedia.org/wiki/Fortune_Global_500; "Hainan Airlines Group Entered the Fortune 500 List of the World's Most Successful Companies," press release, Deer Jet, July 27, 2015, http://en.deerjet.com /content/details16_13543.html.

11. Zeng Qingkai, "Soros Injects Another US$25m into Hainan Airlines," *China Daily*, October 17, 2005, www.chinadaily.com.cn/english/doc/2005-10 /17/content_485469.htm.

12. Emily Feng, "China's New Anti-Foreign Sanctions Law Sends a Chill Through the Business Community," *All Things Considered* (NPR), June 11, 2021, www.npr.org/2021/06/11/1005467033/chinas-new-anti-foreign -sanctions-law-sends-a-chill-through-the-business-communi.

13. See his 2019 annual World Economic Forum speech at Davos: www .npr.org/2021/06/11/1005467033/chinas-new-anti-foreign-sanctions-law -sends-a-chill-through-the-business-communi

14. Soros, *In Defense of Open Society*, 37.

15. Soros, *In Defense of Open Society*, 81.

16. Soros, *In Defense of Open Society*, 89.

17. Soros, *In Defense of Open Society*, subtitle of chapter 3.

18. George Soros, *The Alchemy of Finance*, cited in Tadas Viskanta, "Soros, Fallibility, Reflexivity, and the Importance of Adapting," *Enterprising Investor* (blog), CFA Institute, December 19, 2016, https://blogs.cfainstitute .org/investor/2016/12/19/soros-fallibility-reflexivity-and-the-importance -of-adapting/.

19. George Soros, "Fallibility, Reflexivity, and the Human Uncertainty Principle," introduction to a special issue of *Journal of Economic Methodology*,

GeorgeSoros.com, January 13, 2014, www.georgesoros.com/2014/01/13
/fallibility-reflexivity-and-the-human-uncertainty-principle-2/.

20. George Soros, "Reflections on Death in America," in *Project on Death in America: Report of Activities January 2001–December 2003*, Open Society Foundations, 2004, 6, www.opensocietyfoundations.org/uploads/3373fc83-1a80
-4c71-95d8-381da95d95af/a_complete_7.pdf.

LEON BOTSTEIN / THE CHALLENGE AND LEGACY OF BEING A JEW FROM HUNGARY

1. Henri Bergson, "Les Deux Sources de la Morale et de la Religion" in *Oeuvres*, edited by Andre Robinet (Paris: Presses Universitaires de France 1970) 981–1245, especially 1152–1207.

2. Hannah Arendt, *The Human Condition* (Chicago: University of Chicago Press, 1958), 8.

3. For a concise account of Budapest at the turn of the century, see John Lukacs, *Budapest 1900: A Historical Portrait of a City and Its Culture* (New York: Weidenfeld & Nicolson, 1988).

4. The statistical material used in this chapter derives from the following sources: Ezra Mendelsohn, *The Jews of East Central Europe Between the World Wars* (Bloomington: Indiana University Press, 1983); Bernard Wasserstein, *On the Eve: The Jews of Eastern Europe Before the Second World War* (New York: Simon & Schuster, 2012); Klinga Frojimovics, Géza Komoróczy, Viktória Pusztai, and Andrea Strbik, *Jewish Budapest: Monuments, Rites, History* (Budapest: Central European University Press, 1995); and the entries on Budapest and Hungary in *The YIVO Encyclopedia of Jews in Eastern Europe*, ed. Gershon David Hundert, 2 vols. (New Haven, CT: Yale University Press, 2008).

5. See William O. McCagg Jr., *Jewish Nobles and Geniuses in Modern Hungary*, East European Monographs 3 (New York: Columbia University Press, 1986).

6. See Miklós Konrád, "The Social Integration of the Jewish Upper Bourgeoisie in the Hungarian Traditional Elites: A Survey of the Period from the Reform Era to World War I," *Hungarian Historical Review* 3, no. 4 (2014): 818–49.

7. The now standard revisionist account of the closing decades of the Austro-Hungarian Empire is Pieter M. Judson, *The Habsburg Empire: A New History* (Cambridge, MA: Harvard University Press, 2016).

8. The literature on this issue is extensive. An elegant précis of the matter can be found in "The Making of Austro-Modernism," the introductory

chapter of Marjorie Perloff's *Edge of Irony: Modernism in the Shadow of the Habsburg Empire* (Chicago: University of Chicago Press, 2016), 1–18.

9. György Litván, *A Twentieth Century Prophet: Oscar Jászi, 1875–1957* (Budapest: Central European University Press, 2006), 131–34, 232–55.

10. Tivadar Soros, *Masquerade: The Incredible True Story of How George Soros' Father Outsmarted the Gestapo*, ed. and trans. Humphrey Tonkin (New York: Arcade Publishing, 2011), 20.

11. See William O. McCagg Jr., *A History of Habsburg Jews, 1670–1918* (Bloomington: Indiana University Press, 1989), 129–39, 187–95.

12. These stories, "Der Buchbinder von Hort" and "Die Erlösung," can be found in Leopold von Sacher-Masoch, *Jüdisches Leben in Wort und Bild* (Mannheim: Bensheimer, 1892), 71–84 and 179–90. Translations are my own.

13. Frojimovics et al., *Jewish Budapest*, 361.

14. Frojimovics et al., *Jewish Budapest*, 362.

15. Frojimovics et al., *Jewish Budapest*, 362.

16. Alexander Maxwell and Alexander Campbell, "István Széchenyi, the Casino Movement, and Hungarian Nationalism, 1827–1848," *Nationalities Papers: The Journal of Nationalism and Ethnicity* 42, no. 3 (May 2014): 4.

17. Maxwell and Campbell, "István Széchenyi," 4–8.

18. See William O. McCagg, "Jew and Peasant in Interwar Hungary," *Nationalities Papers* 15, no. 1 (Spring 1987): 90–105.

19. Tivadar Soros, *Masquerade*, 20–21.

20. The discussion of this book is based on the original edition of Mica Josef Berdyczewski, *Die Sagen der Juden* (Frankfurt: Rürten & Loening, 1913) and the posthumous edition published by Schocken Verlag in Berlin in 1935.

21. On Berdyczewski, see Hillel Halkin, *The Lady Hebrew and Her Lovers of Zion* (Jerusalem: Koren Publishers, 2020), 159–98.

22. Tivadar Soros, *Masquerade*, 203.

23. For a recent account of the role of the Arrow Cross in 1944 and 1945, placed in the context of contemporary Hungarian politics, see the 2021 television movie *Monument to the Murderers* (dir. Dániel Acs), which can be accessed at https://youtu.be/4ygZBiMTRR4.

24. See Marsha L. Rozenblit, *The Jews of Vienna 1867–1914: Assimilation and Identity* (Albany: State University of New York Press, 1983), 132–36.

25. On the Viennese context and Popper, see Lisa Silverman, *Becoming Austrians: Jews and Culture Between the World Wars* (Oxford and New York: Oxford University Press: 2012), particularly 176–77.

26. Árpád Göncz, "Hungary and the Open Society," in *The Paradoxes of Unintended Consequences*, ed. Lord Dahrendorf, Yehuda Elkana, Aryeh Neier, William Newton-Smith, and István Rév (Budapest: Central European University Press, 2000), 12.

27. See chapter 5 in Tivadar Soros, *Masquerade*, 31–37.

28. Photographic images of these Orbán campaign slogans, posters, and billboards can be found on Google by clicking "images" under the rubric "Viktor Orban campaign posters."

29. Arendt, *Human Condition*, 8.

Contributors

LEON BOTSTEIN is president of Bard College, where he is the Leon Levy professor in the arts and humanities. He serves as music director of the American Symphony Orchestra, The Orchestra Now, and the Bard Music Festival. He edits *The Musical Quarterly* and has written on the history of music and culture in the nineteenth and twentieth centuries. He serves as board chairman of Central European University and is a member of the Fulbright University in Vietnam board and the Open Society Foundations global board. He holds a BA from the University of Chicago and a PhD from Harvard University. He is conductor laureate of the Jerusalem Symphony Orchestra, where he served as music director from 2003 to 2010.

EVA HOFFMAN grew up in Poland before emigrating to Canada and the United States. After receiving her PhD from Harvard, she worked as a senior editor and writer at *The New York Times,* presented programs for BBC Radio, and lectured internationally on cross-cultural relations, transitions to democracy, and other contemporary issues. Her widely translated books include *Lost in Translation, Exit into History*, and *After Such Knowledge: Reflections on the Long Aftermath of the Holocaust*. She has received major awards for her work and is a visiting professor at the European Institute of University College London. She lives in London.

MICHAEL IGNATIEFF is the rector emeritus of Central European University. Born in Canada and educated at the University of

Toronto and Harvard, he is a university professor, writer, and former politician. His major publications are *The Needs of Strangers, Scar Tissue, Isaiah Berlin, The Rights Revolution, The Lesser Evil: Political Ethics in an Age of Terror, The Ordinary Virtues: Moral Order in a Divided World*, and *On Consolation: Finding Solace in Dark Times*. From 2006 to 2011, he served as a Canadian member of Parliament and then as leader of the Liberal Party. Before taking up his post at Central European University, he was Edward R. Murrow chair of the press, politics, and public policy at the Harvard Kennedy School.

IVAN KRASTEV is the chairman of the Centre for Liberal Strategies, Sofia, and a permanent fellow at the Institute for Human Sciences, IWM Vienna. He is a global board member of the Open Society Foundations, a founding board member of the European Council on Foreign Relations, and a member of the board of trustees of the International Crisis Group. He is the author of *Is It Tomorrow, Yet? How the Pandemic Changes Europe, The Light That Failed: A Reckoning* (co-authored with Stephen Holmes), and *After Europe*.

GARA LAMARCHE is a senior fellow at the Colin Powell School for Civic and Global Leadership at the City College of New York, having previously served as president of the Democracy Alliance, president and CEO of the Atlantic Philanthropies, and vice president and director of US programs for the Open Society Foundations. In his work he took part in some of the events described in his essay and represented George Soros in the Democracy Alliance, though he was not involved in Soros's political activities. (As a foundation official he was barred from such engagement.) A longtime advocate for human rights at home and abroad, he has held various positions with Human Rights Watch and the American Civil Liberties Union, and he has taught courses on philanthropy, public policy, and nonprofit leadership at Hunter College, Bard College, NYU's Wagner School, and the New School.

SEBASTIAN MALLABY is the Paul A. Volcker senior fellow for international economics at the Council on Foreign Relations. He has been a staff writer at *The Economist*, a columnist and editorial board member at *The Washington Post*, and a contributing editor at the *Financial Times*. His works of financial history include *More Money Than God: Hedge Funds and the Making of a New Elite*, a *New York Times* bestseller; and *The Man Who Knew: The Life and Times of Alan Greenspan*, winner of the FT-McKinsey Business Book of the Year prize. His latest book, a history of venture capital, appears in 2022.

PETER L. W. OSNOS is the founder of PublicAffairs, which has published all of George Soros's books since 1998. He had a career in journalism at *I. F. Stone's Weekly* and *The Washington Post* and in publishing at Random House before starting PublicAffairs. He is the author of *An Especially Good View: Watching History Happen*, published by Platform Books in June 2021.

ORVILLE SCHELL is the Arthur Ross director of the Center on US-China Relations at Asia Society in New York. He is a former professor and dean at the Graduate School of Journalism of the University of California, Berkeley. He is the author of fifteen books, ten of them about China, and has written widely for many magazines and newspapers. His most recent book is a novel about the United States and China, *My Old Home*. His nonfiction works include: *Wealth and Power: China's Long March to the Twenty-first Century*, *Virtual Tibet*, *The China Reader*, and *Mandate of Heaven: The Legacy of Tiananmen Square and the Next Generation of China's Leaders*. He is a fellow at the Weatherhead East Asian Institute at Columbia University and a senior fellow at the Annenberg School for Communications at the University of Southern California.

DARREN WALKER is president of the Ford Foundation, a position to which he was appointed in 2013. He was previously vice president at the Rockefeller Foundation and chief operating officer of Harlem's largest community development organization, the Abyssinian Development Corporation. He also had a decade-long career in international law and finance at Cleary Gottlieb Steen & Hamilton and UBS. Educated exclusively in public schools, Darren was in the first class of Head Start in 1965 and is a graduate of the University of Texas at Austin. He is the author of *From Generosity to Justice: A New Gospel of Wealth,* a manifesto intended to encourage donors to move beyond traditional charitable approaches to philanthropy.

Index

Copyright Acknowledgments